GENERAL EDITOR: John Sales, Gardens Adviser, National Trust

Kent, East & West Sussex and Surrey

Tom Wright

In association with the Royal Horticultural Society

B.T. Batsford Ltd, *London*

To my Father and Mother
who first gave me the
opportunity and the encouragement
to garden; and to all gardeners
whose creations have made such
a book as this possible

First published 1978

© Tom Wright 1978

ISBN 0 7134 1281 X O4-11

Filmset by Servis Filmsetting Ltd, Manchester
Printed and bound in Great Britain by
Weatherby, Woolnough, Wellingborough
for the publisher
B.T. Batsford Ltd, 4 Fitzhardinge St, London W1H 0AH

Contents

Contents

Preface

This book covers a reasonably comprehensive selection of gardens normally open to the public on one or more occasions during the year in Kent, East and West Sussex and Surrey, and the descriptions of the gardens and the supplements are largely based on gardens open to the public during the seasons of 1975 and 1976. The great majority of these gardens are in private ownership; the homes of those with an enthusiasm for gardens and plants that they wish to share with others. However, for many reasons, all the gardens referred to in this book may not be open every year and changing circumstances make it essential for the prospective visitor to check the latest edition of the National Gardens Scheme 'Yellow Book' or the Historic Houses, Castles and Gardens publication and others to find out the latest position. Some of the owners have also expressed a willingness to show their gardens, by special arrangement, to interested individuals or groups, given sufficient notice.

The gardens are described in alphabetical order in each county, followed by a supplement of other gardens normally open to the public in that county but not described in the main section. A map is also given for each of the counties to show the approximate location of the main gardens described. The symbols used on these maps are as follows:

- ■ principal towns
- O important gardens open regularly
- • fine gardens open less frequently

For convenience East and West Sussex are treated as one county.

The use of the older 1-inch or the newer 1.50,000 O.S. maps is strongly recommended for those planning an itinerary of visits to gardens.

TOM WRIGHT

Acknowledgements

I would like to acknowledge the assistance of the many people who have helped in the preparation of this book. I wish to record my very special thanks to the following: The County Organizers of the National Gardens Scheme (1977), Mrs Alan Hardy (Kent), Miss Pat Davies-Gilbert (east and mid Sussex), Mrs Nigel Azis (west Sussex) and Lady Heald (Surrey) — their advice and assistance were invaluable.

Mrs Elizabeth Simmons for her painstaking and careful production of the garden plans; Miss Charlotte Cox for her delightful line drawings; all those owners, agents, and, frequently, head gardeners of the many gardens visited for their generous help, hospitality and encouragement; Miss Bridget Cue for the typing of the drafts; and finally my wife and family for their assistance and forbearance during the two years the book was 'evolving'.

The author and publishers would like to thank the following for permission to reproduce black and white photographs: Bernard Alfieri (figs 6 & 18); Cambridge University Collection (copyright reserved) (figs 2, 5, 7 & 8); *Country Life* (figs 3, 16 & 19); Ernest Crowson and the Royal Horticultural Society (fig. 17); Reginald Thompson (fig. 14).

The remaining black and white photographs and all the colour plates are from the author's own collection.

8

List of maps

List of garden plans

List of colour illustrations

(The colour plates are between pages 112–113 and 128–129)

Sissinghurst
Sheffield Park
Northbourne Court
Great Dixter
Denmans
Wakehurst Place
Royal Horticultural Society's Garden, Wisley

List of black and white illustrations

Introduction

There is a high concentration of gardens open to the public in the south-east of England. Those listed in the National Gardens Scheme annual publication total over 60 in Kent, 100 in East and West Sussex and over 40 in Surrey. The gardens of the National Trust and other properties may also be added to this list.

Many volumes could be written about the fascinating gardens to be explored in these counties, especially as some have never really been chronicled in detail, but restrictions have had to be severe to keep this book within the prescribed length. A selection of gardens – based on the author's assessment of the merits and interest of each to the visiting public – has therefore been presented from the many visited. In making this selection, invaluable help has been given by the County Organizers of the National Gardens Scheme. Injustices will abound, one fully accepts, to gardens either omitted entirely from the descriptive sections, or condensed, in an apparently rather subjective way, to mere summaries of gardens of which the owners are immensely proud. The author's apologies to all those so aggrieved.

To simplify the practical use of this book, a standard format has been adopted which varies somewhat depending on the size and importance of the garden.

A brief information section gives the location of the garden with National Grid reference numbers to Ordnance Survey maps, details of ownership and of opening arrangements and any facilities. Then follows a brief summary of the main characteristics of the garden. Next comes an account of the history and evolution of the house and garden, reference to the house being considered important since its evolution is often inseparable from that of the garden. Concise information on the setting, soils and microclimate follows and, finally, the section on the main features of the garden.

Abbreviations and references used in the descriptions are as follows:
Location   *O.S.* Ordnance Survey 1-inch and 1.500,000 series. The

bracketed number after the main reference numbers refers to the current sheet of the 1.500,000 series on which the garden should be found.

Opening   *N.G.S.* National Gardens Scheme. Note this abbreviation is *not* in current use and has only been adopted in this book for brevity. *G.S.O.* Gardens Sunday Organization.

H.H.C.G. The Historic Houses, Castles and Gardens annual publication produced by A.B.C. Travel Guides Ltd.

Climate   All figures are approximate for the gardens described and are mostly taken from the Meteorological Office average for 1941–70. Rainfall as annual averages in inches. Sunshine as daily average figures in hours for the year.

References   *Country Life* publication volume and number. Royal Horticultural Society's (R.H.S.) Journal, now *The Garden*.

The south-east of England has always been the gateway to and from the Continent; the corridor, the living space and the growing place, horticulturally speaking – the Garden of England – for many centuries. Topography, climate and soils have attracted generations of invaders and settlers from the Romans and the Normans to the Flemish Huguenots who began the market garden industry in east Kent in medieval times, to more recent 'migrants' from the north and midlands attracted by the additional magnet of London. The increasing popularity of the south-east as a place to live compared with the rest of Great Britain is demonstrated by the fact that whereas in 1801 23% of the population lived in the area, by 1969 the figure had reached 32%. The great 'wen' of London, as William Cobbett called it even in the mid-nineteenth century, has absorbed much of this population with suburban sprawl and county town expansion having the greatest impact on the counties of Kent and Surrey. Urban development and population pressures in Surrey have created large numbers of smaller gardens but have probably caused the loss of the larger, historic and high quality gardens still to be seen in the rural areas of Sussex and Kent. This trend seems likely to continue in all counties as the problem of upkeep of large gardens increases and the price of land also continues to rise.

Monastic and early feudal strongholds were the first places to have real gardens and hunting parks and farms, and some of the latter have survived. Examples are Penshurst Place and Saltwood Castle.

The growth of London as the cultural, commercial and royal centre of England caused the building in the sixteenth and seventeenth centuries of great country houses for the nobility and gentry who regularly travelled to London from their seats in these three counties. Typical examples are Chilham Castle, Cobham Hall, Hever Castle and Knole House. The restoration of the monarchy in 1660 and Charles II's love of French gardens in the baroque formal style saw the fashion for these influencing the design of gardens and great houses like Hampton Court, Cobham Hall and Petworh House. Most of these geometric designs were to disappear in the next century. The great eighteenth-century landscape movement again changed the styles of many gardens in the south-east, and some exist today largely intact in the style of Lancelot Brown and Humphry Repton at Petworth and Cobham Hall.

The nineteenth century, and especially the late-Victorian period, was the beginning of an epoch-making era for gardens in the south-east and for horticulture throughout the country – an era that lasted until the outbreak of the First World War. A number of large country houses with gardens to match were built in the home counties at the same time as a wealth of new plants from many countries were arriving. This stimulated an expanding Surrey-based nursery industry to supply trees and shrubs to the many affluent customers in the region. Architects like Pugin, Norman Shaw and George Devey, working in Gothic and Jacobean revival styles, created larger, often pretentious, country and suburban houses (Horsted Place and Hall Place) for the middle and upper classes, with gardens echoing a partial return to formalism and Italian styles. Further great impetus to country-house and garden-making followed in the early twentieth century as a result of the work of three famous collaborators whose names appear frequently throughout this book in connection with both the actual design and the inspiration behind many fine gardens:

GERTRUDE JEKYLL (1843–1932)
A cultured, gifted artist and lover of the Surrey countryside, where she lived for most of her life, who later in life became one of the foremost advocates of the naturalistic planting styles – with a talent for colour and textural associations – that are very much in vogue again today. She helped to advise on or design at least 300 gardens in many parts of England, and her collaboration with the architect Sir Edwin Lutyens was highly successful.

SIR EDWIN LUTYENS (1869–1944)
The famous and successful architect whose importance in this book is in the unique series of fine country houses and equally fine gardens that he created or helped create, many in conjunction with Gertrude Jekyll with whom he worked for over 30 years. Two classic examples in this book are Hascombe Court and Great Dixter.

WILLIAM ROBINSON (1839–1935)
A writer, practical gardener and outspoken critic of the then fashionable 'carpet bedding' and formal stereotyped gardens, which to him had 'no more interest than an oil cloth pattern'. He loved wild plants and perennials and the growing of suitable plants in shrub borders, herbaceous borders and wild gardens. He was joined by Gertrude Jekyll and, later, Reginald Farrer in developing this new style of gardening, whose influence continues right up to the present day.

Great collections of trees and shrubs were also being built up in the early decades of this century; especially of the newer introductions from Asia, Australasia and South America, sent back by such great plant-hunters as Forrest, Wilson, Comber and Kingdon Ward. Outstanding examples of these can be seen at Wakehurst, Leonardslee and Borde Hill, all in West Sussex.

No new styles have really evolved since this era, although a number of important intimate and well-planted gardens were created in the Thirties – such as Sissinghurst Castle and Charleston Manor – and from 1945 onwards. In the latter period particularly, most garden owners have had to face mounting problems of costs and scarcity of skilled gardeners and the whole business of maintaining large gardens with dwindling resources. Design and planting is now very much related to these problems (Great Comp).

The geological map for the area shows the remarkable range of topographical and soil types that characterize these three counties, constituting a major reason for such widely contrasting styles of gardens in a comparatively small region. Each garden description includes some reference to the soils and after studying this book in conjunction with visiting some of the gardens described, a picture emerges of groups or categories of gardens lying on the same major geological and soil classes, with similar characteristic landscape settings.

The High Weald A large area of west Kent and east and central Sussex, of undulating hills and deep valleys of predominately acid soils, ranging from the dramatic outcrops of Tunbridge Wells sand-

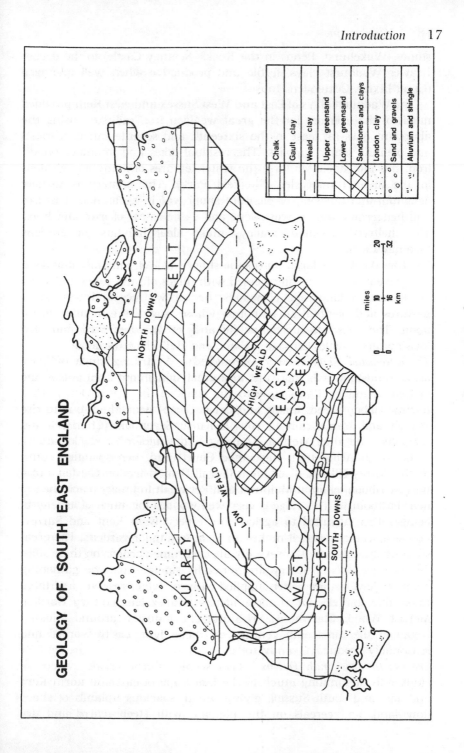

GEOLOGY OF SOUTH EAST ENGLAND

Chalk	
Gault clay	
Weald clay	
Upper greensand	
Lower greensand	
Sandstones and clays	
London clay	
Sand and gravels	
Alluvium and shingle	

SURREY

KENT

NORTH DOWNS

WEALD

LOW WEALD

HIGH WEALD

EAST SUSSEX

WEST SUSSEX

SOUTH DOWNS

miles
0   10   20
0   16   32
km

stones (Wakehurst, Penns in the Rocks, Scotney Castle) to the deeper heavier Wadhurst clays, fertile and productive when well managed (Great Dixter, Crittenden House).

The Wadhurst clays of East and West Sussex and west Kent provided much of the iron ore for the great wealden iron industry, using the abundant oaks (at least in the sixteenth and seventeenth centuries!) and plentiful water supplies. The residual lakes and 'hammer ponds' from this industry often form the water features of many fine gardens in the area (Leonardslee, Sheffield Park). The scenery is usually delightful and unspoilt, of plentiful small woods, permanent pastures and hedgerows and, in west Kent and east Sussex, of fruit and hops. The sheltered woodland valleys make ideal habitats for gardens (Scotney Castle).

The Low Weald   A large horseshoe-shaped belt of generally low-lying heavy weald-clay soils interspersed with ridges of sandstones and some limestones. A landscape of woods, hedgerow trees and permanent pastures and plentiful small ponds whose origin is not fully agreed upon. The soils are mostly acidic and fertile when well managed (Sissinghurst Castle, Penshurst Place and Hall Place Gardens).

The Greensand Ridge (Lower Greensand)   A striking ridge of light, acidic sandstone soils that runs in a great spinal cord from Folkestone in Kent (Sandling Park) close to the chalk of the North Downs as a narrow ribbon (Leeds Castle and Great Comp) near Maidstone to rise steadily and dramatically to Toys Hill near Sevenoaks (Chartwell and Emmetts) and then west to Dorking and Guildford and Godalming (Winkworth Arboretum, Hascombe Court) and then swinging south as the Surrey Hills of Blackdown (Farall Demonstration Gardens) to a narrow ribbon again at Midhurst and Petworth to finally reach the sea near Eastbourne. This ridge is very well wooded for much of its length, being rather unsuited to agriculture, especially in Kent and Surrey, and as a scenic feature it makes an ideal setting for gardens. The great summer drought of 1976 severely affected some gardens on these soils.

The Bagshot Beds of Surrey are generally similar from the gardening point of view, but are better supplied with soil water reserves and these make fine gardens for rhododendrons and azaleas (Wisley Garden, Merrist Wood, Claremont). The nursery industry around Woking began in the nineteenth century on these light, easily worked and reasonably productive sandy soils.

The North and South Downs   Two scenic, characteristic sweeps of chalk hills dominating much of the landscape of east and north Kent and east and south Sussex, giving broad, spacious uplands of sheep downland, and cereals on the plateau, with steep scarps and dry valleys of beech and ash woodlands, with sweet chestnut coppices on the deeper soils. These range from the chalky loams to deeper clay with flints (Withersdane Hall, Telegraph Hill, Charleston Manor).

The favourable climate in the south-east has already been referred to, adding to the attractions of this region as a place in which to live, to work and to garden. Temperature, sunshine and rainfall are all important here and the significance of microclimate is referred to under each garden description, with local weather data. The effect of altitude is also very significant; there is in general a decrease of 20–25 growing-season days in the south of England for every 350 ft rise in altitude (growing-season days as defined by the Ministry of Agriculture are those days in the year when the soil temperature at 1 ft depth exceeds 6°C). The incidence of frosts in frost hollows is another important factor.

Visitors with a particular interest in wildlife and natural history will be fascinated by the numbers and the range of animal, insect and plant life to be found in the larger, less intensively managed gardens described in this book. The ornamental woodlands, shrubberies, lakes and ponds, streams, meadowlands and damp places, and the great diversity of other plant associations, provide many ideal habitats for birds, insects and wild flowers. With the intensification of agriculture and the loss of hedgerows, ponds and many other wildlife habitats today, owners of these large gardens and parks are making a great and often unrecognized contribution in this respect alone. A further important contribution is in the continued cultivation of old garden varieties and hybrids of many plants, now less and less seen in nurseries, which are in grave risk of total extinction unless perpetuated by keen plantsmen and gardeners.

The Gardens of Kent

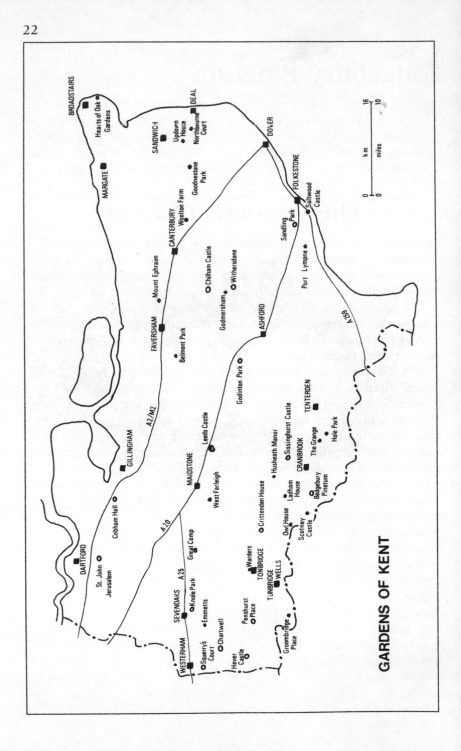

GARDENS OF KENT

Bedgebury Pinetum

TQ 725 335 (Sheet 188) West Kent. Bedgebury Forest. Goudhurst (3 miles to NW), Hawkhurst and Cranbrook. Main entrance well signposted off rather narrow B2079 Goudhurst–Flimwell road. There are two other entrances for walkers from the Royal Oak, Flimwell, and from Tubs Lake between Cranbrook and Hawkhurst. Open normally 10–8 (or sunset) every day of the year. Parking excellent. Toilet facilities are provided but no teas or refreshments.

This world famous pinetum represents one of the most comprehensive collections of conifers in Europe, developed during the last 50 years by the Royal Botanic Gardens, Kew and the Forestry Commission. It is set in the beautiful weald landscape near Goudhurst on acid soils.

The pinetum lies in the former grounds of Bedgebury Park, a mansion in the French style. It was enlarged in the mid-nineteenth century by Marshal Viscount Beresford. The house is now a girl's school and not open to the public.

In 1924 nearly 100 acres of the park were acquired by the Royal Botanic Gardens at Kew, and the pinetum established under the joint auspices of Kew and the Forestry Commission. The first plantings were made in 1925 under the inspired direction of Mr W. Dallimore, the then Keeper of Museum at Kew, who became the first Curator of the National Pinetum. In 1929 an area of 60 acres of trial forest plots was established – comprising over 150 plots, each of 0.25 acres – of all the main species of coniferous and deciduous trees with potential timber value, the object being to assess the relative performance of these species on the Bedgebury site.

Bedgebury lies on the eastern edge of the High Weald, on the Hastings Beds, the soils being largely acid, infertile, Tunbridge Wells sands, silty and free-draining in the upper slopes but overlying acid clays in the valleys and near the lake, where conditions in the winter can be very wet indeed. Most conifers, oaks, beeches and maples like these moist acidic soils. The altitude varies between 210–295 ft, the deep valleys acting as very marked frost pockets, so that there are usually ground frosts recorded in every month of most years. The mean annual rainfall is over 33 inches, sunshine average 4 hrs; a relatively cool, moist microclimate with shelter from the strongest winds.

From the car park (once the great walled garden of the house) there is a recommended route to follow round the pinetum. Before descending the slope into the spruce valley (2), spend a few moments taking in the fine views across beyond the conifers to the fine sheltering backcloth of oak forests, with the parkland of Bedgebury House to the north.

On the slope to the spruce valley is a fine row of *Liquidambar styraciflua*, the Sweet Gum, a maple-like tree from North America that colours scarlet, purple and gold over a long period in the autumn. The spruce collection along Dallimore Avenue (2) and the spruce valley is mostly 40–50 years old, and outstanding are glaucous steely-blue forms of the Colorado Blue Spruce (*Picea pungens* 'Glauca'); the striking group of Brewers Weeping Spruce (*Picea breweriana*); the fine pagoda-like column of the Serbian Spruce (*Picea omorika*), a native of Yugoslavia; the sculptural dark black-green mounds of *Picea mariana*, the Black Spruce, from North America; and, in late spring, the fascinating crimson young cones of the Chinese *Picea likiangensis*.

On the south-west edge of Marshall's Lake (3) is a fine grove of the two deciduous conifers *Taxodium distichum* (the Swamp Cypress) and the remarkable *Metasequoia glyptostroboides*, the Dawn Redwood only discovered in cultivation as late as 1941 in central China.

The cypress valley (4) – tall groves of many cypresses usually seen as 10–13 ft specimens in gardens, here tower up to 50–65 ft, and there is a remarkable collection of the many varieties of Lawson's Cypress, *Chamaecyparis lawsoniana*, probably best seen from the west side of Pine Hill (6). The pine bank and collection of yews (*Taxus*) and related *Podocarpus* and *Cephalotaxus* can be explored in the north avenue. After crossing the cypress valley, looking west up Hill's Avenue (10) notice the beautiful groups of *Tsuga heterophylla*, the Western Hemlock from the eastern United States. The collection of *Thujas* (7) the Arborvitae make an interesting study for the specialist. The great authority on the pinetum, Mr Alan Mitchell, can identify the species of *Thujas* from the pungent scents emitted from the resin-gland on the leaves when bruised. He likens the scents of different species to Dundee cake, apple pie, and even orange peel! Look at the flourishing Wellingtonias (9) (*Sequoiadendron giganteum*) growing very rapidly indeed by the stream. In some 45 years since planting, the largest Wellingtonia has grown to over 80 ft with a girth of 15 ft. The closely related redwoods, *Sequoia sempervirens*, planted on the hill near the cedars, have reached over 90 ft in the same time. There are also some fine Serbian Spruces (*Picea omorika*) beside the Wellingtonias, reaching about 65 ft in 50 years. Notice the rather castellated line of Leyland Cypress, *Cupressocyparis leylandii*, planted in the last 10 years for screening purposes on the skyline to the right and there are also isolated groups, in the spruce

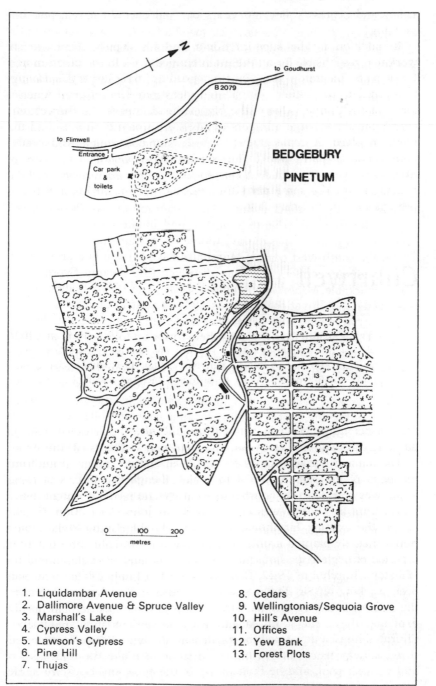

1. Liquidambar Avenue
2. Dallimore Avenue & Spruce Valley
3. Marshall's Lake
4. Cypress Valley
5. Lawson's Cypress
6. Pine Hill
7. Thujas
8. Cedars
9. Wellingtonias/Sequoia Grove
10. Hill's Avenue
11. Offices
12. Yew Bank
13. Forest Plots

valley and cypress valley, 40 years old and over 75 ft tall, and still growing!

In addition to the superintendent and his deputy there are six workmen responsible for all the maintenance work in the pinetum and forest plots, including grass cutting, pruning, tree surgery, spraying, thinning and the rather complicated measurements required when a forest plot is thinned. One of the biggest headaches for the superintendent is labelling. Large numbers of labels are stolen each year and the work involved in replacement is both time-consuming and costly. Compaction of paths due to large numbers of visitors (in excess of 80,000 per year) has made it certain that in the near future it will be necessary to close some parts for remedial action. Mr Westall is the present superintendent.

Chartwell

TQ 515 455 (Sheet 188) West Kent. 2 miles S of Westerham off B2026 Crockham Hill–Edenbridge Road. Owner: The National Trust. Open most afternoons March–November. Current National Trust handbook and H.H.C.G. for full details. Good refreshment facilities available most open days.

The former home of Sir Winston Churchill, now perpetuated with its garden by the National Trust as a living museum to this great statesman.

The name is derived from the Chart Well that gushes its spring from the head of the sloping valley in which the garden lies. A farming estate was created in the fourteenth century and passed through many hands until in 1849 it was bought by a Mr John Colquhuon. He enlarged the existing farmhouse into a formidable Gothic-style gabled house, heavily planted around with evergreens and shrubberies. After a period of neglect the house and 80 acres of land were purchased by Winston Churchill in 1922. Churchill called in Philip Tilden, who had been working on Sir Phillip Sassoon's house at Port Lympne, to alter the rather gloomy house, with the results one sees today. Tilden fully exploited the great south façade with its fine terraces and views. Churchill himself developed the gardens in the late 1920s. He imported three railway trucks of Westmorland stone to make the rock garden and goldfish pool, and he built many of the enclosing brick walls. He also ordered large quantities of fruit trees, his favourites being quinces, damsons, pears, plums, apples and Kent cobnuts. Lady Churchill also played an important part in developing the garden, which probably reached its heyday in the 1930s.

After the war Sir Winston Churchill decided to sell the property. It was bought for the nation by a group of anonymous friends who gave it to the National Trust. It was first opened to the public in 1965 after Churchill's death in January of that year. 150,000 visitors came to Chartwell in that first year.

Chartwell lies on the southern edge of the great Upper Greensand ridge that is such a dominant landscape feature of south-east England, richly wooded and sloping steeply to the south and south-west. The Toys Hill/Crockham Hill scenery is some of the finest in west Kent and the particular setting of Chartwell, with its sheltered combe and fine views, immediately attracted the Churchills in 1922. The head of the garden lies at nearly 655 ft above sea level, exposed to the south and south-west, but protected from the north and north-west by massive banks of beeches and mixed woodland. The soils are light, acid, sandy loams with ragstone exposed near the house, but heavy gault clays on the spring-line and where the streams have been dammed to form the series of lakes. Rainfall average 30.5–31.5 inches.

The finest features of the Chartwell gardens are the terraces and the rose garden; the walls, loggia and summerhouse, richly hung with vines and roses, and the great wistaria on the house itself. The rose garden has a simple collection of roses including 'Pink Favourite', 'Stephen Leyton' and 'Chanelle'.

The rock pools planted with bamboos, maples and hostas backed by massive rhododendron clumps also have atmosphere and character and flow naturally one to the other. On the other hand, the swimming-pool and lakes fit less easily into the lie of the landscape.

Near the house are tall, mature trees and conifers of the pre-Churchill era, including a large Incense Cedar, *Calocedrus* (*Libocedrus*) *decurrens*; a *Cryptomeria japonica*, the Japanese Cedar and several fine limes, *Tilia spp.*

The land falls away to the south-west and from the terrace is a pleasant view of the orchard, Churchill's studio, and cottage buildings. In the large walled garden to the west side (many of the walls built by Sir Winston) lies the more recent golden rose garden and walk, a present to Sir Winston and Lady Churchill from their children on their golden wedding anniversary in 1958. The feature is probably too formal to blend easily into the naturalized landscape on this side of the house, but in detail it is a popular and attractive feature with a collection of yellow roses as standards and bushes associated with lavenders and catmint, the walk leading to a central sundial with seats and circular grass lawn. The roses 'Peace', 'All Gold' and 'Arthur Bell' do particularly well here.

The head gardener, Mr Vincent, has served under the Churchills and was especially concerned with Lady Churchill in the restoration of the garden after the neglect of the war years. He and his staff of five full-time gardeners maintain a high standard of upkeep. This now includes the extensive car park area where large new banks of shrubs and trees are very effective in partially concealing the cars and coaches.

Chilham Castle

TQ 065 539 (Sheet 179) East Kent. Chilham 9 miles W of Canterbury, 8 miles E of Ashford just off the A28 at its junction with the A252. Owner: Viscount Massereene and Ferrard. Open Easter to September or October, usually most afternoons and from late morning in the summer months. Teas and various entertainments are provided as a commercial venture.

The gardens and part of the grounds of this historic Jacobean house are open to the public. There are fine terraces and walks, specimen trees, lawns and an extensive lake. The castle gates open onto the highly picturesque medieval square of Chilham Village.

The present house stands on a Romano-British site strategically commanding the River Stour. Between 1170 and 1214 Chilham Castle was in Royal ownership and King John used to stay here and hunt in the great wooded park. The present house was built by Sir Dudley Digges, Master of the Rolls to James I, between 1603–16, possibly to designs by Inigo Jones, using red bricks made from local clay for the house, garden walls, terraces and flights of steps.

The style of gardens at this time was essentially formal, and these were possibly laid out in the 1630s by John Tradescant the Elder, gardener to Charles I. The massive Holm Oak, *Quercus ilex* on the front lawn and the veteran avenue of Sweet Chestnuts and limes to the south-west of the house probably date from this period. The Colebrook family owned Chilham in the eighteenth century and they called in Lancelot 'Capability' Brown in the 1760s to advise on the improvement of the grounds in the current fashion. He is recorded as paying only a brief visit to Chilham for four days when he probably advised on the siting of the lake, the landscaping of the park and the introduction of the ha-ha. There have since been later additions to the gardens in Victorian and Edwardian periods and the recently restored rock garden near the lake is part of a wild garden and rock garden built in the 1920s. During the period 1918–30 Sir Edward Davis owned the castle and was responsible for a major restoration programme. He employed the architect Sir Hubert Baker to help with the restoration of the buildings. The lodge gates of the main entrance are his work. Sir Hubert was also the original architect of Port Lympne.

On a slight prominence overlooking the Stour Valley and protected from most directions except the south and south-west by mature tree planting, the village and castle lie on a ridge of alluvial soils overlying the chalk 165 ft above sea level. Rainfall and sunshine (see Withersdane).

A nineteenth-century planting of Common Limes, *Tilia* × *europaea*, with Beeches, *Fagus sylvatica*, and mostly Hornbeams, *Carpinus betulus*, form the block of the silent garden on the left as one enters the lime avenue. In autumn, the lime avenue from the main gates is pink with *Cyclamen hederifolium* (*neapolitanum*). All the wooded areas have a remarkable succession of spring bulbs.

The terraces and main borders date from the seventeenth century. Note the reputedly very ancient Judas Tree, *Cercis siliquastrum*, on the wall of the top terrace, possibly 300 years old and flowering every year in May. The three terrace borders were designed with colour themes in mind. The upper border is usually of blues and purples, the lower two being more mixed in effect. Planting against the red brick walls includes the Pomegranate, *Punica granatum*, Trumpet Vine, *Campsis* (*Tecoma*) *radicans*, and a few old roses.

The house walls are richly clothed with a great *Wisteria sinensis* on the east and south-east sides rising up to the topmost windows, and a magnificent Banksian Rose (*Rosa banksiae*), on the south and north walls with 'buttresses' of pyracanthas beneath, their berries turning a fiery orange in the autumn and early winter. The small courtyard on the west side is usually planted with scented annuals in the framework of small box hedges with a central pool and fountain.

The ha-ha is extremely effective, the break in the smooth lawns west of the house to the grazed pastures of the park being almost imperceptible. The trees on this lawn are ancient and stately, especially the great Holm Oak, *Quercus ilex*, the cedars, including *Cedrus atlantica glauca* and Tulip Tree, *Liriodendron tulipifera*. The topiary and curiously shaped yews on the south terrace lawns date from the early 1920s, although some of the oldest may be from the eighteenth century.

The rose garden lies to the south-east of the house below the silent garden. The walls of this garden are splendidly draped with wistaria, Trumpet Vine and a *Magnolia grandiflora* at the east end with massed *Fuchsia magellanica* varieties beneath. These fuchsias have been here for very many years, an indication of the sheltered microclimate.

The lake, rock and water garden is a more remote and relatively wild informal area. The lake is extensive and heavily fringed with trees and shrubs on its south and south-west margins, although recently much clearance has been effected. There is a small island on the north side of the lake on which may be seen the rusty but still surviving machinery of a horse-drawn water pump. Note the massive carp in the lake, and the waterfowl. The rock garden has been neglected for many years, but is now emerging from scrub and undergrowth. Note the 32–50 ft tall *Pinus parviflora, Chamaecyparis lawsoniana* 'Ellwoodii', *C. pisifera* 'Squarrosa' and others. In the woodland fringe near this rock garden is a massive Tulip Tree.

The 36 acres of garden are maintained at present (1976) by two full-time gardeners with some part-time help. This is clearly inadequate for the diversity and scale of activity really needed.

Cobham Hall

TQ 683 689 (Sheet 178) North Kent. One mile E of the village of Cobham and 4 miles W of Rochester, with signposted access off the M2/A2 London trunk road. A picnic site lies near the main gate. Owner: The Westwood Educational Trust. Cobham Hall is an Independent Girls' School. Open in the school vacations as a general rule, which in fact means one week at Easter and 3–4 days per week during the months of July and August. Consult the H.H.C.G. for current details.

A splendid late-Elizabethan red brick mansion, the former home of the Earls of Darnley, standing in a fine park, landscaped by Repton. There are some especially fine trees in the grounds around the house.

The old manor house of Cobham came into the possession of the de Cobham family early in the fifteenth century, but it was in 1580 that the construction of the present mansion was begun by William, tenth Lord Cobham, using red brick and stone. In 1603 the eleventh Lord Cobham fell into disfavour with the monarchy, his title was forfeited and work on the house stopped for 60 years, beginning again under the succeeding Dukes of Lennox using drawings prepared by Inigo Jones. The Blighs (the Earls of Darnley) made further additions to the house in the late eighteenth century and greatly extended the park. James Wyatt carried out much work on the interior of the enlarged house and in 1783 built the pyramidal mausoleum now standing in romantic decay on the south-east edge of the park, but this was never used as a burial place by the family. In 1790 the fourth Earl of Darnley commissioned Humphry Repton to carry out improvements to the park and during the summer of that year he produced one of his famous 'Red Books' for Cobham Hall. Repton included in his improvements 'enveloping the whole of the premises in plantations, shrubberies or gardens'. He also made the south terrace garden, a 'trellis' garden to the south-east, a menagerie on the far side of the original north terrace, an 'irregular modern flower garden' north of the kitchen garden, and, beyond all these, sunk walls, low fences, balustrading or steps to provide a 'nice gradation from the wilder scenery of the park to the more finished and dressed appearance of the gardens'. After 1800, Repton was joined in the work at Cobham by his son John. Three of the original lime avenues which stretched away from the house were removed, but the fourth, still remaining, 1,000 yards long and leading south-west to the village, was preserved. Throughout the park, wide grassy rides were introduced, winding through the plantations.

Looking back on his work here after 25 years, Repton was to feel a justifiable pride in the transformation. From the Red Books: 'The house is no longer a huge pile standing naked on a vast grazing ground', he wrote. 'Its walls are enriched with roses and jasmines; its apartments are perfumed with odours from flowers surrounding it on every side . . . all around is neatness, elegance and comfort.' His achievements were commemorated by a stone seat bearing his name which Lord Darnley had placed in a grove to the northern side of the house.

The Darnleys continued to flourish at Cobham in the nineteenth century, promoting the arts and sport. In 1882 the eighth earl, the Hon. Ivor Bligh, took an English cricket side to Australia and brought back the Ashes to be lodged in Cobham Hall. More additions to the gardens were probably made in the late nineteenth and early twentieth century. The Second World War created problems for the owners, and after a period of decline the house and park were acquired by the Ministry of Public Buildings and Works. After an extensive restoration programme the Hall was purchased by the Westwood Educational Trust for use as an independent public school for girls.

The Hall and its 150 acres of estate lie on the rather exposed chalk ridge of the North Downs some 320 ft above sea level in comparative remoteness and isolation in the attractive undulating downland countryside north of the River Medway so much beloved by Charles Dickens. The M2 now cuts perilously close to the eastern boundary (see the disused and decaying Brewer's Gate near the northbound carriageway) and the sprawling blight of Rochester is only halted short of the park by this modern communication barrier. The soils are mainly clay with flint over chalk. Plentiful woodlands surround the Hall giving valuable screening. Rainfall 27.5 inches.

Nothing remains today of Lord Cobham's Tudor garden. It was probably surrounded by a great hunting park, some of whose ancient oaks and sweet chestnuts still survive today. The great lime avenue of the Restoration style retained by Repton when he improved the park still survives, although renewed in some sections near the Hall itself. It runs west towards Cobham village.

The pleasure grounds today are still essentially those of Repton's making. The most whimsical and evocative lies at the eastern end of the main north terrace and is called the Chinese garden or Lady Darnley's garden. This could have been Repton's 'irregular modern flower garden' in his latter-day gardenesque style. Disposed around the edges of this green grassy glade are such features as the aviary (now in ruins), the cave or grotto, some unusual Dolman stones and the remnants of a long dried-up water garden of a later era. A farm dairy building dates from the early nineteenth century. The main north terrace carries some good specimens of the Judas Tree (*Cercis siliquastrum*) and the False Acacia (*Robinia pseudoacacia*), while the shrubberies around the house are enlivened with massed rhododendrons and azaleas, laburnums and flowering cherries. Great drifts of naturalized daffodils are spectacular in April.

A number of fine trees were planted by Repton and his successors in the grounds around the house, as can be seen by the aerial photograph (fig. 2). Some of these have reached a veteran age and size, and in 1965 many of them were measured by the great tree expert Mr Alan Mitchell. A selection of these is listed here to give visitors some idea of how large trees can grow even up on the North Downs where drifts of deeper soils occur. These trees are not labelled at present, but can be found with some diligence.

The school in fact possesses a most interesting album of photographs published in 1909 entitled *Cobham Hall Trees*, with good photographs of many of the trees still to be seen today.

At present the 50 acres of garden and 100 acres of estate are managed by a staff of three which, although adequate to keep the areas near the buildings well cared for, is well below the minimum that would be required to restore all the ground to the condition maintained by the Darnleys. In those days they employed large numbers of gardeners and additional staff for the woodlands and estate.

		1965	
		RECORDED HEIGHT	
COMMON NAME	BOTANICAL NAME	AND SPREAD	REMARKS
Deodar	*Cedrus deodara*	77 ft × 11 ft 4 in.	
Cedars of Lebanon	*Cedrus libani*	98 ft × 20 ft 6in.	
(4 specimens)	*Cedrus libani*	88 ft × 18 ft	
	Cedrus libani	80 ft × 18 ft 6 in.	
	Cedrus libani	80 ft × 18 ft	
Maidenhair Tree	*Ginkgo biloba*	67 ft	
Wellingtonia	*Sequoiadendron giganteum*	81 ft	
Norway Maple	*Acer platanoides*	63 ft	
Sycamore	*Acer pseudoplatanus*	110 ft	Tallest and finest recorded in Britain
Purple Beech	*Fagus sylvatica purpurea*	85 ft	
Willow Oak	*Quercus phellos*	82 ft × 12 ft	Tallest and finest known in UK
English Limes (2 specimens)	*Tilia × europaea*	98 ft 116 ft	

Crittenden House

TQ 656 435 (Sheet 188) West Kent. 5 miles SE of Tonbridge, 1½ miles N of Matfield, between the B2160 and B2015 that runs NE off main A21 Tonbridge–Hastings road. Owner: Mr B. Tompsett. Open mainly weekends throughout the spring and summer for charities, including the N.G.S. Full details published annually in the H.H.C.G.

A comparatively new post-war garden of about six acres, on acid soils, created out of an old farmstead since 1956. This and the old ponds left by the medieval iron workings provide a fine setting for the rich collection of trees and shrubs and many excellent plant associations for spring and early summer display. All year round interest is an important aspect of the gardens at Crittenden.

The early seventeenth century farmhouse and some four acres of land were acquired by Mr Ben Tompsett in 1955. To quote Mr Tompsett, 'The old farmhouse was barely visible behind a hedge and through a mass of bushes. It had a small lawn in front, confined by a privet hedge, an impoverished kitchen garden at the side and a neglected apple orchard at the back, bounded on the east by a belt of woodland.' Mr Tompsett quickly realized the potential of this site and immediately began the task of turning the wilderness into a garden. A tractor and winch, and even explosives, were used to remove the largest unwanted trees. The background and shelter provided by the coppice and old orchard he wisely left and these have proved invaluable in creating the microclimate and character of the garden. Great care was also taken to preserve the best of the existing native flora, such as primroses, bluebells, foxgloves, spotted orchid, bugle, campion and wild roses and honeysuckles on the trees. The land was then drained where necessary and to increase the depth and quality of soil in some areas, carefully selected top soil was imported from local sources. A landscape gardener was also consulted and the late Mr F.G.T. Manners helped with the design of the main layout. The shapes of the borders, the careful planning of a vista from each window, the formal rose garden and the introduction of the large boulders of local sandstone on either side of the grassy slope down to the front main porch are largely his ideas.

Planting continued over a period of several years, and to add maturity and immediate effects, Mr Tompsett successfully moved a number of large trees and shrubs such as magnolias, birches and even *Acer griseum*. Fifteen years after the purchase of Crittenden, Mr Tompsett was able to give an excellent account of the completed garden in the R.H.S. Journal of February 1960 (vol. LXXXV, Part 2).

Crittenden lies in the undulating fruit and hop growing district of the High Weald of west Kent. The house and garden lie on a small brow facing south-west and about 165 ft above sea level. There is slight exposure to the south-west in the upper part of the garden, but in general the setting is enclosed, intimate and exotic. Rainfall is around 31 inches per annum with daily sunshine average of 4 hrs. The soils are particularly interesting. In the upper part of the garden are acid, well-drained Tunbridge Wells sands, whereas the lower part is Wadhurst clay rich in iron ore. The pools are the result of old iron-ore workings.

The style of Crittenden is essentially a post-war English informal plantsman's garden dominated by shrubs, exotic trees and some perennials, yet with strong design qualities. The carefully restored, listed, Kent brick and tile farmhouse and its associated out-buildings sit comfortably in the Weald landscape and the garden seems to flow into the countryside with no harsh breaks. The garden has been planned on labour-saving lines with hedges largely eliminated, the minimum of grass edges, and no forking-over of beds, which are top-dressed with peat and planted with permanent cover plants. Few annuals and the minimum of biennials are used. The natural and existing features on the site when acquired have been retained and incorporated into the scheme. The fine copse and shelter belt in the north-east corner with its ash, Field Maples, hollies and even a fine Wild Service Tree, *Sorbus torminalis*, offers a shady wooded habitat. The three ponds with their great sculptured rocks and lush planting are very important features in the garden.

Around the house the wide stretch of paving creates interesting planted areas against the building. *Crinum*, *Agapanthus* and *Nerine* grow along the south side. There is also a small intimate formal garden with thymes, rock roses, *Arabis*, aubrietias, stonecrops and prostrate species of *Campanula* spilling over the stones. The rose walk is planted with the fine dark red rose variety 'National Trust'. At the top of the rose garden is a stone seat with statuary backed by shrubs and herbaceous planting. Drifts of the bright yellow self-seeding annual *Limnanthes douglasii* add to the charm of the formal garden in late spring. Good clumps of *Iris* 'Pacific Hybrids' flourish in the rose garden. On the house, clematis, *Fremontodendron* 'California Glory' and the rose 'Madame Grégoire Staechelin' make a fine mixture. The lowest and largest of the ponds have been well planted with strong foliage and textural plants. Massed prostrate junipers, weeping birches, glossy-leaved *Hosta spp.* and the grey foliage of *Phlomis fruticosa*, Jerusalem Sage and many other shrubs should be noted here. From the south side of the pool, a fine reflection of house, plants and sky makes a pleasing composition.

In the upper acid soil areas are bold groups of flowering trees and rhododendrons. At one time Mr Tompsett had over 70 species and 130 varieties of rhododendrons but he has tended to be more selective in recent years to emphasize the softer colours and good foliage. This theme has indeed been followed in much of the planting since the celebrated evenings of *Son et Lumière* (for which Crittenden has quite a reputation) drew Mr Tompsett's attention to the subtle effect of nocturnal illumination on different types of foliage and textures.

Two good associations for such effects are *Magnolia × soulangiana* 'Rustica Rubra', *Rhododendron* (Azalea) *luteum*, Azalea 'Orange Flame' and a compact *Magnolia parviflora* – from spring to autumn this group has attractive shape and colour; and the rich-purple-leaved hazel *Corylus maxima* 'Purpurea', the double white *Philadelphus* 'Boule de Neige', the red floribunda rose 'Elaine', the lacy purple-leaved *Acer palmatum* 'Atropurpureum' and the perpetual yellow-flowered *Potentilla fruticosa* 'Katherine Dykes'.

Other special trees to note: the golden-leaved *Acer cappadocicum* to the south-west of the house measures 35–50 ft; a fine young Handkerchief Tree (*Davidia involucrata*) that flowers freely for a tree of such comparative youth; and among the flowering crab and cherry collection there is the outstanding *Malus* 'Crittenden', a seedling found here, which has proved to be one of the best ornamental small trees for the garden – it has pale pink apple blossom, a pendulous habit, and very persistent bright red fruits that look like large glistening cherries in late autumn and hang throughout the winter. Look also for the May-flowering Judas Tree, *Cercis siliquastrum*, the August-flowering *Eucryphia × nymansensis* 'Nymansay' and the various ornamental thorns such as *Crataegus tanacetifolia* and *C. × lavellei* (*carrierei*).

The herb layer and bulbous plantings are exciting too, from the drift of early Narcissus 'February Gold' in particular, and early *Crocus* like *C. tomasinianus*, *Anemone blanda* and bluebells to the great variety of *Lilium* species and hybrids in which Mr Tompsett has long been interested. Autumn colours of the *Colchicum* genus follow in August and September. In the pools there is scope for waterside planting using Asiatic May-flowering primulas, the dramatic-foliaged rhubarb *Rheum palmatum*, and *Rodgersia* species. This latter group looks splendid when lit up at night and I can recommend a tour round this garden after dark after several sherries and a good dinner; a whole new dimension in planting design emerges!

The six acres are managed entirely by the owner with the help of one part-time man for two or three hours per week. Herbicides are used on the paths and edges but not on any planted area due to the diversity of bulbs and other sensitive species. Mr Tompsett finds the pruning back of shrubs like the brooms immediately after flowering promotes longevity and good form.

Emmetts Garden

TQ 477 525 (Sheet 188) West Kent. 2 miles S of Brasted, 1 mile NW of
Ide Hill, 6 miles SW of Sevenoaks (not easy to find). The best route is
probably on the B2042 Riverhead–Ide Hill road, turn right in Ide Hill.
Owner: The National Trust. Open several days a week during the summer
season, but see H.H.C.G.

A remote and unusual garden of shrubs and trees, many of them rare
and of great maturity.

The large nineteenth-century house with its garden and estate was
purchased in 1893 by the Lubbock family. Some of the present plants
survive from an earlier period c.1870 when many good plants were
introduced. Many of the unusual shrubs and trees came from the sale
of the great Veitch Nursery collection in 1907. The garden and estate
(not the house) were left to the Trust in 1948 and first opened to the
public in 1966. The estate comprises over 100 acres of woodland,
80 acres of farmland and some four-and-a-half acres of garden. The
rich woodland and the acid soil are the home of the increasingly rare
wood ant known locally as 'Emmetts', which could be the derivation
of the name.

This is one of several gardens, including Chartwell only a mile or
so away, lying high up (590 ft) on the great Upper Greensand Ridge.
The acidic sandy loams, comparatively high rainfall (over 31.5
inches) and the presence of springs give a fine scenery and landscape
of wooded hills with magnificent views to the south and north from
the ridge.

The garden comprises two main parts, divided by the approach road
to the car park and house. The garden to the north of the road was
once contiguous with the gardens of the house (which is private)
standing nearby. The area has an interesting detailed collection of low
shrubs and conifers, with winding grass paths, and represents the
first, much older, garden dating from the 1860–70 period. Part of the
area is an old rock garden and former pond. Dwarf *Rhododendron* species,
and other Ericaceous shrubs, some newly planted, thrive in this acid
leafy soil, with massive 80-year-old specimens of azaleas, especially
Rhododendron obtusum 'Amoenum' (*Azalea amoena*), Japanese Maples
and a particularly fine *Chamaecyparis lawsoniana* 'Nana Compacta'.
Spectacular in flower here are venerable plants of *Magnolia stellata*,
Magnolia denudata and the American Mountain Laurel, *Kalmia latifolia*.

This area was mentioned by William Robinson in the 1870s since it was created on the lines of his wild garden. In the wetter hollow of the old rock garden are many waterside plants and particularly noteworthy is the rare Royal Fern species *Osmunda claytoniana*. Beside the house is a fine Blue Cedar, *Cedrus atlantica glauca*, over 100 years old, and the *Sequoiadendron giganteum*, Wellingtonia, soaring to over 100 ft, a landmark that can be seen from as far away as Crowborough Hill and many other places in the Weald. (Note: this area is not open to the public.) The garden south of the road takes the form of a pleasant informal arboretum of groups of shrubs and trees in lightly mown grass. The casual visitor and family groups can stroll through this pleasant place and relax in the glades and grassy banks, while plantsmen and enthusiasts can have an exciting time studying the many fine and unusual trees and shrubs to be found here. Many of these are labelled. A summary only of the principal plants to be found in this area is given here. The majority of these are acid-soil-loving plants.

Acanthopanax ricinifolius (now *Kalopanax pictus*). An exceptionally large specimen of this very unusual tree of the ivy family *Araliaceae*. It has large, lustrous, 5–7-lobed maple-like leaves, prickly branches and large flat clusters of white flowers in autumn. Very few reach this size of 65 ft.

Davidia involucrata, Handkerchief Tree. A fine specimen bearing its white, pendulous 'handkerchiefs' in May and June. *D. vilmoriniana* also growing here is similar, but the tree has a single stem and glaucous leaves.

Liriodendron tulipifera, Tulip Tree. A fine tree up to 82 ft here.

Cercidiphyllum japonicum Two fine specimens of this elegant Japanese tree, which can colour well in the autumn. These at Emmetts, however, seldom produce good autumn colour.

Acer. There are a number of fine maple specimens, including some unusual species. The Japanese Maples, *A. palmatum*, as green- or purple-leaved forms are well represented, but note also *A. circinatum* the Vine Maple, its circular leaves prettily tinted in summer and turning orange and crimson in autumn; *A. henryi* with leaves scarcely lobed, a fine specimen and magnificent in the autumn; *A. davidii*, a Chinese, 'snake bark' species, with conspicuous green or reddish fruits – unfortunately the specimen here is suffering from Honey Fungus (*Armillaria mellea*) infection, a serious disease of many woodland and arboretum collections in this country. Control is difficult.

Parrotia persica, a spreading, low-growing tree from Persia, its leaves turning crimson and gold in autumn. This specimen is about 60 years old.

Styrax japonica, Japanese Snowbell. A beautiful, graceful small tree whose arching branches are clustered with pendular white bells in June. Somewhat similar are the flowers of *Halesia carolina*, the North American Snowdrop Tree. There is a fine 30–50 ft specimen here, a graceful, spreading tree flowering in mid-May.

The flowering dogwoods. A number of magnificent specimens of this group of *Cornus* can be seen here, especially *C. kousa* (possibly the best specimens in the UK, according to G. Thomas) and *C. kousa chinensis* and the taller-growing *C. controversa* with white or creamy-flowered bracts in May. Architectural habit and good autumn colour are some of the fine qualities of these dogwoods.

Other interesting trees include a veteran gnarled *Laburnum alpinum*, the Scotch Laburnum; some good Asiatic *Sorbus* species, especially *S. vilmorinii*; and of interest to propagators a tree of the popular pink cherry *Prunus* 'Kanzan' near the road growing on its own roots. This plant was raised from a hardwood cutting 10–15 years ago. These are normally grafted on to wild cherry stocks.

Flowering shrubs include a massive mound, 23 ft across, of the alpine *Rhododendron ferrugineum* near the entrance gate. This plant is from the original garden and is probably 80 years old; and some more good species of *Magnolia*, *Rhododendron*, *Pieris*, *Hydrangea* and *Camellia*. Search for the unusual Fishtail Camellia, *C.* × *williamsii*, 'C.F. Coates', a deep pink, single variety whose leaves have a peculiar three-lobed apex like a fish's tail; the scented *Abelia triflora*, regrettably all too rare in cultivation; *Cotinus coggygria*, *Eucryphia* (a particularly fine plant of *E. cordifolia*), and many more besides. In spring the whole area is flecked with spring bulbs, including the Dog's-Tooth Violets, *Erythronium dens-canis*, and natural bluebells. Mr Lubbock also records in his garden notes of 1917 the planting of many Australian plants. Most of these have since gone. *Eucalyptus* species have been replanted since and several are growing here.

Visitors should remember that these four-and-a-half acre gardens are managed virtually by one man alone, Mr C.S. Joy, the head gardener, who believes in regular mulching of all plants, and in his hands very few suffered severely from the great summer drought of 1976. Honey Fungus is the main disease problem of this garden, attacking the older trees in particular.

Godinton Park

TR 985 438 (Sheet 189) East Kent. Ashford ½ mile NW of town W off the A20 London–Folkestone trunk road. Owner: A. Wyndham Green. Open most Sunday afternoons from June–September, including the house, and some Bank Holidays. For current details see H.H.C.G.

A romantic red-brick part-Jacobean gabled house standing in a secluded well-timbered park quite close to the expanding town of Ashford. The garden is largely Edwardian and has been developed since then, with topiary gardens, fine trees and a blend of formal and informal planting.

The present park of over 250 acres is undoubtedly medieval or even earlier, with many ancient oaks and sweet chestnuts to the south and south-west of the house. The oldest oak mentioned in Domesday fell on the eventful date of 3 September 1939 (the outbreak of World War II) and still lies as a decaying skeleton near the house.

The house was enlarged by the Toke family in the early seventeenth century in the Flemish-gabled style. Few records of the park survive, but it is known that towards the close of the eighteenth century a certain Mr Driver was employed to lay out shrubberies and deal with the park 'in the improved taste' of that time. Much of his tree planting and some of the shrubberies still survive in the wild garden (12) and around the house. Until the early twentieth century the park appears to have swept up to the very walls of the house itself with no indication of a ha-ha or enclosed formal features.

The Ashley Dodd family purchased Godinton in 1896 and in 1902 called in the architect and garden architect Sir Reginald Blomfield (1856–1942) to renovate the house and create a garden around it. Blomfield was a great exponent of the formal style of garden and he therefore enclosed an area of about 10–12 acres in the form of a large rectangle, with the house located on its north side. His boundaries were established with solid yew hedges planted between 1902–6, which later were trained into the gables and buttresses, echoing the lines of the house. These hedges look magnificent today, 70 years after planting. He also created a formal topiary plat of box in the south-east corner, presided over by the fine statue of Pan (3). (His layout is shown on the plan.) The main axis of the garden still runs south-west from this statue. He enlarged an existing pond into a large formal pool (6), judging by the photographs of it in *Country Life* of 11 May 1907.

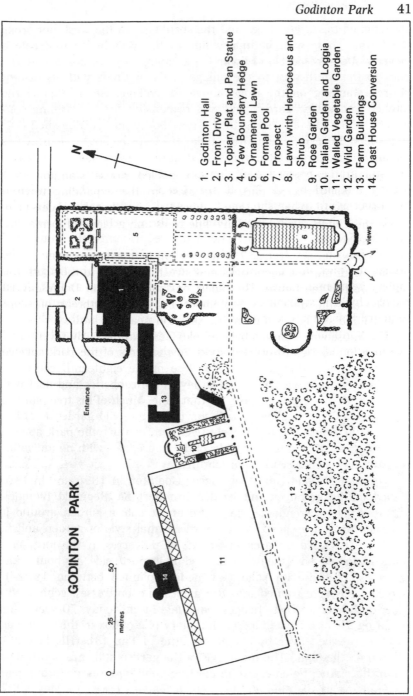

GODINTON PARK

1. Godinton Hall
2. Front Drive
3. Topiary Plat and Pan Statue
4. Yew Boundary Hedge
5. Ornamental Lawn
6. Formal Pool
7. Prospect
8. Lawn with Herbaceous and Shrub
9. Rose Garden
10. Italian Garden and Loggia
11. Walled Vegetable Garden
12. Wild Garden
13. Farm Buildings
14. Oast House Conversion

He retained the largest trees and the shrubbery to the west, but broke the formal south-west boundary line of the yew hedge to create a cleverly sited prospect or belvoir (7) enabling one to look across the park to the south-west to the village of Great Chart with its distant church standing on the ridge above the village. He redesigned the kitchen and walled garden and was responsible for a charming conversion of the old oast house into a new bothy and potting-shed (14) that still looks very contemporary today. In 1916 he produced drawings for an Italian garden near the walled garden, the originals of which are still in the possession of the present owner. His designs were greatly modified by Mr Wyndham Green's grandmother, the Hon. Mrs Bruce Ward, when she rebuilt this garden in the early 1920s (10).

The last phase in the development of the garden at Godinton was after the Second World War. The Army requisitioned the house and property during the war. Although no real damage was done to the house, the park and gardens became neglected, only the hedges and topiary being maintained. The lawns were ploughed up and Mr Green recalls chickens swarming everywhere! All the previous statuary was removed before the occupation to a safe hiding-place in the cellars.

Mr Wyndham Green began a slow process of restoration and modification of the Edwardian design in the early 1950s. He replaced

the neglected grass banks in front of the house with effective brick retaining walls offering good scope for planting. He partially enclosed the pool with willows and a hedge and introduced marginal plants. He planted the small avenue of whitebeams (*Sorbus aria*) and cherries along the gravel drive leading to the prospect, and restored the rose garden using good varieties of red and pink floribundas associated with an attractive blend of pinks, grey foliage and some summer annuals. The long border beside the kitchen-garden wall he softened and re-shaped, planting for foliage and texture, using some ideas and planting themes from Great Dixter.

Godinton is in the upper valley of the Great Stour River that flows through the park. The house stands on a former river terrace. Soils are heavy, weald-clays and alluvial silts. Climate (see Withersdane).

The wild garden (12) is particularly attractive in the spring. For the last century or more bulbs have been naturalized here, and there is now a rich and delightful tapestry of early flowers from March onwards, including, in order of appearance, aconites, *Cyclamen repandum*, snowdrops, *Scilla*, *Chionodoxa*, *Crocus*, Dog's-Tooth Violets, *Fritillaria* and many of the older daffodil varieties, especially 'Golden Spur', 'Emperor' and 'Empress', planted by Mr Wyndham Green's grandfather. Later in the year, primroses and wild strawberries abound in the grass, and in the early autumn *Cyclamen hederifolium* (*neapolitanum*) flecks the turf with pale pink. The management of this area is very critical, being cut in late June with a hay-mower cutter-bar and possibly again in October. There are some especially fine trees in this wild garden.

The remaining features in the garden have been mostly referred to in the previous historical section and are shown on the plan. The trees in the park are also noteworthy, there being an exceptionally large number, many still in excellent health and vigour. Note the large group of Sweet Chestnuts, *Castanea sativa*, on the left as one approaches the house. One of these chestnuts is mentioned in *The Guinness Book of Records* as being the largest in the UK. Other trees include fine examples of London Plane, *Platanus × hispanica*, Red Oak, *Quercus rubra*, Tulip Tree, *Liriodendron tulipifera*, Engliah Oak, limes, Red Horse Chestnut, beeches, walnuts, Sycamore, Hornbeam, maples, red thorns and a fine weeping silver birch, *Betula pendula* (*alba*) 'Tristis'. Most of the magnificent elms that once flanked the park on the Ashford side have now been felled due to Dutch Elm disease.

The 12 acres of garden are at present managed by two full-time gardeners with considerable help and direction from the owner. It normally takes two men over one month to cut the hedges alone!

Godmersham Park

TR 064 510 (Sheet 179) East Kent. Close to the village of Godmersham. 12 miles W of Canterbury, 6 miles E of Ashford. Just N of A28 in a very secluded lay-by that used to be the old road through the Stour valley. Owner: Mrs K. Tritton. Open one or two Sunday afternoons only in spring or early summer for the N.G.S.

A fine eighteenth-century house and park in the beautiful valley of the River Stour between Canterbury and Ashford. A series of walled gardens offer good examples of styles and planting of the pre-Second World War era, with exceptionally well-managed wall fruit and climbers. Unfortunately opening times are very limited indeed.

An ancient site associated with the old Norman monastic church, the now demolished twelfth-century Monks Grange and the earlier Saxon derivation of the name from Godmaer's Ham. An Elizabethan house once stood on the site of the present house, which was built in 1732 by Thomas May Knight. Note his arms on the gate piers and Coade Stone urns dated 1793. Thomas Knight II adopted as his son Edward Austen (Jane Austen's brother). He lived there with his family from this time under the name of Edward Austen Knight and Jane was a regular visitor to the house. She loved the park and is reputed to have written some of her novels here. Later, in the nineteenth century, Godmersham suffered from neglect and the lack of responsible owners.

In 1935 it was purchased by Mr and Mrs Robert Tritton and with the help of the architect Mr Walter Sorrell they embarked on an extensive programme of reconstruction and renovation. New gardens were made in the kitchen gardens to the south-west of the house, including a sumptuous swimming-pool garden with borders designed and planted by the garden designer Mrs Norah Lindsay. An Italian loggia was made at the east end. Little alteration has taken place since that time.

The house and garden are associated with some 3,000 acres of estate and farmland that surround the property. The clear, chalk stream of the River Stour flows through the estate and the North Downs sweep away dramatically to the west and south in the broad valley. There is excellent shelter for the gardens from tree planting to the south-west, west, north-west and north. Soils are alkaline, light loams of the river valley. Rainfall and sunshine see Withersdane.

There are two contrasting styles and elements at Godmersham.

First, the broad expansive parkland setting with the fine house, the mature specimens, groups and belts of trees, the river and the valley and downland landscape, and the classical temple as a focal feature due west of the house; the main tree species to note being the magnificent Turkey Oaks, *Quercus cerris*, on the north-east lawns associated with limes, planes, sycamores and beeches. Secondly, the more enclosed, detailed and intimate walled gardens with good traditional borders, well-managed but rather over-mature wall plants and fruit trees. The walled gardens are (*a*) the kitchen garden, still quite well maintained (1976) with its fine range of old glasshouses and frames, cut flowers and fruits (peaches, apricots) and early vegetables in the frames. (*b*) the tennis court garden leading off from the kitchen garden; the .tennis courts are cleverly concealed by flanking borders of shrubs, perennials and climbers on the netting surround. (*c*) a topiary and rose garden with impressive and well-maintained hedges and sculptured yew blocks enclosing intricate and now rather 'tired' borders of roses. (*d*) the swimming pool garden, a splendid affair with complete protection on the cold north and west sides from great yew hedges and thickets and the high walls to the south and east. There is the fine, boldly planted border on the south side designed by Norah Lindsay; also the loggia with paved terrace and tubs and urns of such exotics as Pomegranate; Lemon Verbena, *Lippia citriodora*; and Myrtle, *Myrtus communis*. Some good climbers here, and two large *Magnolia grandiflora* on either side of the loggia to accentuate the southern European delusion in this garden.

Through tall wrought-iron gates one suddenly emerges into the grassy expanse of the great lawn west of the house and the wide views of the downs and woods beyond the park. The temple lies to the west, approached by a broad, mown grass path. The extensive area of long grass here is thickly naturalized with daffodils. To the north of the house is an effective patio and pool garden. The walls of the entrance drive have an interesting blend of well-managed planting, including *Camellia, Cotoneaster, Vitis*, Morello Cherries, plums and other fruits.

A high standard is still achieved by the staff of five under the able and experienced direction of the head gardener, Mr Elgar. He has been at Godmersham for many years and his wealth of experience and intimate knowledge of the gardens cannot easily be replaced.

Goodnestone Park

TR 255 545 (Sheet 179) East Kent, 2 miles S of Wingham, 9 miles E of Canterbury, close to the village of Goodnestone. A good map is helpful in finding this rather secluded park (Pronunciation 'Gunston'.) Owner: Lord and Lady FitzWalter. Open several Sunday afternoons in late spring and early summer for the N.G.S. (Details in the 'Yellow Book'.)

A remote romantic park and series of 'old-fashioned' gardens around the eighteenth-century classical house and its walled enclosures. A cordial personal welcome from the owners' family and their friends is an additional pleasure to the visitor here.

Much of the present house was built in 1709 by Sir Brook Bridges on the site of an earlier house. Later, Jane Austen's brother, Edward Austen Knight of Godmersham, married the daughter of the second Baron Bridges. In 1959 a serious fire destroyed the two top floors of the house.

Goodnestone Park covers some 3,000 acres of parkland and farms generally at about 165 ft above sea level in this rather flat and gently undulating open agricultural countryside of east Kent. The soils here are mostly alkaline light to medium loams overlying the chalk that underlies much of the east Kent peninsula. In the woodland area to the north of the house the soils are locally more acidic, allowing the growth of some rhododendrons. Shelter is provided by woodland and tree belts from the north and north-west and the walls of the enclosed gardens themselves. The front terraces are rather exposed to the south and south-west. Rainfall 24.6–25.6 inches. Sunshine 4.5 hrs.

There are probably three main periods of gardening styles and planting to look for here. First, the surviving elements of the landscape planting and layout contemporary with the eighteenth-century house: the fine parkland trees, the Holm Oaks, *Quercus ilex*, in particular beside the house, and the rather overmature cedars to the north; the terraced and walled gardens, and the more distant parkland and woodlands. Secondly, the remnants of an important garden planting period from 1914–20 undertaken by the aunt of the present Lord FitzWalter. She planted a number of unusual trees and shrubs, notable of which are the cut leaved *Alnus glutinosa* 'Imperialis' close to the front portico of the house, the mature wall-climbers such as *Abelia triflora* (deliciously scented in mid-summer) and *Jasminum × stephanense*, and in the woodland unusual trees such as *Nothofagus*. Finally, the new gardens and plantings over the last 10–15 years by Lord and Lady FitzWalter and their head gardener, Mr Wellard, who has concentrated on creating a series of delightful old-world garden and plant collections with an especial emphasis on old roses, pinks, and grey foliage perennials.

The front lawns and terraces are south-facing with panoramic views across the park. This area is still being re-designed. A new effective foliage and mixed border in front of the yew hedge to the west of the house has a blend of roses, old-fashioned pinks, and grey and blue foliage including *Ballota*, *Ruta* and *Senecio* 'Sunshine' (*greyii*). The north drive, lawns and woodland area – a sweeping circular drive to the main portico of the house is backed to the north-west with amphitheatre-like terraces of grass and flights of steps leading away to the tennis courts. On the lawn immediately to the north-east of the house is a fine specimen of the Smoke Bush *Cotinus coggygria*, 'disappearing' in a haze of pinky buff 'smoke' of inflorescences in July, followed by good autumn colour. Nearby is a fine tree of the winter-flowering cherry *Prunus subhirtella* 'Autumnalis'. The cut-leaf alder lies behind these plants. The rugged, rather battered cedars (1939–45 war damage!) dominate the lawn on the way to the woodland area. A most effective rose walk has been created by Lady FitzWalter, linking the house with the woodland garden. Here old-fashioned roses are trained on pillars in a narrow border mass-planted with a fine collection of pinks. This border looks splendid in mid-June. The woodland area is still being reclaimed and re-planted. It offers a pleasant cool contrast from the rest of the garden.

The walled gardens are probably the most attractive and nostalgic features of Goodnestone, enhanced by the distant glimpse through a series of ancient brick archways of the old grey tower of Goodnestone church. The luxuriant wall plants are a magnificent feature of these walls and mention has already been made of the 50-year-old *Abelia triflora* (why is this plant not grown more today?), jasmines and other climbers. The tumbling masses of old roses are superb here in June, and other climbers include the mauve *Solanum jasminoides*, several vines *Vitis spp.*, honeysuckles *Lonicera spp.* and clematis. New borders selected by Lady FitzWalter have been made in this area with sensitive and delightful plant association, perfectly in keeping with the setting and atmosphere of the place.

The owners have no illusions over the maintenance problem of this large garden and estate and a great deal of restoration work still lies ahead. With one full-time gardener, one part-time, and what help the family are able to give, a realistic and appropriate standard of upkeep is achieved for most areas of the gardens. In fact, the achievement with such a limited staff (there used to be five full-time gardeners here) is very commendable.

The Grange

807 326 (Sheet 188) West Kent. Benenden (close to the church). 8 miles W of Tenterden, 7 miles E of Goudhurst. Owner: Captain Collingwood Ingram. Open usually two or three Sunday afternoons in April for the N.G.S. to coincide with the main displays of flowering cherries, magnolias and many other unusual trees and shrubs.

A medium-sized, unusual garden of an informal, woodland and shrubbery type with a large and extraordinary collection of trees and shrubs, of especial interest and fascination to the plantsmen and knowledgeable gardeners, representing a lifetime's collecting and hybridizing by this famous horticulturist. Unfortunately very few plants are labelled.

The large, rather gaunt house was formerly the home of Lord Cranbrook, who built the Grange about 1898 in open farmland, planting some trees around the house for shelter. The magnificent eucalyptus near the house was planted at this time. Captain Collingwood Ingram bought the house in 1919 and found it 'to all intents and purposes without a garden'. He made an immediate start on the first part of the garden on the south-west side of the house, and much of the finest tree planting here dates from the early 1920s. The garden gradually grew in size and interest, and being a passionate and highly energetic traveller, explorer and plant-hunter, Captain Ingram brought back to this garden a steady stream of unusual plants from many countries of the world, some of them new species to cultivation. The visitor should read his book, *A Garden of Memories*,* before, or certainly after, visiting this garden.

The garden lies at about 230 ft above sea level in the high weald. Shelter is provided by an abundance of mature planting, particularly to the north-west and north and very favourable conditions are created in the woodland-type glades created over the last 50 years.

* Collingwood Ingram, *A Garden of Memories*, H.F. & G. Witherby, 1970.

Soils are of the acidic fertile wealden-clay loams, producing fine growth of many woody plants. Rainfall average over 33 inches.

The style of the garden is essentially very informal. To quote Captain Ingram from *A Garden of Memories*:

'From the outset I kept in mind the realization that in a purely natural landscape there is neither precise symmetry nor any perfectly straight lines – even the sea's horizon is in fact slightly curved! From the start my aim was to reduce to an absolute minimum the unavoidable artificiality of a man-made pleasaunce destined to contain not only native, but mainly exotic, trees and shrubs. To achieve that aim I endeavoured to reproduce as nearly as possibly a succession of *sylvan glades* . . . these all had one thing in common, each was designed to terminate at its furthest end in a sharp bend, the purpose being to close every vista in order to intrigue the eye and to make a stranger wonder what new treasures awaited him round the hidden corner.

Fifty years later one can judge the success of these aims and appreciate the sense of the planning. There are, broadly speaking, four main areas to the garden which have differences in quality and planting: the main lawns, shrubberies and tree specimens around the house; the shrubbery and woodland garden; the orchard; and the approach drive area. However, there is such a profusion of plants throughout the garden that without a conducted tour by the owner himself (a fascinating experience) the precise location and description of all the plants would need a book in itself. This account therefore concentrates on some of the more unusual and outstanding groups of plants. The *Eucalyptus* by the house, now over 80 years old, is thought to be of a hybrid of the name *E.* × *whittinghamensis*. It has survived the many very cold winters of the century. Its height in March 1976 was measured at over 80 ft. The flowering cherry collection – Captain Ingram has had a life-long interest in cherries that began with his visits to Japan 70 years ago. He earned the nickname 'Cherry Ingram' as a result, and is the author of *Ornamental Cherries*,* which has been the standard work on the subject ever since. Most of the cherries at the Grange are now between 30 and 50 years old and some are becoming over-mature. Others have already been grubbed. The longevity of cherries is of great interest to the owner, who has concluded that for general purposes a life span of between 40 and 50 years is about the maximum for many of them. The visitor should look for the following outstanding

* Collingwood Ingram, *Ornamental Cherries, Country Life*, 1948.

hybrids and species, hopefully flowering well in April, provided the bullfinches have not ravaged the buds:

Prunus 'Kanzan'. A number of slightly different forms of this very popular variety are still growing well at Benenden, although many of them aré now nearly 50 years old. According to Captain Ingram this variety is not popular in Japan.

Prunus 'Tai Haku'. Captain Ingram's first choice of all single white-flowered ornamental cherries. There are many fine mature trees of this lovely variety still looking very healthy and vigorous.

Prunus serrulata spontanea, 'Japanese Hill Cherry'. A very popular and long-lived variety in Japan, a prototype of most of the hybrid cherries from Japan with single white or pinkish flowers, rich coppery red young foliage and a graceful spreading habit.

Prunus 'Kursar'. Raised at Benenden by Captain Ingram and a fine small tree. It is very early-flowering, in March or early April, flowers rich deep pink with reddish bronze foliage. The autumn colours are good.

The *Malus* collection, ornamental 'crabs'. Another group of flowering trees to attract Collingwood Ingram's attention. There are many unusual species here over 40 years old. On the main lawn is a selected gnarled and very attractive fine-flowering form of the Japanese Crab, the most lovely white-flowered small *Malus floribunda*, a mass of pink-budded, pale flowers in April, followed in autumn by masses of tiny red fruits. There is also a very tall and rare *Malus baccata mandschurica*.

Other unusual trees to be found include tall specimens of *Nothofagus dombeyi* and *N. obliqua* (75 ft) planted in 1920, some exceptionally fine eastern European pears (a spectacular plant of *Pyrus amygdaliformis* with creamy-white flowers in April, and silvery willow-like leaves); many rhododendrons and azaleas, a real 'catchplant' in one of the glades is a large mound of the willow-leaved evergreen azalea, *Rhododendron macrosepalum* 'Linearifolium', long cultivated in Japan; many different magnolias; a good collection of *Berberis*, particularly of the evergreen Asiatic species, and the rare Chilean Holly-leaved Barberry *Berberis ilicifolia*. Spring bulbs abound also, and here again there are unusual forms of hardy cyclamen, especially *C. repandum*; several rich blue *Iris histrioides* hybrids; and groups of *Scilla*, *Narcissus* and *Fritillaria*. There is also a fine collection of *Hepatica*.

Mid-April is usually an ideal time to visit the Grange and if there is a chance to meet Captain Collingwood Ingram and have a conducted tour of the gardens this will indeed be rewarding for those fortunate enough to enjoy this experience. The garden is maintained very effectively, mostly by Captain Ingram and one other gardener.

Great Comp

TQ 633 566 (Sheet 188) Mid Kent. 8 miles W of Maidstone, 2 miles E of Borough Green, off B2016 that leaves the A20 at Wrotham Heath. Owner: Mr and Mrs R. Cameron. Open Fridays and Sundays from mid-May–mid-October for the N.G.C. and G.S. Teas are available.

An outstanding example of a large informal private garden developed over the last 20 years by the present owners on the modern concept of bold, effective planting associations, abundant ground cover and rationalized maintenance.

Great Comp is a seventeenth-century house, the name being derived from the Saxon word for fortification. Some minor modifications have taken place in recent years. A fine garden apparently existed here before the First World War, and the larger trees to the north-west of the house are certainly of this period or even earlier. The Camerons bought the house in 1957 with four-and-a-half acres of garden, rough woodland and paddock, to which they have since added a further 2 acres or so bought in 1962. Most of the gardens have been developed from 1958 onwards.

In the Lower Greensand fruit-growing belt between the chalk downs and the Weald, the garden lies some 360 ft above sea level on a gentle south-east slope. Mature limes and other trees give shelter and protection from the west, north-west and north and young permanent planting of conifers and broad-leaved trees like oak, birch and maple are having a significant effect on the microclimate. Rainfall is about 29.5 inches. Sunshine 4.25 hrs. Spring frosts are liable to be damaging to emerging new growth of many shrubs and the devastating frost of 29 April 1976 will be long remembered by the Camerons. The damage was heartbreaking and aggravated by the long and memorable drought that followed. Soils are essentially light, fertile acidic loams of the Hythe, Sandgate and Folkestone beds that all occur on the site. There is a distinct graduation from light sandy, free-draining soils on the top of the garden to rather deeper, moister soils in the south-west corner. An intensive and very thorough programme of soil improvement has been carried out by the Camerons.

This is a large garden created in the tradition of the English post-war plantsman's style with strong influences of Jekyll and Robinson and, more recently, the writings of Charles Eley, Graham Thomas, Christopher Lloyd and also the gardens of Hidcote, Sissinghurst, Wisley and many others. To quote the Camerons, 'The plan of the present garden grew from the existing walls, paths, hedges and mature trees. The design has developed over the years with few plans on paper. It has been carried out by the owners themselves who gladly acknowledge the influence of many gardens they have visited.'

Spatial division lines have been achieved by irregular, well-grouped blocks and drifts of shrubs within a framework of fine mature trees and a generous planting of the pioneer shelter species such as Scots Pine, larch, birch and spruce. These were mostly planted in the exposed south-east and south area by 'reclaiming' open intensive market garden land in the early 1960s. They have been progressively thinned since to give a woodland effect, and provide most valuable shelter and screening. A digest of the main planting associations and outstanding specimens follows here to accompany the plan:

The north gardens lying between the house and Comp Lane (3). Magnificent lime trees, *Tilia × europaea*, flank the drive (13). Well-managed lawns slope upwards away from the house to a focal feature of steps and a small terrace. Note the background massing of shrubs *Viburnum plicatum* 'Lanarth', Tree Peonies, cotoneasters including *C. bullatus* and *C. salicifolius*, Mahonias, many shrub roses, especially the deep purple 'Zigeunerknabe', the brilliant orange 'Austrian Copper', *Rosa foetida* 'Bicolor' and the deep yellow *Rosa ecae* from Afghanistan. Flanking the steps are bold massing of shrubs and herbaceous plants including the purple *Berberis thunbergii* 'Atropurpurea Nana', *B.t.* 'Rose Glow', *B.t.* 'Aurea', *B.t.* 'Erecta', *Corokia virgata*, forms of *Hebe* and *Cistus*, the silver of *Artemisia ludoviciana* and the gold and silver of *Potentilla arbuscula* 'Beesii' (*P. fruticosa* 'Nana Argentea'), *Dictamnus*, *Stipa gigantea*, *Geranium* and *Erodium*. A delightful ground-work of many plants can be discovered in this area – notably the white and blue forms of *Viola cornuta*; also *Hosta*, *Geum*, *Gillenia*, *Chrysogonum virginianum*, Bowles' Golden Grass and the variegated London Pride.

In the tree and shrub groups to the east can be found many interesting plants, mostly selected for their preference for acidic, organic soils; most of these were planted in the mid 1960s. Here there are several North American and Chinese trees: the Fringe Tree, *Chionanthus virginicus*, the Hop Tree, *Ptelea trifoliata*, *Evodia* (*Euodia*) *hupehensis*, *Styrax japonica*, *Styrax obassia*, *Idesia polycarpa* and *Amelanchier asiatica*.

The *Magnolia* collection includes *M. × proctoriana*, *M. × loebneri* 'Merrill', *M. × l.* 'Leonard Messel', *M. × soulangiana* 'Lennei' and *M. × s.* 'Picture'. Azaleas and rhododendrons are prolific in this area and drifts of groundcover like *Geranium sylvaticum Album* and *G. macrorrhizum* and many others add to the natural effects. There is a good

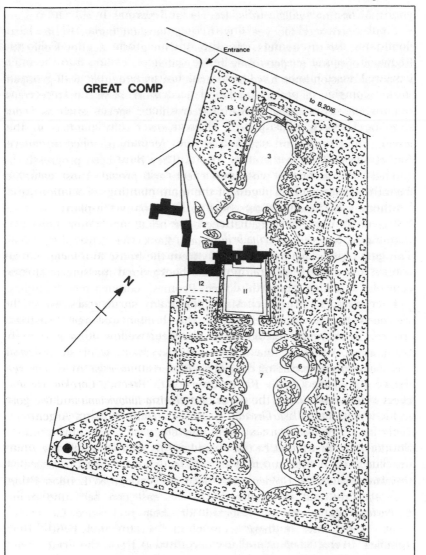

GREAT COMP

Entrance

to B.2016 →

N

1. Great Comp House
2. Drive
3. Front Lawn and North Gardens
4. Terrace and Steps
5. Beeches
6. Bog Garden
7. Open Vista
8. Heather Beds
9. New Woodland Glade
10. Chilstone Temple
11. Walled Garden and South Terrace
12. Tea Gardens/Toilets
13. Limes

young *Metasequoia glyptostroboides*, Dawn Redwood, in this area.

South terrace (11) — a fine *Eucalyptus gunnii* planted in 1961 dominates this area and note the unusual form of the California Redwood, *Sequoia sempervirens*, beside the steps leading into the main garden. Massed planting in front of the house, and a pleasant intimate formal complex of paths and small gardens west of the terrace are reminiscent of Sissinghurst. Note the two fine Dawyck Beeches, *Fagus sylvatica* 'Dawyck' ('Fastigiata'), *Quercus robur* 'Fastigiata' and *Acer lobelii*, and also in this area the ancient Medlar, *Mespilus germanica*. *Malus tschonoskii* here is notable for autumn colour.

The most spectacular vista down the main sweep of the garden is from the terrace, across peninsulas and promontories of many massed heathers, and low growing shrubs (7), with vertical pinnacles of fastigiate conifers and the further masses of many shrubs and trees: *Cornus alba* 'Spaethii', *Rosa rubrifolia*, *Staphylea colchica* and Purple Nut. The emphasis is again a complete groundcover, textural and colour contrasts and simplified maintenance. Some of this section is reminiscent of the Wisley Heath Garden.

Four large mature beeches (5) dominate the central area of the garden with underplanting of natural grasses and many bulbous species. An old pond has been filled in and turned into a bog garden (6) and planted with good foliage plants such as ferns, *Ligularia*, *Rodgersia* and even teasels and Angelica. The paths wander informally through the young wooded glades (9) in the south of the garden, the natural effect being achieved by bold and simple massing of woodland floor, shade-loving plants like *Geranium endressii*, *Lamium galeobdolon luteum* (only for very difficult areas), *L. maculatum*, many ferns, including the Shuttle-cock Fern, *Matteuccia struthiopteris*, *Onoclea sensibilis*, many hellebores, *H. corsicus* and *H. orientalis*, Lenten Rose, *Hosta*, *Polygonum*, foxgloves, *Euphorbia robbiae*, and many more. A striking combination is *Sedum* 'Autumn Joy' with *Anaphalis triplinervis*. Lily species like *L. martagon* have been naturalized in this area.

In the extreme south-west corner of the garden is a 'Chilstone' Temple (10) erected on a small area acquired in 1975, thus lengthening the vista. The deep soils here are ensuring rapid growth of fine specimens of Red and Scarlet Oaks, *Nothofagus*, *Pinus radiata*, *Pinus coulteri* and a particularly fine *Abies grandis* planted in 1962. There are exciting effects here from massed plantings of the golden green mantle of *Alchemilla mollis* and the tall decorative grass *Stipa gigantea* with magnificent flowering spikes, and a large grouping of *Telekia speciosum* and varieties of *Filipendula*.

The seven acres of garden are managed almost entirely by Mr and

Mrs Cameron on their own. The only occasional part-time help is in the small nursery area, to produce plants for sale on the open days. Hard paths are treated annually with herbicides, and the grass paths and lawns also with selective weedkillers. Edges are cut with a 'Spin Trim' machine. Curves of borders and paths are designed to allow easy mowing.

Groombridge Place

TQ 535 378 (Sheet 188) West Kent. 4 miles SW of Tunbridge Wells at the village of Groombridge on the B2110. Owner: Mr Mountain. Open one Sunday afternoon in July for the N.G.S.

A fine unspoilt moated house of the mid-seventeenth century with much of the formal gardens of this period existing today.

A fortified manor house has stood on this site since the time of Edward I. The Wallen family created a moated house here but it was Philip Packer who rebuilt the house in the late 1640s or early 1650s. A great friend of the family was John Evelyn, who visited the site and advised on the layout of the formal enclosed garden. The house passed into chancery hands and was subsequently owned by the Saint family in the nineteenth century. There are good descriptions of the house in *Country Life* of 1897 (vol. XII, p. 624) and 1902 (vol. CXIX, p. 986) and December 1955.

In the wooded, fertile and well-watered valley of a small tributary of the River Medway that has been used to create the moat and an attractive lake. The garden lies on a gentle south slope above the house some 145 ft above sea level. The site is well-sheltered with woodland to the north and north-east but rather open to the east across what were the old jousting and tournament water-meadows. Soils are light alluvial river soils with the acidic Tunbridge Wells sandstones nearby. Rainfall and climate similar to Penshurst.

The unique character of Groombridge Place and its gardens are well-summarized in the 1902 *Country Life* account: 'What governs the character of the gardens here is the time-consecrated architecture and the house fixed with its moat in the hollow. The garden looks as if it belongs to the house.' This is exactly the impression the visitor has today. The main features are the clipped topiary and yews, grass paths and alleys with terminal vistas of old wrought-iron gates, urns and peacocks, of which there are over a dozen in the gardens today. There is little evidence of new or unusual planting and the owner, being somewhat elderly, has not attempted to modernize it or change many other of the traditional features of the garden. There are some fine lime trees near the house and a Wellingtonia between the house and the lake.

There are three full-time gardeners under the leadership of Mr Ben Charmen who has been with the family for over 50 years. He will be retiring shortly. He and his staff achieve a high standard of meticulous maintenance in the traditional style. There is also a large kitchen garden.

Hall Place Gardens

TQ 545 465 (Sheet 188) Mid Kent. Leigh. 4 miles W of Tonbridge on the B2027 Tonbridge–Penshurst Road. Owner: Mr G.H. Hope-Morley. Open seven Sundays, four in May, three in June for the N.G.S. and other charities. The number of visitors is increasing after the first opening to the public in 1965. A gratifying feature is the good labelling of many plants in the garden.

A good example of a high-Victorian mansion and gardens in a landscape park with a great lake, fine trees and impressive formal and kitchen gardens.

The mansion was built in 1871–72 in the high-Victorian style by the architect George Devey who was probably influenced by the arts and architecture of the Elizabethan style after his first great commission, the restoration of Penshurst Place, in 1850. Hall Place was the largest house Devey built in the Tudor style, built for Samuel Morley MP. At the same time the extensive gardens and park were laid out to a scale to match that of the house. The east and west neo-Tudor gateways from the road are a foretaste of the opulent seat that used to exist here. The present owner is descended from Samuel Morley. In a programme of essential and realistic rationalization of the property he has reduced the size of the great house considerably by removing one wing, thereby creating some effective courts and walled gardens out of the old rooms of this feature. He is also carrying out an extensive restoration of the large and scenically beautiful gardens with the aid of his excellent garden staff.

Hall Place and the village of Leigh are about one mile north of the

River Medway and the setting is similar to Penshurst Place. The stiff clay loams respond well to good management (see kitchen garden). The gardens are some 130 ft above sea level and reasonably well sheltered. Rainfall 29.5 inches. Sunshine 4.25 hrs; the incidence of air frost averages over 30 per year, which is high compared with Emmetts or Chartwell on the nearby sandstone ridge.

The gardens and park extend to nearly 30 acres, of which 11 are occupied by the lake. The formal gardens include a rose garden, with an outstanding pergola, and a very well-maintained vegetable garden. There is also a wild garden to the south of the house with fine rhododendrons, flowering dogwoods, and other shrubs. The great feature for visitors at present is probably the lake and the planting associated with it. There is a pleasant perimeter walk of nearly a mile in length on which one encounters features and interesting planting and good views back to the house. Rustic stone bridges visible from the house (there are three in all), cross small inlets, one of which has been made into a Japanese-style water garden, probably in the last century. There are good specimens of Japanese evergreen azaleas, green and purple-leaved forms of *Acer palmatum* 'Dissectum', while wistaria wreathes itself romantically over the parapet of another bridge. A large selection of waterfowl on the lake enlivens the scene here. New planting of waterside foliage plants like *Hosta, Rodgersia* and others is in progress. There are islands on the lake, and as on the north and north-east edges they are planted with good tree cover – willows, alders and some conifers forming a fine back-drop to the lake when viewed from the house. At the west end is a bog and water garden. On the lawns in this area are some fine cedars and Wellingtonias planted about 100 years ago. Between the lake and the house is what is known as the spring garden, a feature created in the 1920s by Lord Hollenden, uncle of the present owner. It takes the form of large, informally-planted groups and islands of shrubs for early season flowering, examples being the bold masses of *Viburnum, Berberis*, azaleas and some crabs and cherries. Note the fine group of *Rosa* 'Nevada' and *R. moyesii* grouped around the great Copper Beech here. New planting is taking place here using large groups of *Hosta* and *Euphorbia* and ground cover of *Geranium* species. Trees in the grounds include a large gnarled *Arbutus menziesii*, a Pin Oak, *Quercus palustris*, near the lake, large specimens of *Calocedrus* (*Libocedrus*) *decurrens*, *Pinus nigra maritima* (*calabrica*), *Pinus radiata, Pseudotsuga menziesii, Betula pendula* 'Dalecarlica' and *Fraxinus excelsior diversifolia*. Do not miss the magnificent specimen of the Wild Service Tree, *Sorbus torminalis*, on the left of the drive on the way out.

Maintenance is so often taken for granted by the visitor and at Hall

Place the achievements of remarkably few staff deserve special mention. Three full-time men manage the 20 acres extremely effectively by means of an efficient, intelligent approach to the organization of their work. Under the able direction of the present head gardener, Mr Peter Beagley, they adopt the following policy: (*a*) All paths and hard surfaces are given one application per year of the granular herbicide Dichlobenil. Most grass edges have been reduced to the minimum. (*b*) The many areas of grass are managed in three ways: The extensive parkland grass areas away from the main lawns are cut by a local farmer as a hay crop under contract. He usually does this in late June and in 1975 he made 200 bales of hay from the grounds. This treatment allows for naturalizing of bulbs and also promotes a pleasant hay meadow flora as developed at Great Dixter. It also accords with the conservation role of such parks. The main lawns and grass areas near the house are cut with tractor-mounted gang mowers which reduce cutting time very drastically compared with conventional motor mowers. Detailed prestige areas, where access is difficult with the gang mowers, are cut with smaller cylinder motor mowers. (*c*) All borders and cultivated areas are heavily mulched, with leaf-mould or other organic matter. Peter Beagley can see many benefits here since, apart from moisture conservation and weed reduction, it produces a friable tilth which makes hoeing very simple. (*d*) General efficiency and forward planning.

Hearts of Oak Benefit Society Convalescent Home

TR 395 695 (Sheet 179). Extreme East Kent on Isle of Thanet in Callis Court Road. Broadstairs. 1 mile from town centre. Margate 6 miles to N. Owner: Hearts of Oak Benefit Society. Open a few Sunday afternoons in early and mid-summer generally for the N.G.S.

Extensive gardens and pleasure grounds of this convalescent home laid out in the last 40 years and containing a fine collection of unusual and well-grouped trees, shrubs and perennials suited to seaside gardens. A visit is strongly recommended.

Formerly a private residence, known as Callis Grange, of the early twentieth century, of which some of the original layout, and particularly the very important shelter belts of trees and shrubs, still remain. The Hearts of Oak Benefit Society purchased the property in 1938 and extended the house during the next 30 years or so. The gardens were also enlarged and re-designed to provide a pleasant, secluded place for the 50 or so inmates, as well as furnishing fresh vegetables and fruit for their consumption.

This is the most maritime of all the gardens described in this book, being less than a mile from the English Channel and North Foreland Point, that easternmost tip of Kent that juts out into one of the most exposed stretches of the Channel. There is virtually unbroken sea between here and Jutland! The rigorous, bracing climate of Broadstairs and the Isle of Thanet attracted the attention of health-seeking Victorians like Dickens, and one of his seaside homes, Bleak House, is not far away. These gardens lie some 130 ft above sea level on shallow chalk cliffs above the North Foreland lighthouse (it can be seen from the viewpoint on the walls of the kitchen garden). Soils are light, alkaline, alluvial loams, free-draining but fertile and productive when well managed.

The gardens cover some 11.2 acres, of which about two-and-a-half acres are walled kitchen gardens. There is also a small sheltered orchard planted in 1950. The special feature of the garden is the fine and well-maintained collection of trees and shrubs and perennials. This collection was largely built up by the former head gardener, Mr Carter, now retired, who deserves full praise for his achievement in such a dry, windy, seaside garden. There is a very good selection of the genera *Hebe*, *Olearia*, *Helianthemum* and shrubby *Salvia* species and among the perennials, grey-foliaged *Helichrysum*, *Artemisia* and also the more exotic *Agapanthus* and *Phormium*. One of the most successful areas is the fountain and pool garden. The planting is rich and colourful here. On the pergolas are a purple vine *Vitis vinifera* 'Purpurea', deep yellow flowered *Fremontodendron californicum*, climbing roses, wistaria and honeysuckles; while the borders around the pools are equally exotic – with gold-variegated *Buddleia davidii* 'Harlequin', the grey *Teucrium fruticans*, the delightful lavender-blue *Hebe hulkeana*, an unusual dwarf form of *Ceratostigma willmottianum*, *Coronilla glauca* 'Variegata' (usually a conservatory plant!) and *Olearia* 'Waikariensis'. Also in this area look for the splendid and unusual perennial *Lobelia tupa*, an exotic, half-hardy Chilean species with great spikes of deep red claw-like flowers on stout stems in mid-summer. The four pools are well planted with aquatic and marginal plants, including some fine water lilies.

In the less formal, southern area of the gardens are shade and shelter trees forming a woodland boundary, and here, in spring, are massed daffodils and other early flowering bulbs followed in late summer by the charming pink-flowered hardy *Cyclamen hederifolium* (*neapolitanum*). There is a well-placed group of autumn colouring trees and shrubs here, including *Acer griseum, Amelanchier, Euonymus alatus,* various cotoneasters and shrub roses. Note also the Blue Cedar *Cedrus atlantica glauca* planted about 17 years ago. The superb kitchen gardens to the extreme south-east of the grounds grow prolific crops in splendid condition (1976) and are reminiscent of that great era of estate walled gardens that were once the proud centre of a head gardener's empire.

On the exposed eastern flank of the garden there are massed shelter trees, shaped into dense, rounded bushes on the windward side. Pines, elms and sycamores are the main species (some of the elms are regrettably now diseased) and the almost forgotten hardy evergreens of seventeenth-century gardens, *Phillyrea spp.,* of which *P. angustifolia* is an excellent seaside evergreen. Around the main buildings are good examples of summer bedding. The lawns are not shorn too close and this, and the use of limited herbicides, has encouraged the colonization of the charming little August- and September-flowering wild orchid, the 'Autumn Ladies Tresses', *Goodyera repens.*

The 11 acres are managed by six full-time staff under the able head gardener, Mr Albert Davis, a progressive, experienced and very knowledgeable man who is to be congratulated on his achievements at Hearts of Oak.

Hever Castle

TQ 478 454 (Sheet 188) Mid Kent. 6 miles SW Tonbridge, 2 miles S Penshurst between B2026 and B2027 roads. Owner: Lord Astor of Hever. Open certain days of the week from late March to late September. Full details in H.H.G.S.

An early twentieth-century garden conceived on a lavish scale by the first Lord Astor around the restored and enlarged original of the historic Tudor castle, once the home of Anne Boleyn.

The earliest part of Hever Castle was built in the late thirteenth and early fourteenth centuries by William de Hever, an ancestor of a Norman baron who came to England during the Conquest. The central

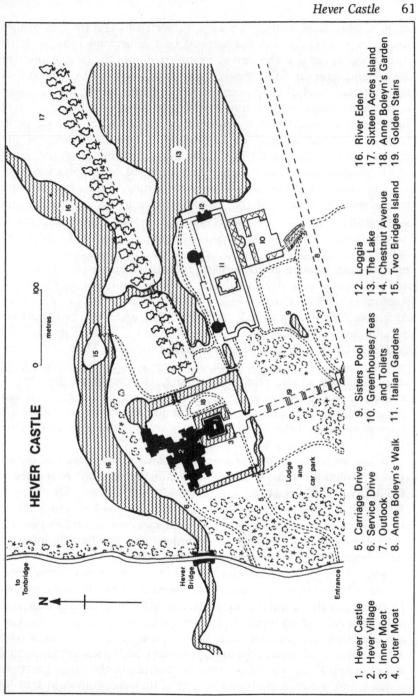

HEVER CASTLE

N

to
Tonbridge

Hever
Bridge

Entrance

Lodge
and
car park

17

13

16

16

12

11

10

9

8

19

18

16

15

14

metres
0　　　100

1. Hever Castle
2. Hever Village
3. Inner Moat
4. Outer Moat

5. Carriage Drive
6. Service Drive
7. Outlook
8. Anne Boleyn's Walk

9. Sisters Pool
10. Greenhouses/Teas
　　and Toilets
11. Italian Gardens

12. Loggia
13. The Lake
14. Chestnut Avenue
15. Two Bridges Island

16. River Eden
17. Sixteen Acres Island
18. Anne Boleyn's Garden
19. Golden Stairs

keep, machicolated walls, gateway with portcullis and the two square towers survive today, still surrounded by the original moat with its drawbridge approach. The stone was quarried from the local Tunbridge Wells sandstone. In 1462 Hever Castle was acquired by the famous Bullen family and they proceeded to turn the castle into a more comfortable Tudor manor house. There is little surviving record of Hever at this time, but it is presumed to have had a hunting park, farm and formal gardens in keeping with the importance of the Bullens' position at Court. Hever came into Royal hands on the death of Sir Thomas Bullen and then slowly declined in importance. Subsequent owners included the Waldegrave family in the sixteenth and seventeenth centuries and the Meade Waldos in the eighteenth and nineteenth centuries. The small moated manor house became a modest farmhouse for a succession of tenant farmers and was maintained in good repair. In 1903 Hever Castle and 640 acres of land were purchased by William Waldorf Astor, recently emigrated from America and naturalized as a British subject. William Astor had wealth and a passionate love of Europe, much of it derived from his period as American Ambassador to Italy. Between 1903 and 1907 he undertook an ambitious and ostentatious restoration and expansion programme for Hever Castle and its grounds. With the architect Mr F.L. Pearson, he fully restored the moated castle, preserving with faithful detail every fragment of the original structure. He conceived the idea of creating a Tudor-style 'village' of houses of individual and random medieval design to house his staff and friends. He also created a second outer moat around the castle. A force of over 1,000 men worked on this conversion project for over four years.

At the same time, the gardens were devised and laid out on an equally ambitious scale, drawing on a fanciful mixture of medieval, Renaissance and romantic eighteenth-century styles. The site at Hever is low lying, poorly-drained and liable to flooding and a major drainage scheme was necessary to create as dry a setting as possible for the restored home and the new garden. This involved draining all the surrounding land, diverting the River Eden and creating a large 35-acre reservoir and balancing lake that is now a fine ornamental feature of the gardens. The lake was created in about 19 months from the signing of the original contract, using 800 men, six steam diggers and seven miles of an internal railway system linked to the main line. The lake depth was excavated to 3–10 ft, and the bed reinforced with concrete where necessary. The famous nursery and landscape gardening firm of Joseph Cheal was responsible for laying out the 50–60 acres of gardens and grounds at this time. The rather romantic and fanciful names attached to many of the features of these new gardens must presumably be attributed to William Astor's fertile imagination. They certainly appeal to visitors today. William Astor became Baron Astor and then Viscount Astor of Hever Castle in 1917. The present Lord Astor is the third in this line. He has embarked on an ambitious programme of restoration and renovation of the gardens in particular. In 1970, a modern range of glasshouses was installed with automatic, labour-saving equipment, providing plants for the gardens and surplus stock sales to visitors. The need to increase the income from visitors to maintain Hever Castle and its garden is evident in the attractions and facilities being provided. The success of their policy is evident to anyone going there on a peak day in the summer months.

Hever lies in the moist fertile valley of the River Eden – a tributary of the Medway that joins the main river at Penshurst – at 147 ft above sea level. Sheltered and thinly wooded to the east; extensive mixed woodland to the south and west on the high ground beyond Anne Boleyn's walk. The microclimate of walls in the garden is favourable to an exotic range of shrubs. Rainfall 29.5–31.5 inches. Sunshine 4.25 hrs.

The soils are mostly acidic and weald-clay in the low-lying areas around the house and lake. There is light Tunbridge Wells sandstone to the south, and an outcrop of this can be seen in the quarry beside the Golden Stairs.

The plan shows the main features of the gardens summarized here. It also indicates the rather detached nature and the pastiche of styles used by Astor to create something of a show garden in that period of transitional and revivalist garden-making when many different styles and a whole range of new plant introductions did not always rest so easily in one harmonious composition. There are probably two distinct styles and areas of gardens to be distinguished:

(1) FORMAL AREAS

The castle courtyard and terrace and the Tudor-style gardens, including Anne Boleyn's Garden (18) – The walls of the castle have been used to good effect. Note the lustrous vine *Vitis coignetiae* in the castle courtyard that colours deep crimson and purple in the autumn; white wistaria; clematis varieties; *Jasminum nudiflorum*; many climbing roses and such exotic species as the New Zealand yellow-flowered *Sophora tetraptera*. Anne Boleyn's Garden was laid out in 1906 and includes a maze of yew, a small well-planted herb garden around a central sundial, and a recent Silver Garden commemorating the 1970 silver wedding anniversary of the present Lord and Lady Astor. A well-selected blend of silver and grey plants here remind one of the White Garden at Sissinghurst. A Chess Garden and Fountain Garden may also be explored. Note the good selection of climbers on the pergolas surrounding these gardens: laburnum, wistaria, honeysuckle, roses, jasmine, clematis and the unusual *Akebia quinata*. The moats are well-planted with collections of red, pink, yellow and white water lilies at their best in July and August.

The Italian gardens (11) – The concept and scale of these are impressive as a complete contrast to the Tudor complex. They were originally designed to house Astor's considerable collection of antique statuary and sculpture from Rome and many parts of Italy, and the view from the loggia at the eastern end of these gardens across the lake is also quite dramatic. The Pompeiian Wall of golden sandstone that runs as a northern boundary to the gardens offers a series of warm, south-facing bays for a combination of good exotic planting among the statuary. Outstanding wall plant associations noted in 1976 included white *Clematis montana*, the purple-leaved vine *Vitis vinifera* 'Purpurea', silver variegated *Euonymus fortunei* 'Variegatus', yellow *Sophora tetraptera*, lilac-purple wistaria, pink *Magnolia × soulangiana* 'Lennei', blue *Ceanothus* species and such fragrant plants as Lemon Verbena, *Lippia* (*Aloysia*) *citriodora*, lavenders, roses and many others. Seats here provide a warm basking place on sunny days. Note the huge *Wisteria floribunda* 'Macrobotrys' (*multijuga*) over the loggia. Elsewhere in this Italian Garden there is much to explore and the written guide is helpful; the rose garden, the pergolas, the pools and grottos inspired by the Villa d'Este near Rome, and many other features. This garden should be a place for meditation and peace, an atmosphere encouraged by the moss-clad figures and the romantic urns and sarcophagi. Unfortunately, the recent trend to introduce refreshment kiosks, tea pavilions and a flood of visitors into this classical place can have a disturbing effect for the discerning visitor.

The Blue Corner and rose garden can also be found to the south-east of the Italian Garden. The Blue Corner is really a bold attempt at rock gardening using huge pieces of stone originally brought from Chiddingstone Causeway, and now planted with blue-flowered shrubs such as *Rhododendron* 'Blue Diamond' and *R.* 'Blue Tit', blue hydrangeas, and blue perennials and bulbs, etc. The rose garden occupies the site of a conservatory demolished in the 1920s; some good wall-planting in this area, including the yellow-flowered Californian *Fremontodendron californicum*, the rare and tender South African *Freylinia lanceolata*, camellias and the Chinese honeysuckle *Lonicera tragophylla*.

(2) INFORMAL AREAS AND THE LAKESIDE – Away from the formal enclosed areas, one can climb the Golden Stairs (19) up the Tunbridge Wells sandstone-outcrop, noting the azaleas and rhododendrons

1 Great Comp, Kent: the bold informality of the Great Comp garden. The backdrop of mature trees north-west of the house shows well here

2 Cobham Hall, Kent: an aerial view from the south-west. The fine trees standing in part of Repton's pleasure grounds to the north of the house are well illustrated

3 Crittenden House, Kent: looking north across the lower pool – rich textural plantings in sympathy with the house and waterside

4   Groombridge Place, Kent: a prospect drawn in 1874, now in the possession of the owner, showing the seventeenth-century moated house and the symmetrical terraced gardens that still survive virtually intact today

5   Hever Castle, Kent: an aerial view from the south-east. Note the River Eden north of the house; the lake and chestnut avenue; the Italian Garden, and the maze close to the castle

6   Royal Horticultural Society's Garden, Wisley, Surrey: Seven Acres in winter – the frozen lake

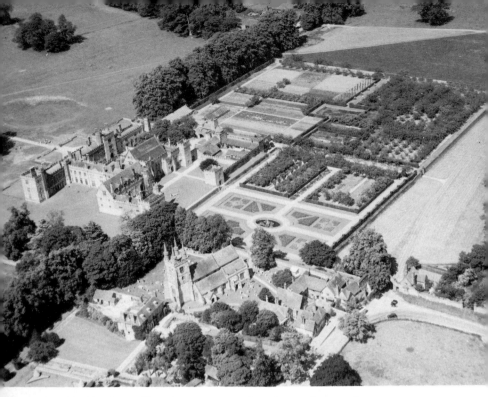

7   Penshurst Place, Kent: a view from the south-west taken some years ago, showing clearly the compact formal enclosures of the Elizabethan garden and the expansive parkland beyond. The village of Penshurst lies bottom centre

8   Scotney Castle, Kent: Edward Hussey's picturesque composition of ruined castle, lily-mantled lake and exotic trees and shrubs, as seen from the air

9   St John Jerusalem, Kent: the intimate enclosure and well-planted borders of the walled garden. The fine willows in the background grow beside the moat surrounding the garden

10 The Badeslade engraving of Squerrys, ('Squerries') Kent, dated 1714, showing the once famous formal gardens around the house, which has survived intact to the present day. A few remnants of the formal garden can be traced to the south and west of the house

11 Charleston Manor, Sussex: a delightful border of chalk-loving shrubs and perennials against a rose-clad wall west of the old manor house

Petworth Park, Sussex: two contrasting views
12   (top) Lancelot Brown's magnificent lake in the park seen through the boles of ancient Sweet Chestnuts

13   (bottom) the romantic temple in the Pleasure Grounds close to the giant Cedar of Lebanon (not seen)

14　Leonardslee, Sussex:　massed rhododendrons and azaleas in a dramatic woodland setting beside the lake. These provide a brilliant spectacle in late May

15　Polesden Lacey, Surrey:　Richard Sheridan's superb terrace walks extending nearly 500 yards in a southerly direction from the house. There are delightful views of the Surrey countryside over the parapet hedge to the south-west

16 Vann, Surrey: the woodland garden originally designed by Gertrude Jekyll. Like the rest of the garden at Vann, it retains many of the characteristic qualities of her style of design and planting

17 Sunte House, Sussex: the Big Pond seen from the south windows of the house. Skilful selection and siting of the planting here makes this one of the finest features of the garden

18 Royal Horticultural Society's Garden, Wisley, Surrey: the Alpine Meadow in early April

19 Vann, Surrey: the Old Field Pond; a tranquil setting for the house. The skilful, sensitive waterside planting reflects the quality of this garden

20   Great Dixter, Sussex:
the visitor's first impressions of the
garden near the front porch (left) of
the old Hall House. The richness and
quality of the fine old buildings is
superbly matched by the planting

21   Horsted Place, Sussex:
the Rose Walk in the redesigned
Victorian garden

massed on either side, and from the top there is a fine prospect (7) where one can look down and across the castle gardens and lake to the distant landscape beyond. The Chestnut Avenue (17), however, looks incongruous, to my mind, in the 'lake' landscape it bisects. The park-like effect on either side of Anne Boleyn's Walk (8) is mainly due to the very diverse tree collection in lightly mown grass. Mature, specimen beeches and oaks are outstanding here, but there are many more trees and shrubs from the 1906–10 era to be seen in this area and, indeed along the lake. There is a fine walk that extends round the lake for those who wish to find peace and tranquillity. The guide to the gardens at Hever Castle recently written by Lord Astor is strongly recommended for those wishing to know more about this place. Visitors who would like to enjoy the plants and planting should try to go to Hever in early summer or in September on off-peak days, since visitor numbers are enormous in July and August.

A high standard of maintenance is achieved.

Hole Park

TQ 832 325 (Sheet 188) West Kent. 2 miles W of Rolvenden off the B2086 Rolvenden–Cranbrook road. Owner: Mr D.G.W. Barham. Open several Sunday afternoons in April, May and October for the N.G.S.

An extensive garden in the undulating High Weald, surrounded by parkland, pastures and hops and fruit. The Georgian brick house stands on a somewhat exposed plateau some 250 ft above sea level with fine views to the south and east across the Weald. The gardens that are open to the public mostly lie to the north and east of the house.

The soils are acidic weald-clays and sandstones, enabling the owner to grow many fine acid-loving trees and shrubs. Rainfall averages 31.5 inches.

The gardens consist of two distinct parts disposed in a large horse-shoe shape to the east and north-east of the house. The main drive up to the house forms the boundary of the southern arm of the horseshoe and here there are a series of formal, enclosed and intimate gardens, including a rose garden. The yew hedges are shaped and beautifully trimmed into rather unique configurations and the planting is restrained. Groups of large mature trees give character and some shelter to these rather exposed sites, noticeably some fine oaks

Quercus robur and Monterey Pine *Pinus radiata.* The horseshoe then curves around an open paddock to descend into an attractive wooded valley garden that runs east–west on the northern arm of the horseshoe. The gentle descent passes through a heather garden with informal drifts and groups of many different species and varieties of *Erica* and *Calluna.* Daffodils are naturalized here in plenty and look especially attractive in April. The wooded dells and glades of the valley garden are partially shaded by the canopies of several fine 'standard' oaks, with clear trunks running up to 30 ft before the crown branches emerge. There are many species and varieties of rhododendrons, camellias, Asiatic maples and other trees and shrubs. There is also a comprehensive collection of conifers. The size and maturity of some of the slower-growing conifers at the west end of the garden is impressive. There are particularly good specimens of the weeping *Tsuga canadensis* 'Pendula' and the unique *Picea breweriana*, Brewers Spruce, standing to the left of the gate that leads into the bluebell wood.

Recommended times of the year to visit the garden are: April for the woodland garden: early shrubs, bulbs, primroses, cowslips, etc. May for rhododendrons, azaleas, bluebells. October for autumn colour.

The maintenance standards are very high indeed.

Husheath Manor

TQ 758 408 (Sheet 188) Mid Kent. 4 miles NE Goudhurst, E off B2079; or 3 miles SW of Staplehurst off A229. Owner: Mr and Mrs P. Maitland Smith. Open one or two Sunday afternoons in early summer for the N.G.S.

A cleverly-designed and well-planted garden in an early twentieth-century anglo-Italian style, around a magnificent historic timbered manor house.

On a greensand ridge in the High Weald, looking north-east towards the Medway Valley and Tonbridge. The house lies on comparatively steeply sloping ground at some 145 ft above sea level. This ridge is exposed to the cold north-east winds, but important shelter trees fringe the garden, a blend of Black Poplars and Hedge Maples, with strategic 'windows' giving fine views of the Weald. The soil is light, acidic greensand of the Weald series, an excellent forest soil as evinced by the oak and ash woods that enclose the house to the west and south-west. Rainfall 29.5 inches.

The manor house at Hushheath was built in 1534 by a master weaver, this area being an important centre for sheep farming and the associated wool industry. The garden of some three-and-a-half acres was made about 40 years ago by a Mr Bower who was strongly influenced by the Italian styles of gardening when he laid out Husheath. Peter Coats in his description of the gardens at Husheath in his *Great Gardens of Britain** notes: 'The garden is fascinating in that it is such a happy blending of the Italian and English styles. English with its traditional borders, its roses and its topiary; Italian with its statues, and terraces and general architectural feel.'

One approaches the house and garden from a quiet, narrow, country lane (parking very limited) by climbing up ancient steps, through a charming Tudor-style gazebo/gatehouse. The fine north façade of the house (the best-looking side of the house) faces one and looks over a cool, green lawn decorated with topiary. An encircling bank slopes up a hillside around this lawn. The bank is studded with flowering bulbs in March and April. Steps lead away up the slope to a circular enclosure surrounded by a castellated cypress hedge. From here, on top of the ridge well above the house, the longest axis of the garden runs as a long avenue of yews. Cool green woodlands lie mysteriously to the right as one walks down the romantic paved walk, and to the left one gets glimpses of the gardens and house below. The yew walk ends with a marble statue of a mysterious veiled woman. Another walk runs parallel to this, a paved, very atmospheric walk with stone pillars, old roses and climbers and ending in wrought-iron gates and old walls. A wild wooded valley falls away below this walk, thick with bluebells in May. To the south of the house is another charming sunken lawn, the retaining walls beautifully planted with carpeting ground cover associations of *Alchemilla mollis*, *Geranium* species, and *Viburnum davidii*. Near the terrace of the house stand two fine columnar Italian Cypresses, *Cupressus sempervirens*, at least 30 ft high, with a fine Weeping Willow, *Salix × chrysocoma* (*alba tristis*), on the corner of the house. This tree looks singularly correct here and it helps to soften the disturbing effect of a rather dull brick extension presumably added to the house in the 1920s. The many changes in contours in this garden are given the same sensitive treatment of cool, careful planting, good detailing of steps, statuary and urns, the latter beautifully planted. A dell lies to the south-east of the garden, its central pool being planted with strong

---

* Peter Coats, *Great Gardens of Britain*, Spring Books 1970.

foliage and textural plants like *Hosta, Rodgersia, Gunnera, Astilbe* and Japanese irises in bold groups and drifts. Ferns abound everywhere in the garden. One can leave the main garden and cross into a charming old-world kitchen garden. One picturesque feature of this vegetable garden is the selection of old-fashioned shrub and climbing roses trained up tripod 'wigwams' of poles on either side of the long central path and edged and interplanted with chives.

This remarkable garden of three-and-a-half acres is looked after most successfully by one gardener, Mr Turner, who has designed many subtle techniques for maintaining the character and interest of the gardens with little extra help. A talk with him is most revealing and inspiring.

Knole

TQ 540 543 (Sheet 188) Mid Kent. 1½ miles SE of Sevenoaks off A225 Sevenoaks–Tonbridge Road. Owner: The National Trust. Open: the Park is open throughout the year, but the house and gardens are open on a more limited basis. See H.H.C.G.

One of the largest private houses in England, dating from the fifteenth century and standing in 1,000 acres of parkland. The enclosed gardens include a wilderness and some formal planting. They are of rather limited horticultural interest.

The excellent guide produced by the National Trust gives fascinating details of the development of this great house and its associated park. A summary only is relevant here. The first reference to Knole is in the reign of Edward I, but the medieval elements of the present building date from the fifteenth century when Archbishop Bourchier of Canterbury built a fortress-like house on the site. He is known to have enclosed a smaller park, but Henry VIII and later owners gradually added to its size. Some of the oldest oaks and sweet chestnuts may date from the medieval period. Knole remained in Royal possession and in 1603 it was bought by Thomas Sackville, a wealthy statesman, and remained in his family for the next 300 years or more. The title of Sackville-West was assumed in the mid-Victorian period. In 1946 the fourth Lord Sackville, Major-General Sir Charles Sackville-West, gave

Knole to the National Trust with an endowment. Vita Sackville-West, the novelist, of Sissinghurst Castle spent her youth at Knole.

The park is the finest landscape feature of Knole. It extends to over 1,000 acres and its undulating contours on acidic weald-clays have given rise to fine trees, wooded slopes and a smooth heath-like turf grazed by rabbits and the herds of fallow and Japanese deer. A golf course is located in the park. There are fine Sweet Chestnut avenues on the south-east edge of the park and a long avenue of oaks known as the Duchess Walk. In the eighteenth century some sham ruins and a small Gothic bird-house were built in the park, possibly to house Lord Amherst's ornamental pheasants. A former ice-house once existed in the mound called Ice House Hill. The kitchen gardens lie to the east.

The garden covers about 26 acres and are completely enclosed by a high wall of ragstone, built in the mid-sixteenth century. The actual plan of the garden dates from the seventeenth century. There is a formal area of shrub borders and square orchards and a wooded area with winding paths known as the Wilderness. The present condition and treatment of the garden is rather unimaginative and of very limited interest to plant lovers and gardeners. It has a considerable potential to use the old basic plan to create an exciting garden worthy of the great house it embellishes.

Ladham House

TQ 735 389 (Sheet 188) West Kent. 1 mile N of Goudhurst off B2084. Owner: The late Sir George and Lady Jessel. Open several Sunday afternoons in late spring, early summer and in October for the N.G.C.

A well-designed garden of some 40 years maturity, with contrasting areas of formal and informal planting. There are fine collections of flowering shrubs and plenty of autumn colour. Arrangements for visitor days are extremely well-organized.

Sir George inherited the partly Georgian and partly Victorian house in 1930 with some 15 acres of land and he and Lady Jessel have developed the garden since then. The garden lies in the High Weald, the house being set on a small plateau some 230 ft above sea level, with a gentle slope to the north-east and north and sufficiently elevated to offer distant views through the trees and parkland of the River Beult valley towards Headcorn and the distant North Downs beyond. Fine perimeter belts of mixed deciduous and evergreen trees provide important screening and shelter to the garden. The climate here tends to be slightly cooler and wetter than the eastern areas of Kent, and with the combination of light tree shade and the deep retentive lime-free soils, offers good conditions for rhododendrons and many unusual trees and shrubs. Rainfall 29.5–31.5 inches. Sunshine 4 hrs. Soils are of the Wealden series being acidic light, sandy loams with some clay near the house. They respond well to good management and organic matter.

The garden really consists of two quite contrasting areas. The larger part is the informal area to the east of the house and approach drive where one can find the main collection of trees and shrubs. From the car park in the stable yard area walk to the east side of the house (having paid your entrance fee first!) and pause on the terrace. Note the climbers on the house – Banksian Roses, *Rosa banksiae*, the white and yellow forms; wistaria; and great masses of *Choisya ternata* against the walls. The style of these gardens lying to the north-east and east of the house is a blend of parkland with stately trees, and drifts and informal blocks and masses of exotic shrubs and some unusual trees. The specimen trees on the main lawn include limes, oaks and beeches, some exceeding 82 ft, and a young Tulip Tree, *Liriodendron tulipifera*. Note the very important screening and shelter belts of spruce and fir and deciduous trees to the south-east. Bold shrub islands lie in the main 'sea' of the lawns in this direction composed of massed rhododendrons, the tabulate, white tiers of *Viburnum plicatum* 'Mariesii' the autumn colouring *Enkianthus campanulatus* and various *Berberis* species. Beyond these islands lie the main wealth of mixed plantings. One large area beneath a fine group of mature Scots Pine, *Pinus sylvestris*, is a 'heath' of low carpeting and shrubs and unusual plants. Dominant are many varieties of *Erica* and *Calluna*, *Rhododendron* dwarf species and hybrids and other ericaceous shrubs like *Pernettya mucronata* with its shining green foliage and red and purple berries in late autumn. There are groups of 30–40-year-old specimens of such beautiful trees as the Japanese Snowbell, *Styrax japonica*, the Snowdrop Tree, *Halesia monticola*, and some exceptionally fine flowering dogwoods, including the white-flowered *Cornus florida*, the rich pink variety *C. florida rubra* and the Japanese *Cornus kousa*. All these flower in mid to late May. Note the fine young specimen of the Chilean Fire Bush, *Embothrium coccineum*, with brilliant orange-scarlet flowers in early June. Foliage effects are enriched with well-sited specimens of Japanese Maples, *Acer palmatum*, ending the season in a flame of autumn colour, and a continuity of winter effects follows with massed planting of various evergreens, including good holly varieties, and some conifers, noteworthy being the unmistakable drooping form of *Picea breweriana* planted some 30 years ago.

The garden falls gently to a small wooded dell where a former old pond has been cleverly planted with a lush and leafy collection of waterside perennials like the Royal Fern, *Osmunda regalis*, *Rodgersia*, *Peltiphyllum* and various *Iris* species. On the fringe of the dell are more masses of *Viburnum plicatum* (*tomentosum*) 'Mariesii' and a fine symmetrical plant of the Dawn Redwood, *Metasequoia glyptostroboides*, up to 50 ft. Look for the unusual grey-leaved thorn *Crataegus orientalis*, a fine Japanese Crab, *Malus floribunda*, some good autumn colouring trees like *Parrotia persica* and *Liquidambar styraciflua* and Colorado Blue Spruce, *Picea pungens glauca*. Beside the tall beeches nearer the house are effective boundary 'hedges' of the sterile-flowered form of the Guelder Rose, *Viburnum opulus* 'Sterile'. Background planting is enriched here with dense, glaucous-green masses of the Japanese White Pine *Pinus parviflora*. Behind these lie the rock garden which is a deeply excavated, rather gloomy, labyrinthine affair dating from that era 50−60 years ago when even the most fantastic creations in stone could be constructed with cheap labour and plentiful materials. A mysterious adventure-type of rock garden with deep, winding paths, craggy rocky steps, a rustic arch or two and dark tunnels beneath great canopies of vast, mature, 'dwarf' shrubs rather than true alpines or rock plants. Look out for the fine gnarled dwarf Japanese Maples *Acer palmatum* 'Dissectum', great spreading masses of *Rhododendron obtusum* 'Amoenum' (*Azalea amoena*) and other rhododendrons and azaleas, dwarf conifers, *Pieris*, *Arbutus*, *Arctostaphylos* and many carpeting ferns, small bulbs and Lily of the Valley.

The formal gardens: to the west of the house are the formal gardens, probably created from part of the former kitchen gardens. Two fairly narrow borders divided by a wide grass path lead away from the west door of the house to a focal corner seat set in a cool green corner flanked by two splendid *Magnolia × watsonii*, each over 30 ft high, their richly fragrant white saucer-shaped flowers appearing in June and July. Some fine late July and August flowering *Eucryphia* species grow here. In the two borders is a profusion of carefully selected foliage and flowering plants in grey, white, pink and yellow. Old shrub roses, peonies, the grey-leaved *Senecio* 'Sunshine', *Cistus*, *Potentilla fruticosa*, *Artemisia*, fennel and many others make a most effective blend. A walled enclosure to the north side of these borders encloses a delightful rose garden of brick paths and a careful selection of roses. Note the spilling mass of wall plants: *Lonicera periclymenum* 'Belgica' (Early Dutch), *Ceanothus* × *veitchianus*, *Clematis montana* 'Rubens' and the very attractive blue and white forms of *Abutilon vitifolium*. A small pool and garden-house in the north-west corner of the rose garden has also been well planted. Two good shrubs, *Kolkwitzia amabilis* (pale pink) and *Azara serrata* (yellow), look well here in early summer. The kitchen garden leads off on the south side of the two formal borders. It is large, splendidly stocked and very well maintained, a pleasure to behold.

Maintenance standards are very high throughout the gardens at Ladham and very sympathetic to the style and range of plants grown.

Leeds Castle

TR 836 534 (Sheet 188) Mid-East Kent. 5 miles SE Maidstone close to Leeds village. Main entrance is off A20 London–Folkestone Road, *not* from the village. Owner: Leeds Castle Foundation. Open: A recently opened property. For latest details see H.H.C.G.

A superbly sited historic moated castle; possibly one of the finest settings in England, standing in an extensive, well-timbered park overlooking the secluded, green valley of the River Len. The gardens are of limited interest at present.

The very first Saxon castle on this site was followed by a more substantial stone building in 1119. The castle grew in size and importance, with particular enlargements carried out by the two ambitious monarchs Edward I and Henry VIII. Full details of this important historical story are to be found in the well-illustrated guide available on open days. An important restoration programme was undertaken in 1822 and again in the second decade of this century, when the castle and estate were acquired by the late the Hon. Lady Baillie. From 1926 onwards she carried out a full and careful restoration of the castle fabric and also developed the gardens and parkland. The Wood Garden is her creation and she replanted much of the woodland on the estate. She also introduced many unusual wildfowl to the lakes and water gardens. A nine-hole golf course was also laid out around the lake. On her death in 1976 the castle was left as a trust and centre for medical research and the arts.

Visitors will find little of formal or intimate enclosed gardens at Leeds Castle, and interest to plantsmen and connoisseurs is therefore rather limited. The outstanding feature is undoubtedly the setting of the castle standing in the hollow of the moat. Tree planting has clearly been kept clear of the lake margin, but note the fine groups of beech, oak, lime and especially the great cedars romantically sited around the lake. The colouring of the more remote area of the park with its pine, oak, larch and bracken is fine in the autumn.

The wood garden gains its character from several streams that drain eventually into the River Len, meandering among willows, alders and other trees; a cool, pleasant place with touches of the exotic from mass plantings of such waterside foliage perennials as *Gunnera*, *Peltiphyllum*, *Ligularia*, *Astilbe* and the scarlet-stemmed clumps of Red-barked Dogwood, *Cornus alba*.

The potential for extending these gardens is considerable partly as a means of distributing the large number of visitors who are now coming to the castle in its first years of opening.

Northbourne Court

TR 338 524 (Sheet 179) East Kent. Between Deal (3½ miles) and Sandwich (5 miles), lying at the northern end of the village of Northbourne. Owner: The Lord Northbourne. Open on several Sundays in the summer in aid of the N.G.C. and other charities. See their publications for full details.

A compact series of enclosed walled gardens and terraces around the historic and attractive Court, providing a setting of diverse and very sensitive planting by the present owner.

Northbourne Court is said to have been on the site of a palace or hunting-lodge of Eadbald, son of Ethelbert, the Saxon king of Kent. In 618 it came into the possession of the monks of St Augustine's Abbey, Canterbury. After the dissolution, Henry VIII gave the manor to Archbishop Cranmer and later, Elizabeth I gave it to her foster-brother Edward Saunders; finally, James I gave it to Sir Edwyn Sandys who built a large house in the Jacobean style facing the three tiers of the garden terraces which provided the raised walk and 'prospect' or 'mount' that the Elizabethans and Stuarts regarded as very important features of their gardens. These terraces still survive. The house was burnt down in 1750 and the ruined hall can still be found today at the eastern end of the pool garden. In the lower garden the sixteenth-century coach-house with Flemish gables and a two-roomed gate-keeper's lodge also remain. Do not miss the fine Elizabethan gateway, at the end of a green walk to the south, which was long ago the main entrance to the old house. Since the Sandys left in 1750, Northbourne Court has belonged to various owners until bought by the second Lord Northbourne in 1895.

One of the most easterly gardens in Kent, in the rather flat, exposed tip of east Kent close to the Isle of Thanet and only three miles or so from the English Channel. It lies only 50 ft above sea level and slopes gently to the south-east. A key feature to note is the fine, ancient planting of belts of evergreen or Holm Oaks, *Quercus ilex,* and other trees to the west and north-west of the house, providing good shelter to the gardens and a distinct character to the house and buildings (compare with similar situations at the nearby Updown House and Goodnestone Park). Rainfall is low − 23.5−24.5 inches and, despite the cold east and north-east winds that can blow in late winter and early spring, the presence of the sea confers a tempering effect on the microclimate. Sunshine averages 4.6 hrs per day. The garden lies in the chalk belt that runs out to sea at Deal and Dover, and the soils are for the most part a light alkaline loam, although the antiquity of the site has caused the accumulation of vegetable and organic soils to some depth, and lime-free soils have been locally introduced to create habitats for calcifuge plants.

The old gabled house and the great Holm Oaks foretell the character of Northbourne Court before one has moved far from the car. One normally enters the garden through two charming and intimate courts. The first court is brick and stone paved and planted in a theme of grey, white and pink with a delightful carpet of great spreading mats and many long-lived plants. Here are trailing masses of *Zauschneria, Juniperus sabina tamariscifolia, Dianthus* and a 'maquis' of lavenders and dwarf shrubs. There are some splendid tubs which are, like the whole garden, planted with great refinement and artistry. In the second court is a small raised bed of lime-free soils for *Meconopsis* and other acid and shade-loving plants. Note here also the charming pale blue *Viola cornuta* seedlings raised by Lord Northbourne.

The pool garden is the largest open space of the garden. Apart from the central pool and fountain, its main features are the delightful borders and a large Irish Yew thought to be a remnant of the formal

Jacobean garden. There is a large Corsican Pine at the western end. This is a sunken garden and the enclosing walls are also splendidly planted with a restrained selection of species in keeping with the style of the garden and Lord Northbourne's highly personal taste. The plantings of the three borders are fine examples of this: The south-facing border is in a theme of soft pinks, greys and mauves, mainly achieved with perennials and some annuals and is a delicate and delightful blend of *Avena candida* (now called *Helictotrichon sempervirens*), Cardoons, smokey-grey strains of poppies, *Salvia turkestanica*, *Geranium rectum album*, *G. anemonifolium* and *G. psilostemon*, *Allium christophii* (*albopilosum*), Cotton Thistles *Onopordon acanthium*, *Pimpinella rosea* and the delicate and attractive annuals *Omphalodes linifolia*, *Nemophila maculata* and a very dark purple strain of old-fashioned (and very sweetly scented) sweet pea. The north-facing border has stronger blues and bolder forms with delphiniums, *Hosta spp.* and shrub roses against the background of the old walls which are also draped with plants. The narrower east-facing border beneath the shade of trees has soft-foliaged *Alchemilla mollis*, *Brunnera macrophylla*, *Geranium* species and the summer flowering blues of *Campanula lactiflora*. Here and elsewhere in the garden is the old cottage-garden, scented Sweet Rocket or Dames Violet, *Hesperis matronalis*. On the main walls are

large old specimens of the white and lilac forms of the Persian Lilac, Banksian Rose, *Rosa laevigata*, *R.* 'Dr Van Fleet, *R.* 'William Lobb' and *Wisteria floribunda* 'Macrobotrys' (*multijuga*).

The terraces afford charming views of the garden. They are edged with lavender and rosemary and are planted distinctively with different seasonal colour schemes. On one, gazanias, day-lilies and hardy *Agapanthus* predominate; on another, yellow and flame *Helianthemum* cultivars with Japanese Anemones and Michaelmas Daisies on the shady side. Here also are rose 'Blairi No 1' and *Paeonia lutea ludlowii*, and the unusual *Bupleurum fruticosum*. The banks and steps descending at the southern end of the top terrace are mantled with a delightful blend of *Cotoneaster conspicuus* 'Decorus', the pink and white daisy *Erigeron mucronatus*, and the pure pink Mediterranean bindweed *Convolvulus tenuissimus*. In the lower garden are drifts of peonies, iris, many shrubs and a richly scented form of the Mock Orange, *Philadelphus delavayii*, very floriferous and far more shapely than many of these varieties. Here there are many old-fashioned roses, including 'Charles de Mills', 'Fantin Latour', 'Rosa Mundi', *R. californica* 'Plena'. The Chinese shrub *Xanthoceras sorbifolium* grows here, with attractive pinnate leaves and white horse-chestnut flowers in May. It enjoys a chalky soil. In mid-summer, the Spanish Broom, *Spartium junceum*, adds to the abundance of scents and colours in the lower garden. Here the old buildings, brick walls, and the Tudor gateway enrich the character of the garden.

Remarkably enough, this three-acre garden is maintained by one full-time experienced gardener and one assistant and occasional part-time help, with the guidance, help and close supervision of the owner. Hence the great quality and character of Northbourne Court.

The Owl House

TQ 665 374 (Sheet 188). Mid Kent. 1 mile from Lamberhurst SW off A21 on a narrow road in the village. 8 miles SE Tunbridge Wells. 2 miles from Scotney Castle. Owner: Maureen, Marchioness of Dufferin and Ava. Open: Gardens only open all year on Mondays, Wednesdays and Fridays, also some summer weekends 11–7. See H.H.C.G.

An extensive informal woodland-style garden with attractive ponds and planted glades and a contrasting formal well-planted garden around the sixteenth-century house.

The origins of the house may go back to the pre-Dissolution days and links with nearby Bayham Abbey. The present sixteenth-century tile-hung half-timbered house was used by smugglers from the coast known as 'owlers', from which the house derives its name. It was acquired by the Marchioness of Dufferin in 1952 and the gardens have largely been developed since then. The setting is in the fruit and hop growing area of the Weald, very like that of Crittenden House and Ladham House which lie not far away to the north-east. Soils are acidic Wealden Tunbridge Wells sandy loams, as at Scotney Castle. The gardens lie on a south-west facing ridge over 320 ft above sea level. From the house there are fine views across the wooded Weald to the west and south-west.

There are two distinct styles and areas to this garden. Around the house are flagged paths, terraces and richly planted borders as a setting to the attractive old house. A pergola leading to a pool is clad with roses and clematis and there is an attractively planted terrace. The owl motif occurs frequently here and one can see, for example, stone owls on the pillars of the main entrance gates. The house itself is clothed with scented climbers – clematis, honeysuckles, and old roses.

Away from the house to the north-east and east across a great expanse of lawn one can find the 15 acres of woodland and wilderness garden, the acidic heathland soils being ideal for the collections of rhododendrons and azaleas and other rare shrubs that have been planted in the glades and walks. The woods are of oak and birch and vistas have been created to great effect. Daffodils are naturalized in vast numbers here and one can also explore a series of former hammer ponds now developed into romantic planted lakes. Good associations of waterside perennials and such trees as Japanese Maples add atmosphere, with well-placed seats and access paths.

Two to three gardeners are employed to maintain these gardens, which include a private swimming-pool area and enclosed garden south-west of the car park.

Penshurst Place

TQ 527 440 (Sheet 188). Mid Kent. In Penshurst village 5 miles W of Tonbridge on B2176, 32 miles from London. Owner: Viscount De L'Isle, VC, KG. Open April to September, usually 5 days per week, but for current details see H.H.C.G. and excellent literature produced by Penshurst Place.

Undoubtedly one of the finest and best-preserved historic complexes of this period to be found in the south of England. The gardens are a blend of contemporary and traditional styles within the formal structure which has its origins in the Middle Ages. New designs and planting are still in progress in the general spirit of the place.

The detailed history of the house is well summarized in the comprehensive guide available to visitors to the house. A brief summary is given here relating the evolution of the house to the gardens and parks. A house of this size and importance has stood at Penshurst since Domesday (1085). Sir John de Pulteney, a wool merchant and four times Mayor of London, bought the manor in 1338. Surviving from this period is the superb Great Hall, with its lofty roof of sweet chestnut over 60 ft high, considered to be one of the finest remaining examples of the work of masons and carpenters of the fourteenth century. The local sandstone was used for the main walls. John de Pulteney almost certainly would have created the park around the house for hunting deer, and there would have been farms, fishponds and woodlands to match the importance of this house. The famous Sidney Oak to the north of the park beyond the lake is a magnificent, slowly dying, sculptured 'ruin' of a once mighty tree, thought to be a remnant of the former great oak forests that were heavily felled in the fifteenth and sixteenth centuries for construction, ship-building and iron-smelting. In the fifteenth century Penshurst Place was bought by Henry V's brother, the Duke of Bedford, from Pulteney's successors. He added the block containing two further rooms of state. The third duke entertained Henry VIII at Penshurst in 1521 and shortly afterwards lost his head! The house passed by gift from Kind Edward VI

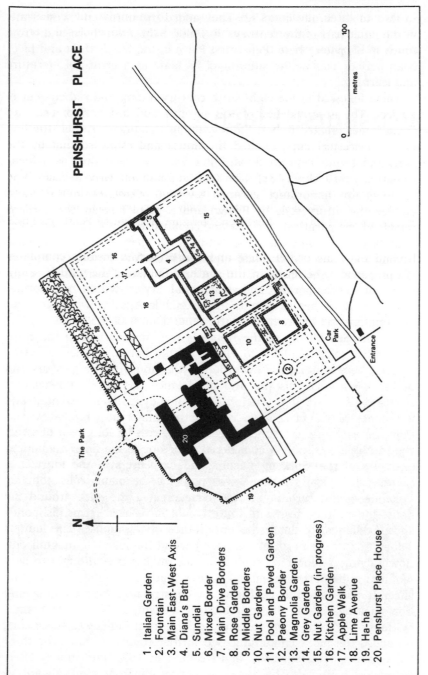

PENSHURST PLACE

N

The Park

Car Park

Entrance

0   metres   100

1. Italian Garden
2. Fountain
3. Main East-West Axis
4. Diana's Bath
5. Sundial
6. Mixed Border
7. Main Drive Borders
8. Rose Garden
9. Middle Borders
10. Nut Garden
11. Pool and Paved Garden
12. Paeony Border
13. Magnolia Garden
14. Grey Garden
15. Nut Garden (in progress)
16. Kitchen Garden
17. Apple Walk
18. Lime Avenue
19. Ha-ha
20. Penshurst Place House

to the Sidney family in 1552. They added the north and west fronts
in the latter part of the century. Sir Philip Sidney was born and wrote
much of his poetry here. Penshurst Place in the Elizabethan and Jacobean periods was at the summit of its fame as a centre of literature
and learning.

There followed in the eighteenth century a long and sad chapter of
neglect. The improvidence of the seventh and last Earl of Leicester
(King James created Robert Sidney, Philip's younger brother, the first
Earl of Leicester) impoverished the house and estate so that by the
early nineteenth century it was described by one visitor as a 'near
romantic ruin'. This is probably one explanation why a house and
estate of this importance escaped the 'improvements' in the grand
eighteenth-century style by Brown and Repton. Instead, the gardens
remained comparatively modest and confined within their rectangular
boundary walls. Only the park to the north opened up the landscape
beyond the house. In the late eighteenth century Penshurst became
the property of the Shelley family. A programme of restoration begun

by John Shelley Sidney was to extend over several generations. John's son, Philip Charles Shelley Sidney, was created Lord De L'Isle and Dudley in 1835. George Devey, who specialized in Elizabethan-revival architecture, worked at Penshurst from the 1850s onwards. He also designed nearby his great Elizabethan-style house, Hall Place at Leigh. The ha-ha, separating the west and north lawns from the park, dated from this time. The present Lord De L'Isle inherited Penshurst in 1945 and he is combining the work of restoration and development of the house, garden and estate with great dedication, enthusiasm and efficiency. An impressive list of improvements to the garden completed between 1965 and 1975 led to a well-deserved Architectural Heritage Award for 1975.

The village of Penshurst is close to the house, derived from the medieval, feudal integration of manor and village.

Penshurst lies in the fertile, well-wooded upper Medway valley, some 98 ft above sea level with the sheltering Lower Greensand hills to the south and west. The soils are rather heavy weald-clays, improved by centuries of good management, and having a pH with neutral and slightly acid reaction. Rainfall about 31.5 inches; sunshine 4.25 hrs.

The plan shows the present layout and components of the gardens. Their relationship to the house and the parkland to the north is well illustrated by the aerial photograph (fig. 7) taken several years ago. One can see the tight, formal structure of the gardens, based on the sixteenth and seventeenth-century format before gardens tended to be opened up and allowed to lead into the surrounding countryside. Much of this area would, in previous ownerships, have been orchards and kitchen gardens. In the post-war period, and more especially in the last 10–15 years, Lord De L'Isle, with the help of professional garden architects and an able garden staff, has added a further series of distinct gardens and special features to those established last century, all enclosed by well-managed hedges of yew *Taxus baccata* and retaining where appropriate an extensive canopy of mature fruit trees of apple, pear and some plum, so that one has the impression of being in an early monastic orchard with the old walls and hedges offering sanctuary and repose.

The Italian garden (1) is the greatest open space in the gardens, taking the form of large *parterre* on the south side of the house and providing a fine viewing platform from which to view the splendid south elevation of the building. The garden's geometric designs were laid out on Devey's advice in the middle of last century by the second Lord De L'Isle when he had succeeded his father. Low, clipped, box hedges enclosing beds planted throughout with the red polyantha rose 'Karen Poulsen' preserve the form of the Victorian garden, itself a reflection of a seventeenth-century style. The central oval fountain (2) looks deceptively round when viewed from a distance. Note the bold, raised walks and terraces on the west and north side of this garden, offering a good prospect of the gardens and at the south-west end a delightful 'window' in the brick wall from which one can look down on the everyday world of Penshurst village. The 'plat' on which the Italian garden was formed is largely artificial, having in the late sixteenth century been contrived by 'cut and fill' out of the south-east slope, where the ground runs gently away from the westernmost tower of the south front down into the Medway valley. Along the raised, shaded, western terrace are regularly spaced, mature specimens of Japanese Maples, *Acer palmatum*, with white clematis on the walls. Penshurst church lies just over the wall.

The main axis of the garden (3) runs obliquely across the natural slope from the west side of the Italian garden in front of the house, a long alley between yew walks, and across Diana's Bath (4) to the terminal sundial against the east wall (5). Notice the attractive, mixed border (6) on the south wall of the terrace below the house along this impressive walk to a design by Lanning Roper using a blended planting of shrubs and perennials on the colour theme of gold, blue and silver. The main drive borders (7) flank the main entrance from the south. Access is through the fine iron gates at the entrance. The borders are boldly planted with great drifts of such striking perennials as *Acanthus*, *Paeonia*, *Iris* and *Hemerocallis* and collections of late-flowering Michaelmas Daisies. Behind the borders on either side of the drive runs a row of well-pruned, spreading, mature apple trees, giving a most pleasing effect, especially when in full blossom in early May. Another most effective feature to note here is the use of the flagged stone paths between the drive and the borders, replacing grass paths. This not only cuts down maintenance, but provides a sympathetic composition of stone, perennials and apple trees.

Three distinctive and pleasant gardens lie to the west of the main borders and next to the Italian Garden, combining the ideas and planting schemes of the garden designers John Codrington and Lanning Roper working separately within the overall themes suggested by Lord and Lady De L'Isle. The head gardener, Mr Maurice Clarke, has, with his staff, carried through these designs with much skill and energy. These three gardens retain in part the formal patterns of the old orchard fruit trees, making a perfect setting for the design and planting.

The rose garden (8) is a simple, effective design of bush and standard roses in pink 'Elizabeth of Glamis' and red 'King Arthur', underplanted with the silvery carpet of *Stachys byzantina* and the steely-blue aromatic rue *Ruta graveolens* 'Jackman's Blue'. Two highly unusual polyhedron sundials stand on either side of the garden. The outer beds are edged with the purple-leaved dwarf *Berberis thunbergii* 'Atropurpurea Nana'. Paths lead to seats among a bower of clipped bushes of English lavender.

The middle borders (9) are very effective mixed borders of foliage, flower and textures planted to Lanning Roper's designs. Some of the many good plants used in this border in 1976 are noted here: *Salix repens argentea* (silvery-leaved); *Juniperus sabina tamariscifolia* (deep green, aromatic, low-growing); *Phlomis fruticosa* (the grey-green-leaved, yellow-flowered Jerusalem Sage); *Senecio* 'Sunshine' (*greyii*) (grey-leaved); *Rosa rubrifolia* (bronze-red foliage, red flowers and fine autumn hips); *Cytisus × praecox* (early creamy-yellow-flowered broom); Many shrub roses, including the white-flowered 'Iceberg'; *Cornus alba* 'Elegantissima' (silvery-green variegation and red winter stems); *Buddleia fallowiana* (grey-leaved, white flowers); *Crambe cordifolia* (huge heads of white flowers from bold foliage in June). Also in this border were many good frontal and ground cover perennials.

The nut garden (10) is a most restful, pleasant, cool garden re-introducing cobnuts as formal, pleached 'walls' beneath ancient pear trees and underplanted with a cottage-garden blend of spring and summer bulbs and annuals.

Note the small pool and paved garden (11) at the junction of the two main axes. The four clipped purple-leaved Myrobolan plums stand in old paving with beds of pale blue violas. Three trained gnarled wistarias stand in front of the yew hedges here. *Fuchsia magellanica gracilis* tumbles over the pool from the wall above. The pool is well planted with various ornamental aquatic species, notably *Aponogeton distachyos*, the Water Hawthorn.

To the east of the main approach drive on the north–south axis are a series of gardens that are still being developed. The most established is the north-facing paeony border (12) running eastwards from the wrought-iron gates with bold groups of mixed peonies alternating with large groups of the hybrid Canadian lilac *Syringa* 'Bellicent'. A new magnolia garden (13) has been created from an area of old sunken greenhouses and pits. A grey garden (14) is already looking effective with silver and grey mats of prostrate growing plants in formal red-brick paving agreeably patterned from material saved on site. A new nut garden is being created (15) in an area once part of the kitchen garden, and developments are planned for another enclosed garden to bring interest in August and September. Diana's

Bath (4) is not, it now appears, an ancient feature, perhaps to the regret of historically inclined visitors. This, and the other ponds and pools in the garden, probably existed from the earliest periods but were re-designed last century when the second Lord De L'Isle carried through his bold scheme of recreation. Water was brought to the garden through hollow wooden pipes from the man-made lake in the park as early as the fourteenth century.

The park – from the kitchen garden (16), a new walk through apple trees (17) leads through a gate in the north wall into the park. The limes avenue (18) running along this boundary of the garden is about 250 years old. The park is being developed sympathetically for quiet visitor enjoyment. The extensive lake, parkland, trees, and the ancient Sidney Oak are some of the features to explore.

The gardens of 11 acres are managed by three full-time gardeners with some additional help under the able leadership of Mr Maurice Clarke. The standards achieved are high, although any new developments in the main garden will have to be related to staff limitations and maintenance problems.

St John's Jerusalem

TQ 560 705 (Sheet 177) North Kent. Sutton-at-Hone. 3 miles S of Dartford on A225 Dartford–Farningham Road. Owner: The National Trust. Open: April–November, Wednesday afternoons 2–5.

A most interesting house and unusual moated garden, tending to escape the notice of all but discerning explorers. A visit is well worth while.

An ancient moated site in the valley of the River Darenth, a division of which has been used to fill the moat. The original manor belonged to the Knights Hospitallers of the Order of St John of Jerusalem. In 1234 there is reference to Henry III providing oaks to roof the new chapel (open to the public). After the Dissolution in 1540 much of the old building was destroyed and eventually a Mr Abraham Hill built the present late-seventeenth-century house within the moated garden of the old manor. Later, the famous Kent historian, Edward Hasted, lived here from 1755–76. Sir Stephen and Lady Tallents became the owners in this century and in 1943 they gave the property to the National Trust.

A site in the chalk valley of the River Darenth; sheltered and secluded, despite the general despoilation and development that have changed this once charming valley in the last 20–30 years. Soils are alluvial, silty loam, chalky in places, normally moist and occasionally flooded. The converse was the case in the great summer drought of 1976 when the River Darenth dried up completely from June to October with the complete loss of fish and aquatic life and the dispersal of the wildfowl that are normally a feature of the river and moat at St John's Jerusalem. Rainfall averages 24.5–25.5 inches. Valley frosts risk in the spring.

The house and gardens stand in a green, almost miniature park with scattered specimens and groups of native trees of about 50 years old. Some protective woodlands lie to the south-east. The form of the gardens is contained within about five acres bounded by the rectangular moat. The space enclosed must at one time have been more formal and geometrical in design, consistent with the age of the house. A pleasing car park beneath trees (a good cedar here) leads one over the moat to the south-east front of the house. A strong axial line as a walk runs parallel with the house past the chapel into the walled garden with its terminal view of large weeping willows on the moat borders to the east. The walled garden has some attractive traditional borders of mixed herbaceous and summer flowering species. Away from these more sophisticated areas one can wander through an old orchard with grassy walks beside the moat. There are some ancient Medlars, *Mespilus germanica* here and a nut plat. Some ornamental trees and shrubs have been planted beside the moat, including a willow collection of varying age and species. A large Crack Willow *Salix fragilis* and the several weeping willows *Salix × chrysocoma* (*alba tristis*) make a fine background to the moat and garden. Pollarded red-stemmed willows *Salix alba* 'Chrysostella' are attractive in the winter months. At the front end of the main lawn is an informal group of weeping cherries, walnuts and thorns. There are also some large Horse Chestnuts and a Copper Beech in this shaded, woodland-type area. In the park there is a collection of Walnut cultivars.

The five acres of garden are maintained to a very high standard by one full-time gardener and a very active and extremely well-informed tenant, Mrs T.C. Mallik, who is an authority on historic architecture and buildings.

Saltwood Castle

TR 162 360 (Sheet 179) East Kent. Saltwood. 2 miles NW of Hythe.
Owner: The Hon. Alan Clark, MP and Mrs Clark. Open 5 days per week
throughout June, July and August (not Mondays and Saturdays). Current
details see H.H.C.G.

Saltwood Castle has a long and fascinating history dating back to the
Roman period. It was largely restored earlier this century under the
distinguished medieval revivalist architect Sir Philip Tilden. It was
strategically placed some 295 ft above sea level to command the coast
near Hythe and the inland routes to Canterbury. Despite its closeness
to Hythe and the teeming south-east coast of Kent, the castle is today
surprisingly secluded and hidden away in well-timbered parkland on
the same wooded ridge as Sandling Park. The soil here is light, sandy
loam.

The present gardens are a simple and sympathetic setting to the
romantic complex of old buildings and ruined walls which offer an
ideal home for many vigorous climbers like *Clematis montana* and
other species, old roses and the vigorous *R.* 'Wedding Day', honeysuckles, wistaria, and many more. The borders alongside the walls
are simply planted with herbs, perennials and shrubs in keeping
with the ancient site and the setting. A walk along the old battlements
gives a magnificent series of views of the landscape of this area, and
a bird's-eye view of the castle grounds. The remote and tiny secret
garden in the heart of the castle can be seen from up here; a cool,
leafy retreat, very easily missed.

Restful mown lawns, well-placed seats and the serving of delightful
home-made teas in an old stable building beneath the shade of several
fine old sycamore trees add to the charm and sense of welcome and
homeliness of this place. Peacocks usually strut around the grounds to
give a final touch of aristocratic splendour.

The tea break is an ideal time to study the excellent guidebook to
the castle produced by the Clark family. Sir Kenneth Clark lived here
for many years and wrote most of his books, including the *Civilisation*
series, at Saltwood. His son is the present owner.

Sandling Park

TR 144 367 (Sheet 179) East Kent. 2 miles NW Hythe. S off A20 Ashford–Folkestone trunk road at Sandling, Folkestone 7 miles. Owner: Major A.E. Hardy. Open last four Sundays in May and first Sunday in June, for the N.G.S. Details in H.H.C.G. and the N.G.S. publications. Good parking and well-organized arrangements.

A large, 30-acre woodland garden on acid soil, being part of the ancient forest of Westenhanger. Such gardens are rare in east Kent where the soils are predominantly chalky. Open for spectacular displays of rhododendrons, magnolias, primulas and many other flowering plants in a pleasant, informal setting with very fine specimen trees.

The mansion that once stood on the site of the present house was built in 1796 by the Italian architect Bonhommi for the Deedes family. The park was probably fenced for deer at this time and many of the fine beeches and oaks of the present day would have been growing in the park then.

There seems to have been an important era of planting more exotic trees in the middle of the nineteenth century, along with other estates of the same period. A diary presented to the Hardy family contains invaluable information and records that many of the existing fine conifers were planted in 1846. The woodland was planted in 1854 with *ponticum* rhododendrons, along with another noted garden nearby – the Garden House, Saltwood – by a local churchman and keen gardener, Archdeacon Croft, rector of Saltwood. In 1897 Sandling Park was bought by the present owner's father, The Rt Hon. Lawrence Hardy, MP. He was responsible for much of the landscaping in the garden and park from 1900 onwards. He had a good eye for vistas and planned some of the first woodland walks. The very first coloured hybrid rhododendron, R.'Cynthia', was planted in 1900 and is still growing today. So from the turn of the century came the gradual development of the garden, with the R. *ponticum* giving way to allow space for the planting of more exciting specimens. However, they have not been banished completely and still form a very helpful shelter belt around the perimeter of the wood, flowering well each June.

Three generations of the Hardy family have applied their energies and keen gardening interest to making this woodland garden a continual source of pleasure, concentrating on trees and shrubs that enjoy the rich, acid, forest soils, exploiting the moist dells, and streamside planting with Asiatic primulas and other water-loving plants. Much use has been made of all types of woodland plants, along with the natural flora — primroses, bluebells and ferns grow in abundance. In spite of the awe-inspiring forest trees and the great banks of rhododendrons and azaleas, visitors often say that the garden has a young feeling about it. Perhaps this is due to the continual addition of new plants, constant re-appraisal and striving for improvement.

Sandling Park, as the name might suggest, lies on a gentle south—south-west slope of a Lower Greensand ridge, at about 260 ft above sea level, the soils being acidic sandy loam, rich in organic matter from their forest origin and the annual leaf-fall. The surrounding area is scenically attractive and the sea can be seen from the lawn by the house through a convenient gap in neighbouring woods. The gardens are generally well-sheltered by mature trees which occasionally suffer gale damage. Rainfall averages 27.5—28.5 inches.

The present house was built by Major Hardy under post-war restrictions, the original being destroyed by enemy action in 1942. The imposing creeper-covered gate-posts and the stone balustrade around the lower terrace are reminders of the earlier stately home. There are two distinct parts of the garden for the visitor to explore. The greater part is the informal woodland garden already referred to and a large walled garden, described later.

The first impression which strikes the visitor is the spacious, well-kept, rolling lawn below the house. This is dominated by fine specimen trees and the rugged conifers of the 1846 planting. The most massive specimen is a Monterey Pine *Pinus radiata*; note also the Douglas Fir *Pseudotsuga menziesii* and tall Sitka Spruce *Picea sitchensis*, some fine cedars and a Monkey Puzzle, *Araucaria araucana*. One of the most impressive trees is a Tulip Tree *Liriodendron tulipifera*, a large specimen with its characteristic oddly-shaped leaves, flowering in July. Also two beautifully grown *Magnolia* × *soulangiana*, planted 1900, each standing in a specially cut niche in the yew hedge, the dark-green background a perfect foil for the gleaming white flowers in early May. Large informal beds of massed Kurume azaleas are spectacular in pinks, whites and reds, also in May. Here one cannot miss the symmetrical pile of cannon-balls cast for the Siege of Sebastopol by a previous generation of the Hardy family from the Lowmore Foundries in Yorkshire. The massive ball on the top weighs one-and-a-half tons and a mortar was never found large enough to hurl this! The smaller balls weigh a mere five cwt each. Descending gradually into the woodland past a fine Cut-leaved Beech, *Fagus sylvatica heterophylla*, one traverses a series of glades, following a winding figure-of-eight path, the light shade coming from the great beeches and oaks above. There are rhododendrons of all ages, a vast and comprehensive collection including many different species with their distinctive types; old-fashioned and much-loved hybrids; also modern hybrids with their fabulous colour range; and many of Major Hardy's own raising. Azaleas are well represented; *Rhododendron luteum*, the well-known common fragrant yellow azalea, scents the garden deliciously. There are also evergreen Kurumes, deciduous varieties, including the Ghent hybrids, the soft-coloured and larger-flowered mollis, and many modern Exbury and Knap Hill varieties in glowing colours. Magnolias are also a feature, with many different varieties, including the strongly scented *M. wilsonii* with its nodding cup-shaped flowers, stained purple at the base. Camellias have earned well-deserved respect and are now included in much of the new planting. Some of the early plants have formed large bushes; there is a fine 23 ft specimen of *C. × williamsii* 'J.C. Williams', and the spectacular variety *C. × w.* 'Donation' flourishes. There is an under-carpet of woodland flowers everywhere; bluebells and *Claytonia* which create much interest. Another great feature of Sandling Park are the Lilies of the Valley at their best in early May.

Sandling Park is fortunate in having many streams and watercourses that drain the slope running down through the garden – a perfect setting for the flowering meads of Asiatic primulas of the candelabra type, ferns, the intriguing Bog Arum, *Lysichitum americanum* and *Rodgersia* spp. Primulas seem to be able to withstand a fair degree of drought, though it can seriously affect a garden such as this, as the mains water springs from the chalk and so cannot be used, being deleterious to ericaceous and allied plants. In March and April daffodils are everywhere, particularly in the daffodil walk in the lowest part of the garden. Some intriguing log seats carved from fallen timber afford a pleasant resting place. In the area are some of the finest Japanese Maples, both green and purple-leaved varieties from the early planting period. There is one outstanding tree in the wood which should not be missed. This is a giant alder, *Alnus glutinosa*, thought to be over 250 years old and standing with a clean trunk and high canopy, like a great oak (unusual habit for an alder), over 85 ft high. It is featured in the *Guinness Book of Records* as the largest recorded tree of this type in Europe.

One leaves the woodland by the gentle slope along magnolia walk, where the white flowers seem to illuminate the whole garden in May. On reaching the lawns again you may lose yourself under the Weeping Beech, *Fagus sylvatica* 'Pendula', with its great long arms running horizontally towards the daylight. Returning to the area around the house is the second part of the garden. Mrs Hardy has concentrated on the more formal features, her main interests being perennials, roses and wall-top gardening. The rose garden is enclosed by an unusual curving yew hedge planted in 1900, and climbing roses are trained along swinging chains giving the impression of great swags of flower in June, a most intriguing method. The great walled garden is one-and-a-quarter acres in extent, and note how the walls are built to rise and fall with the slope. This garden is most efficiently run as a market garden where crops mature early on the light sandy soil, and it always looks in splendid shape. The lean-to houses were replaced a few years ago with well-built aluminium structures, and here one can see the best traditions of large garden horticulture, with the wall peaches and vines being beautifully trained.

Two gardeners manage the walled garden and glasshouse area; one gardener tends all the lawns and the woodland garden. Major and Mrs Hardy's dedication and energy have resulted in a fine example of a well-planted woodland garden, with a very comprehensive collection of trees and shrubs used in the natural way. They are fortunate in that their son Alan and his family are equally enthusiastic – he is dedicated to the genus *Rhododendron* and allied plants. Although the gardens are only open for five Sundays, many thousands of visitors flock to Sandling Park annually, evidence of the justifiable popularity of this fine garden.

Scotney Castle

TQ 685 355 (Sheet 188) West Kent. 1 mile SE Lamberhurst. Left off A21 London–Hastings road. London 40 miles, Tunbridge Wells 8 miles, Hastings 20 miles. Owner: The National Trust. Open April–October, usually 5 days per week (not Mondays or Tuesdays). Full details in National Trust literature or H.H.C.G. Teas are available.

Apart from Leeds Castle, Scotney has the most dramatic and romantic setting, a ruined castle in a lake, surrounded by woodland gardens on acid soils. There are many fine trees and shrubs.

A site of early English origin, the manor being in the possession of the de Scoteni family in the twelfth and thirteenth centuries. The

picturesque moated castle (now a ruin) was built about 1378–80 by Roger Ashburnham who constructed a fortified house of a similar style to that of Bodiam Castle in East Sussex. Only one corner tower survives. For 350 years the castle was held by the Darell family who considerably enlarged the old house and also incorporated numerous secret hiding-places. In 1778 Scotney Castle was acquired by the Hussey family who remained at Scotney until the property passed into the hands of the National Trust in the 1960s. The third Edward Hussey, born in 1807 and an only son, had agreed with his mother that the old castle was too damp and low-lying to be healthy, and in the period 1835–45 Scotney was transformed by the building of a fine new country house on high ground to the north-west; the development of a romantic, natural and picturesque garden; and the deliberate and careful partial-demolition of the old castle to complete the evocative garden landscape composition. In creating the house, garden and 'ruin', Edward Hussey was considerably influenced by the 'Picturesque' school of writers and gardeners of the late eighteenth and early nineteenth centuries, Uvedale Price, Richard Payne Knight and the Rev. Gilpin. The present house was designed in a neo-Elizabethan style by the architect Anthony Salvin (1799–1881).

The house is not open to the public, but visitors can well assess the strategy of the site chosen, with its magnificent views down through the garden to the moated ruin and away to the hills beyond, a landscape of parkland and distant woods. Exotic trees and shrubs were planted, particularly the newly introduced American conifers like Lawson's Cypress, *Chamaecyparis lawsoniana*; Wellingtonia, *Sequoiadendron giganteum*, and Incense Cedar, *Calocedrus decurrens*, and such American shrubs as *Kalmia* and the Smoke Bush, *Cotinus coggygria*. The quarry from which stone was used to build the new house was ingeniously developed as a rock garden, just below the house, adding to the picturesque character of the garden.

The story can be brought up to date with the arrival at Scotney of the writer, the late Mr Christopher Hussey, who succeeded his uncle, Edward Windsor Hussey, in 1952. He carried out a much-needed long-term restoration programme of the house, castle and gardens, and developed a deep love and understanding of this beautiful place. For 18 years, until his death in 1970, he worked to this end, aided by his wife, who has a comprehensive knowledge and equal love of plants and gardens. She still lives at Scotney and takes an active part in the management of the gardens and estate, in association with the National Trust.

About 35,000 visitors per year now come to Scotney.

Scotney lies on the eastern side of the High Weald in richly-wooded, farming, fruit and hops countryside like many other fine gardens in this area of Kent (see Bedgebury, Ladham, Sissinghurst). The house stands on a promontory 230 ft above sea level, the garden falling away to the south and south-west to the River Bewl and the old moated castle in its valley. Much of the garden is well sheltered by mature tree planting and the topography of the land form, providing warm, secluded south and south-east slopes. Rainfall 29.5–31.5 inches. The soils are acidic, wealden Tunbridge Wells sands with the iron-rich deposits that made this area once famous for its iron-smelting industry. The railings round St Paul's Cathedral were forged at Lamberhurst. In the 'quarry' rock garden area can be seen ancient sea-bed ripples of the sandstone rock, and, for those who are prepared to look carefully, the footprints of the giant Iguanodon lizards that once trod the sandy beaches of the great Wealden Sea in the lower Cretaceous period. These moist acidic soils favour the growth of many fine trees and shrubs.

Essentially an informal, extensive woodland 'wild garden' developed from the early nineteenth-century concept of the picturesque with some later planting of exotic trees and shrubs. The setting and genius of the place are the outstanding features, rather than the complexity or variety of the planting. From the car park near the house one descends gradually through glades and paths among masses of mature rhododendrons and azaleas and bold groups of *Kalmia* spp., *Cotinus coggygria* and other shrubs. Fine beeches, limes and oaks add to the woodland scene, and to the right one looks out into open parkland and pasture. In the spring daffodils are massed everywhere and in the old quarry are large mature mounds of white *Magnolia stellata* and many rhododendrons and azaleas, with a fringe of heathers and other shrubs. Japanese Maples, *Acer palmatum*, are everywhere a magnificent sight in autumn, and near the moat are sculptural specimens of the American conifers referred to previously.

One can cross the moat to the old ruined castle and this has been used as a setting for many old-fashioned plantings appropriate to the period. On the old walls are tumbling masses of old roses such as 'Rambling Rector'; a semi-double, scented, creamy-white *Rosa multiflora* variety of unknown date; 'Blushing Lucy', a pink rambler; and the North American *Rosa californica* 'Plena' with rich pink blooms in early summer. There are beds of herbs here and border plants like *Phlox*, *Sedum*, *Geranium* and summer scented Heliotrope, Tobacco Plants and varieties of *Pelargonium*. There are fine masses of waterside perennials – *Osmunda regalis*, Royal Fern; *Ligularia*, *Gunnera* and *Hosta* species around the moat and pools. Cool, shady walks offer further pleasant relaxation and contrast along the moat and the boundary streams. A thatched tent-shaped ice-house can be seen at the north-east end of the garden.

The garden is managed by three full-time staff and one part-time. The standards of upkeep are good, and sympathetic to the style and character of the place. No plants are labelled.

Sissinghurst Castle Garden

TQ 807 384 (Sheet 188) Mid Kent. 1½ miles E Sissinghurst, 3 miles NE Cranbrook off A262 Goudhurst–Tenterden Road. Tunbridge Wells 15 miles. Maidstone 17 miles. London 45 miles. Owner: The National Trust. Open: Generally most days from 1 April–mid-October, noon to early evening. Check current edition of H.H.C.G. or National Trust literature.

These world famous gardens were created by Harold Nicolson and Vita Sackville-West in the 1930s. A series of enclosed gardens evolve around the romantic ruins of the old castle and its gatehouse buildings. There are fine examples of plant associations for colour, site and mood.

In brief, the site was originally a moated medieval manor belonging originally to the de Saxenhurst family from whom the name Sissinghurst is derived. It then came into the hands of the de Berham (or Barham) family. Only a part of the moat survives from this period. In the late fifteenth century, Sir John Baker bought the manor, and after demolishing most of the older buildings, he built a new courtyard house on slightly higher ground to the west. His son, Sir Richard Baker, carried out further major alterations in the 1560–70 period, the most notable feature being the building of the tower and main west courtyard, much of which can still be seen today. The surrounding estate was enclosed by a park fence said to be seven miles in length, containing hunting parks with grazing animals, including deer, enjoying the rich pastures. Fine oak woodlands embellished the house. The Bakers' fortunes suffered during the Civil War and by the end of the seventeenth century their wealth had been largely dispersed and the Sissinghurst estate split up. Mismanagement and the decline of Sissinghurst continued throughout the eighteenth century. In 1756 it became a prison and was heavily mortgaged. The house was still standing intact

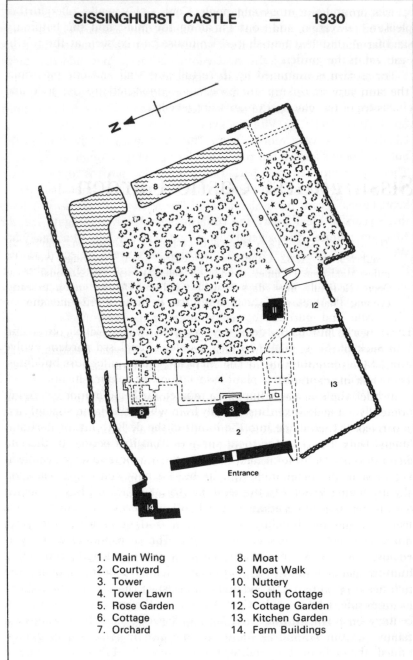

SISSINGHURST CASTLE — 1930

1. Main Wing
2. Courtyard
3. Tower
4. Tower Lawn
5. Rose Garden
6. Cottage
7. Orchard
8. Moat
9. Moat Walk
10. Nuttery
11. South Cottage
12. Cottage Garden
13. Kitchen Garden
14. Farm Buildings

at that time, although very dilapidated. The prison camp was disbanded in 1763, leaving a shattered house whose only assets were the park and farmlands. The famous Kent family of Cornwallis owned the ruins and estate for most of the nineteenth century. They added a large Victorian farmhouse to the estate (opposite the car park) and managed the farm very successfully. Some minor repairs were done to the tower.

Sissinghurst was on the market for two years before being bought on 4 April 1930 by Vita Sackville-West and her husband, Harold Nicolson, for a very modest sum. They had immediately realized the potential of this forlorn but romantic place as a future home and garden. Then followed a ten-year period of making the gardens and restoring the house, tower and buildings. The story is fully related in Anne Scott-James' recent book *Sissinghurst: The Making of a Garden.** It took three years to clear away the rubbish before planting began. Harold Nicolson planned the several vistas and walks while Vita Sackville-West clothed his ideas with a profusion of cleverly selected plants. By the outbreak of war in 1939 the garden was largely finished in its main essentials, and since that time it has matured into perfection. Vita Sackville-West died at Sissinghurst in June 1962 and she left the castle and garden to her younger son, Nigel Nicolson, who continues to live at the castle. In April 1967 the castle and garden and most of the surrounding farmlands passed to the National Trust. Nigel Nicolson continues to live there and to administer the property on behalf of the Trust.

In the Weald of Kent, the gardens are located on a shallow plateau some 130 ft above sea level with some exposure to the north and north-east. Woodland belts to the south-east and south have value as shelter belts. The soils are derived from the weald-clay, heavy, retentive neutral loam. Drainage was a problem but this has been improved in recent years. The climate is equable and less important generally than the series of microclimates created by the enclosing walls and hedges. The tower and the archways in the walls can, however, make it a draughty garden at times, especially in the top courtyard. Rainfall averages 31.5–32.5 inches and being on a plateau site there is relative freedom from valley radiation frosts. Sunshine 4.3 hrs. The more tender plants are covered over in winter and the run of fairly mild winters up to 1976 has given some borderline subjects a chance to get established.

Between them, Harold Nicolson and Vita Sackville-West realized a happy and ingenious compromise of garden styles and planting,

---

* Anne Scott-James, *Sissinghurst: The Making of a Garden*, Michael Joseph, 1975.

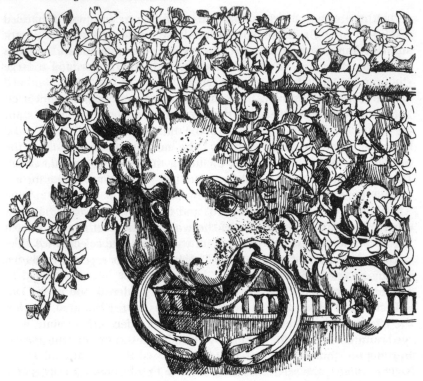

between the formalism of the neo-Elizabethan revival, with a suggestion of influences from Italy, France and Spain, and the natural rich and apparently spontaneous plantings advocated by Gertrude Jekyll and William Robinson (Vita Sackville-West knew and admired Robinson). Vita Sackville-West summarizes the atmosphere perfectly: 'Though very English, very Kentish, it had something southern about it, a Norman Manor House perhaps, a faint echo of something more southern.'* The style at Sissinghurst is essentially one of a series of separate rooms and sub-sections, each with its own personal character of planting, form and quality, linked by a strong overall design. The plan shows the essential components of the gardens. A summary of the main planting characteristics in each area is given here. Many of the plants are well-labelled and as in all gardens change is inevitable, not all the species and varieties noted by the author are included in this summary. Some may well have been replaced or modified since this book was written.

* Alvilde Lees-Milne, *RHS Journal*, September 1966.

The entrance (1) – The four urns standing in the forecourt came originally from Bagatelle, the famous rose garden near Paris. In the summer months a small, but always interesting plant-stall usually stands by the gate, where one can buy well-grown plants of some of the unusual kinds found in the garden.

The tower courtyard (2) – From the entrance, a broad path of old London paving stones leads to the Elizabethan tower. Irish Yews stand on either side of the path. Note the fine vigorous red rose 'Allen Chandler' over the inner archway. The east-facing walls of the court are well-clothed with climbers, including the vigorous annual *Cobaea scandens* with its large, purple, square, bell flowers; the white form is usually here also. Other good climbing plants include *Solanum crispum* 'Glasnevin', *Ceanothus* 'Southmead' and *Lonicera splendida*. Troughs of dwarf plants grow at the foot of the wall. At the northern end is the purple border where the majority of the plants are selected for their purple, magenta and lilac colours. This border looks especially effective in August and September.

The rose garden (17) – In this delightful garden is one of the best collections of old-fashioned and shrub roses in the country. In June the effect is magnificent. The quality of this garden and its planting is well summarized in the article by Alvilde Lees-Milne on the garden in the R.H.S. Journal for September 1966:

The colours, the scent, the hue, billowing pink roses with intriguing French names, such as 'Chapeau de Napoléon', 'Hippolyte', 'Nuits de Young' and many more . . . produce an intoxicating effect . . . None of the stiff garish-coloured hybrid teas is to be seen here or indeed anywhere at Sissinghurst. However, Vita Sackville-West saw no reason for not incorporating other plants among the roses. Following in William Robinson's footsteps she underplanted and interplanted profusely. No bare earth might be seen. Irises carefully selected as to colour are grouped along the broad flag-stones; tulips are in bold clumps, and *Allium albopilosum* (*A.christophii*) looks particularly well massed at the foot of the purple roses. *Acanthus, Kolkwitzia amabilis*, lavender, *Desmodium*, and countless other plants, with pansies tucked in wherever there is a gap, create a sense of voluptuous beauty hard to equal. Also in this garden is a group of immensely tall *Eremurus robustus* growing in front of the dark yew hedge – a highly successful piece of planting. Again, an exuberance of climbers scrambling up and over the walls.

In the centre of this garden is the rondel (18), a circular green room of immaculately cut yew hedges, the name deriving from that given to the round floor of the oast houses so common in the Weald of Kent.

From the centre of the rondel one can look back through a charming archway across the tower lawn to the distant gate leading into the white garden, one of the many internal vistas cleverly marked-out by Harold Nicolson.

The lime walk (14) — is another long vista and a delightful formal feature, looking especially colourful in April and early May. During the winter of 1976–77 the Common Limes were being replaced with a more suitable species, York paving was laid in place of the old concrete block paths and some of the thousands of spring bulbs for which this garden is renowned were carefully replanted. The terra-cotta garden pots from Tuscany are usually planted with trailing clematis. Many other plants are woven into the spring tapestry of the garden. From this walk one can look out into the surrounding country-side to the lake and the woodlands so much beloved by Vita Sackville-West.

The cottage garden (15) — The delightful south cottage building was once part of the end of the long south wing of the Elizabethan house. This garden is planted with 'a controlled untidiness'. The colours are essentially bright, warm and lively. The theme is mainly reds, oranges and yellows. A fine central copper container is usually planted with tulips followed by *Mimulus* (*Diplacus*) *glutinosus* or other summer flowering plants, and formal Irish Yews stand as if guarding it. The paths are paved with old bricks and stones. Red dahlias, orange and yellow species of *Kniphofia*, red and yellow tree peonies, rock roses, iris and evening primroses are only a few of the riot of colourful plants thriving here. On the walls of the cottage is a splendid plant of the white rose 'Madame Alfred Carrière' and also the early-flowering, yellow climbing rose 'Lawrence Johnston'.

The nuttery (13) — or nut platt represents one of the few original features found by the Nicolsons when they bought Sissinghurst. Plantations of Kent cob-nuts were a regular feature of most farms and country houses of the Weald and crops in some years could be prolific. Vita Sackville-West underplanted the nut copse with a great collection of primula polyanthus varieties and seedlings and for many years these were a fine sight in April or May. However, increasing problems of disease have affected many polyanthus stocks everywhere in recent years, and in 1975 it was decided to remove them and replace with bold drifts of shade-loving perennials and ground-cover plants. These have grown well in the last 2–3 years. Note especially the fast-growing purple-magenta-flowered *Geranium procurrens*, Woodruff *Asperula odorata*, *Epimedium*, *Euphorbia* and many shade-loving bulbous plants such as *Erythronium* and *Trillium*.

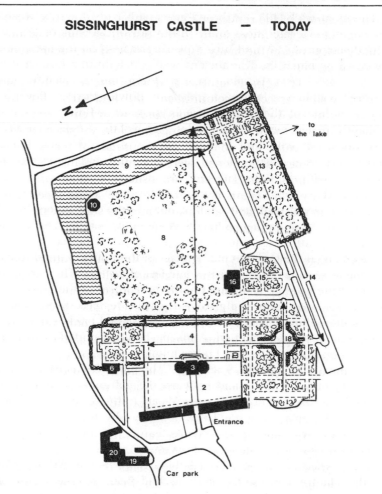

SISSINGHURST CASTLE — TODAY

to the lake

Entrance

Car park

1. Main Wing
2. Tower Courtyard (1931-32)
3. Tower
4. Tower Lawn (1930)
5. White Garden (1946)
6. Priest's House/Delos
7. Yew Walk
8. Orchard (1938)
9. Moat
10. Gazebo

11. Moat Walk (1930)
12. Herb Garden (1938)
13. Nuttery
14. Lime Walk (1932-33)
15. Cottage Garden (1931)
16. South Cottage
17. Rose Garden (1933-34)
18. Rondel
19. Tea Rooms and Shop
20. Farm Buildings

The moat walk (11) — A broad grass path runs down between the old wall of the former moat on the north side and a bank of deciduous, brightly-coloured May and June flowering azaleas on the opposite side colonized by bluebells. The ancient wall is delightfully furnished with Hart's Tongue Fern *Asplenium scolopendrium* and the woody, purple-flowered wall-flower *Erysimum linifolium* 'Bowles Purple'. Beyond the wall is a line of the cherry *Prunus sargentii*, whose leaves colour brilliantly in September. Unfortunately, some of these trees have already been killed out with that dreaded disease of gardens and arboreta, Honey Fungus *Armillaria mellea*. The vista north-east down the moat walk ends with the statue of Dionysus beyond the moat.

The herb garden (12) — Note the attractive and unusual thyme lawn in a paved setting near the moat before one enters the herb garden. This was another of Vita Sackville-West's ideas, and although undoubtedly attractive and appealing, the head gardeners have no illusions about the maintenance problems, the hours of hand weeding, and the losses due to the caresses and feet of visitors. The herb garden is one of the most popular and charming features of the gardens. The original concrete paths and grass paths were replaced some years ago with a more durable but extremely well-designed brick, stone and tile path in the best local tradition. A marble bowl supported by three lions standing on an old millstone makes a fine focal feature.

The moat and orchard (9 and 8) — The moat lies along the eastern boundary of the gardens and between the old gnarled oaks along its borders one can look out across the Weald to the distant North Downs 15–20 miles away. The moat has been here for over 500 years. The old orchard was another surviving feature of the neglected castle gardens in 1930 and Vita Sackville-West conceived the idea of growing a careful selection of vigorous climbing roses up the old apple trees. As the old trees die some of them had been replaced with other flowering ornamental trees so that the effect of an orchard was tending to be lost. However, a policy now being adopted is to plant more apple trees of older varieties on standard stems to recreate the orchard effect. The grass is thick with daffodils and other bulbs in the spring. and becomes a pleasant flowering hay meadow in the early summer. In early autumn *Colchicum* spp., Autumn Crocus, come into flower. Note the charming bed of old roses at the west end of the orchard against the yew walk hedge. There are massed mingling groups of hybrid musk rose 'Kathleen', a delightful single pale pink; the old rose that was found in the gardens, *R. gallica* 'Sissinghurst Castle', deep double purplish-red; and bold clumps of pale blue *Campanula lactiflora* flowering at the same time as the roses in mid–late June.

The yew walk (7) – The longest and most dramatic north–south axis of the garden. The hedges had become increasingly wide over the years, making movement by the great number of visitors more difficult and, more important, overshadowing the base of the hedges and causing much dead growth, with a gradual weakening of the upper parts of the hedge. In 1969 a drastic programme of cutting back the hedges to their original width was begun. First, the drainage of the area was improved and the hedges fed with fertilizer for a year or two in advance. The insides and top were than cut hard back in the first operation, followed by the outsides six years later. The hedges are treated annually with dressings of spent hops and rotted manure. This policy is now being undertaken with other yew hedges in the garden where 'middle-age spread' has become a problem.

The white garden (5) – Described by Vita Sackville-West as the 'grey and white garden, essentially a garden to sit in on a warm evening, because it looks so cool and unaffected by the long hot day'.* The garden has the charming setting of the priest's house, and is divided by low, neatly-trimmed box hedges. Really a miniature *parterre* with the many enclosures having different communities of mostly white or grey plants. Nigel Nicolson designed the graceful arched iron canopy in the centre over which grows the vigorous scented, *Rosa longicuspis*. A list of some of the more outstanding plants noted in the garden in the summer of 1976 is given here: *Stachys byzantina* 'Silver Carpet'; *Salvia argentea*; *Phlox* 'Norah Leigh'; *Gillenia trifoliata*; *Crambe cordifolia*; *Geranium rectum* 'Album'; *Delphinium* 'Galahad' (one of the Pacific strains raised from seed); *Senecio leucostachys*; *Campanula persicifolia* 'Alba'; *Campanula burghaltii*; *Artemisia ludoviciana*; *Jaborosa integrifolia*; *Ballota pseudodictamnus*; *Macleaya cordata*; *Zantedeschia aethiopica* 'Crowborough'; *Nicotiana* 'Lime Green'; *Nicotiana sylvestris*; *Helichrysum petiolatum*; *Helichrysum microphyllum*; *Pyrus salicifolia* 'Pendula'; *Silybum marianum*; *Galega* × *hartlandii*; *Rosa* 'Iceberg' underplanted with *Pulmonaria* 'Sissinghurst White'; *Hosta sieboldiana elegans*; *Tiarella cordifolia*; *Iris* spp.; *Eremurus himalaicus* and many others.

Delos (6) – To the west of the priest's house is a very effective, and often overlooked, recently planted area of ground cover, shrubs and bulb species in delightful and original associations. Note the large bushy plant of the Mediterranean Kermes Oak, *Quercus coccifera*, looking here like a dense spiny-leaved holly. There is also a good Strawberry Tree *Arbutus unedo* near the well, underplanted with the autumn-flowering *Cyclamen hederifolium (neapolitanum)*. There are many early

---

* Vita Sackville-West, *RHS Journal*, November 1953.

spring bulbs such as *Eranthis, Hepatica* and *Anemone*. Look for the highly unusual *Polygonum equisetiforme* beside the path.

The management and maintenance of these superb gardens are under the joint direction of the two head gardeners, Pamela Schwerdt N.D.H. and Sibylle Kreutzberger. They both trained at the famous Waterperry Horticultural School and came to Sissinghurst as head gardeners to Vita Sackville-West in 1959. They thus had two years working with her before her death in 1962. Under their inspired leadership and direction the personal touch and unique individuality that was such a feature of these gardens in her day have been largely retained. This is all the more remarkable and praiseworthy when one learns that 90,000 visitors come to the gardens each year. Four other gardeners are also employed, and some of their work must inevitably be repair and renewal work due to the wear and tear on grass and edges and plants by the enormous number of visitors. There have been as many as 2,500 visitors in one day, and to quote Harold Nicolson, 'they innocently destroy what they have come to see in the serenity of Sissinghurst.' To really enjoy these gardens in an atmosphere of peace and tranquillity, choose a weekday in April, May or early June, or later in September, and arrive soon after opening or in the early evening. A visit under these conditions is unforgettable.

Updown House

TR 315 535 (Sheet 179) East Kent. 4 miles S of Sandwich off A256, 1½ miles SE of Eastry on a minor road to Northbourne. Deal and the sea are 4–5 miles to the E. Owner: Major A. James. Open usually every Sunday afternoon in May and June for the N.G.C.

A delightful and romantic garden hidden away in well-timbered grounds in this rather exposed and treeless part of east Kent. The main gardens were created over the last 25–30 years in two large walled gardens. There is a very good collection of shrubs and old roses and many other fascinating plants.

The house is on a site of considerable antiquity, although the present house, built by the Factor family, is mainly of the 1720 period with further additions in the early nineteenth century. A small park surrounds the house and there are many magnificent mature trees, notably beeches, around the delightful cricket ground beside the main drive. Major and the late Mrs James acquired the property in 1939 but were unable to develop the garden until the post-war period. The present garden was developed from 1956 by Major and Mrs James who concentrated their attentions on the large, enclosed walled gardens of about three acres which, when they began, included many old fruit trees and a very badly neglected kitchen garden. The paths and terraces were carefully designed by Mrs James and built almost entirely with her own hands. Notice the pleasing and harmonious mixture of brick, York stone, and pebbles collected from the nearby seashores. Much of the York stone came from Cadogan Place in London.

Shelter to the gardens on most sides is provided by the mature trees and the walls – a critical factor in this relatively exposed area. The gardens lie some 130 ft above sea level. The soil is a good brick earth with a generally neutral pH (overlying chalk). Rainfall 23.6–24.6 inches.

The style of the main gardens within the walls shows some influences of the Jekyll/Sissinghurst school, but the enclosures are less well-

defined by hedges or intervening walls, being created from banks of shrubs and some trees and other plantings. The entrance drive from the main road is rather concealed and unassuming, to say the least, with little indication of the pleasures to come. Informal parking beneath the trees on the edge of the cricket ground allows a delightful place for visitors to picnic or meditate or perhaps watch the cricket before or after visiting the gardens.

The small entrance gate to the left of the house, where one pays the entry fee, opens onto a large mown lawn with trees and shrubs to the left. If visiting the gardens early in May notice the unusual Formosan Cherry, *Prunus campanulata*, with dark rose-red pendulous clusters of flowers. This normally needs a very mild sheltered place and is a fine indicator-plant of the very favourable microclimate of these gardens. The curtilage of fine tall trees to the east is broken by a ha-ha which allows an unbroken view away across the fields to a distant view of the Channel near Deal. This is the direction of the cold, biting winds that can blow across east Kent in severe winters. Through the old wrought-iron gates in the wall one enters the main gardens and another world. The main axis of these gardens runs east–west from the gates, through flanking borders of old roses and massed shrubs to a distant seat backed by woodland and fine trees. From this seat one can look back through the gardens to the gates and to the countryside beyond. In the first walled garden one enters there are luxuriant masses of old shrub roses, looking splendid in late May and June, particularly the hybrid musks like 'Penelope', 'Buff Beauty' and 'Fantin Latour'. Perimeter borders and the walls here offer homes for *Carpenteria californica* on the south wall, *Abelia × grandiflora, Sophora tetraptera* and several magnificent columnar specimens of *Daphne mezereum*, some of the oldest plants I have ever seen. In June there are masses of spectacular Fox Tail Lilies *Eremurus* spp. in pale pink, white and yellow. There are also many good shrubs like *Deutzia* and *Kolkwitzia* flowering in June. The southern part retains some of the old apple trees and the quartered division of the old kitchen garden layout. Peonies grow well here, especially the Chinese *P. lactiflora* varieties and some fine groups of the cool lemon-yellow *P. mlokosewitschii*. The walls are draped with clematis, honeysuckles and many other plants. Seats and comfortable folding chairs are usually dispersed around the gardens – a very nice touch indeed!

The second garden is more shaded with old fruit trees and orna-mental trees like Judas Tree *Cercis siliquastrum, Magnolia campbellii mollicomata*, lilacs *Syringa* spp. and others. In spring, masses of small bulbous species like *Fritillaria, Crocus* and *Erythronium* are profuse and colourful in a fascinating groundwork of planting. A rather overgrown rock garden has a profusion of regenerating plants of many kinds, many of them quite rare, including a fine, sprawling plant, *Daphne blagayana* 6 ft across, and in a paved area nearby another fine prostrate *Daphne cneorum*. Daphnes seem to thrive at Updown. Look out for *D. × burkwoodii* and the small evergreen *D. tangutica*. Figs grow in abundance in the walls here, and one shaded border has a delightful naturalized area of unusual tulip varieties, many of them the 'broken' or multicoloured kinds. Behind and around the seat on the north-west side are shade-loving woodland glade plants like foxgloves, *Geranium* species, *Helleborus* and drifts of pink, white or purple Honesty *Lunaria biennis*. Beyond and to the south of the walls one can wander through an arboretum-like area of great trees (cedars and limes reach 80–90 ft here), winding grass paths and woodland glades. Masses of the evergreen Holm Oak, *Quercus ilex*, add protection to the garden on this side.

Maintenance has been an increasing problem since the death of Mrs James. One gardener with part-time help now manages the gardens.

Warders

TQ 595 465 (Sheet 188) West Kent. In East Street, Tonbridge, on N side of the town. Owner: Dr T.S. Dewey. Open one or two Sunday afternoons for the N.G.S.

A fascinating, secluded, plantsman's garden close to the centre of Tonbridge, where a most exciting range of well-labelled trees, shrubs and other plants can be found. Warders is an outstanding example of the clever design and planting of a small site to create interest, surprise and seclusion all the year round with the minimum of maintenance.

Dr T.S. Dewey bought the house in the late 1930s and began developing the garden immediately after the Second World War, most of the present planting dating from the early 1950s with a special planting year in 1955. Most of the main tree and shrub planting is therefore between 20 and 25 years old and visitors should remember this.

The solid, brick and stone detached house originally stood on the edge of open country at the beginning of this century, with a ha-ha across the middle part of the present garden. Cattle grazed beyond this on the water-meadows of the River Medway that lies to the south. The ha-ha now survives as a sunken garden and some of the water meadows are now enclosed by poplar and willow planting at the bottom of the garden. Warders is one of several such houses in East Street with long rectangular gardens to the rear, typical of the Edwardian and Victorian period. The soils are fertile, rather heavy, acid clay loam of the Hastings Beds, Wealden series, which Dr Dewey has greatly improved with organic matter, mulches and good cultivation. Rainfall averages 29.5–30.5 inches.

The visitor should note the clever transformation that Dr Dewey has achieved from an undistinguished rectangular town garden to an intimate, secluded and delightfully planted retreat, where the sight and sound of the town seem far removed. He has first carefully concealed the adjoining houses with dense, strategically placed tall hedges and screens of conifers like *Thuya plicata*, Western Red Cedar, *Picea omorika*, Serbian Spruce, and other species, now up to about 25 ft. Specimen trees and shrubs against this dark background wall add to the enclosure and also show up well in front of it. Within this boundary, the style is essentially of informal, winding paths between dense plantings of shrubs and ground cover selected and sited for variety of texture, colour, seasonal effects, mood and atmosphere.

Dr Dewey finds the ingenious use of sawdust paths helps with maintenance. Herbicides are applied occasionally, the sawdust is comfortable and clean to walk upon, and desirable creeping plants can colonize it if required. In fact, there is no grass turf anywhere in the garden except for the small lawn near the house and a small circular glade at the far end of the garden. Around the house area is an attractive terrace, an excellent rock garden and shrub heath of mature, beautifully grown dwarf rhododendrons, heathers, conifers and many others. Note the fine *Carpenteria californica* and wistaria on the house. Beyond this area the garden slopes down to the main tree and shrub collection where the visitor can enjoy exploring a rich collection of rare and unusual plants. Outstanding specimens about 20 years old can be found of the following: *Metasequoia glyptostroboides*, *Styrax obassia*, *Styrax japonica*, *Halesia carolina*, *Eucryphya* × *nymansensis* 'Nymansay', *Picea breweriana*, *Acer pseudoplatanus* 'Brilliantissimum', *Chamaecyparis nootkatensis* 'Pendula' and many others, mostly 20–25 ft high. Note also the rich selection of ground planting of a cool, shady, herb layer; *Geranium* and *Hosta* species, bulbs and the fascinating creeping 'Cornel' *Cornus canadensis* (now called *Chamaepericlymenum canadense*). In the lowest part of the garden are more areas planted with heathers and uncommon herbaceous plants and there is a fine weeping willow as a terminal background feature planted by the owner in 1938. There is a small, beautifully planted pool on the east side of the garden.

Dr Dewey manages the two acres of garden largely by himself with the help of one man for one or two days per week.

Withersdane Hall

TR 062 465 (Sheet 179) South-East Kent. 1 mile S of village of Wye. 3 miles E Ashford. 12 miles SW Canterbury. Good bus and rail access. Owner: University of London, Wye College (enquiries to the estates bursar). Open: Normally 3–4 Sunday afternoons throughout the summer for the N.G.S. and G.S.O. scheme. Visits at other times may be made by previous arrangement with the estates office at the college.

Post-war gardens of about five acres created in the grounds of a small country house acquired by the University of London in 1946 and now used for undergraduate and postgraduate teaching and pleasure gardens as part of Wye College. The gardens are particularly effective in mid and late summer. Many of the plants are suited to the chalky soils of this area.

At the time of purchase Withersdane Hall was a comparatively small, unprepossessing Gothic-style building dating from about 1815, but very cleverly sited on a gentle south-west facing slope with fine views across the Stour Valley and the farming country to the south-west. The present gardens were, for the most part, created from the grounds, and especially the extensive former kitchen gardens, of the old Hall during the period 1948–55. Some original features of these grounds were retained as essential elements of the new gardens. At the same time as the gardens were being developed great changes were taking place to the original building. In 1951 two large hostel blocks for students were added and a conference hall and reception building (known as Swanley Hall to commemorate the merging of the former girls' college of horticulture at Swanley, Kent with Wye College in 1946). In fact, one of the former lecturers in decorative horticulture from Swanley, Miss Mary Page, was largely responsible for the early development and design of the Withersdane gardens on her arrival here in 1946.

The Holm Oak, *Quercus ilex*, that is now surrounded by the newer and original buildings was intentionally 'built' into the new scheme. It also dates from the last century. In 1975 a new building was erected on the south-east end of Withersdane Hall. This is the Centre for European Agricultural Studies and its intrusion into the former gardens on the site has been less damaging than was at first feared. All these new buildings have provided habitats for wall plants and a range of ornamental species that enjoy the protection of walls. With the combined problems of reduced maintenance budgets and the over-maturity of some of the original planting, the next few years will see a gradual renewal of some of the main planted areas of these gardens, allowing for the demonstration of new types of planting with reduced maintenance requirements.

The gardens lie at the western foot of the North Downs that rise up to nearly 590 ft to the south of the village. A landmark for many miles is the crown cut in the chalk in 1902 by staff and students of the college to commemorate the coronation of Edward VII. The gap in this long range of chalk hills where the River Stour cuts through at Wye does create something of a wind funnel effect from the prevailing southwest winds, and cold north-east winter and early spring winds blowing down the Stour valley can also be damaging to plant growth at times. Hence the strategic nineteenth-century planting of the copses and shelter groups of trees so valuable to the gardens today. Generally the microclimate at Wye is favourable to gardens and a wide range of plants can be grown, allowing for the limitation of the naturally calcareous soils. The reasonable proximity of the sea (about 12 miles to the south) tempers severe extremes of weather and temperature and apart from occasional severe easterly-type wintry spells, the climate is in general very good. Rainfall 33.5 inches. Sunshine 4.4 hrs. The soils are essentially calcareous and well-drained, rather shallow in places, but with areas of deeper drift and brick earth over the chalk. A century or more of cultivation and management has built up a good soil fertility in the garden. Springs from the chalk hills flow beneath the gardens and drought is seldom a serious problem.

The accompanying plan shows the main features. The style of Withersdane Gardens is very much like that of a number of early-twentieth-century gardens described in this book which followed or were influenced by Sissinghurst and Great Dixter and the Jekyll/Robinson school — of hedged enclosures with different themes of planting and design, a blend of formal and informal areas confined within a strong framework of hedges, trees and buildings.

The approach drive is still disappointing since it is really the old service road and tradesmen's entrance to the old Hall. However, new landscape treatment is in progress and the general impression of woodland and informality as one drives or walks through the shelter copses of beech, Turkey Oak, ash and sycamore will be accentuated in the future. The Centre for European Studies Court (Kate Barratt Garden) (14) is the first enclosed garden one enters. The *Paulownia tomentosa* tree (*a* on plan) should be noted, remembering that it was planted in 1951 as a seedling. The beech hedges that enclose two sides of the court are 25 years old and a series of rock terraces and rock garden are being restored or renewed in this area. Note the climbing hydrangeas *Hydrangea petiolaris* on the shaded east wall of Swanley Hall. The main gardens can be reached by climbing the steps that lead through an arch in the beech hedge. The attractive Japanese Pagoda Tree, *Sophora japonica*, (*b* on plan), with elegant compound foliage, was planted in 1954. The peony border (8) near here is colourful in May and June, and additional effects have been achieved by inter-planting various species of *Helleborus* for winter and spring interest and a *Viburnum* collection of unusual species. The three enclosed gardens have distinctive planting. The sundial garden (4) has recently been planted with a theme of gold, silver and blue foliage perennials, shrubs and some conifers, with a few contrasting plants to add effect and colour in the summer. The herb garden (5) has been a feature of these gardens since their creation. In the centre is a Kilmarnock Willow, *Salix caprea* 'Pendula', planted in 1973. The lily pond garden (6) looks especially attractive in May and June with its collection of *Geranium* and *Yucca* species, irises, asphodels, and pinks. Note in the east corner of this garden a fine dwarf crab apple that is ideal for small gardens, *Malus sargentii*. The long border (7) used to have the famous Withersdane collection of Flag Irises. They provided a magnificent but regrettably short display in late May and June. They were always expensive to maintain and after many years became diseased and over-mature. In their place have been planted associations of more exotic foliage plants to provide all year round interest. Outstanding are two Arizona Cypresses, *Cupressus glabra* 'Pyramidalis', fast-growing and intensive silvery-blue columnar habitat. They were planted in the spring of 1970. Also in contrast are large, bold clumps of New Zealand Flax, *Phormium tenax*, including the purple and variegated varieties. Collections of ornamental grasses, the sun-loving *Cistus*, *Hebe*, *Potentilla fruticosa* varieties and many more plants grow in this south-west facing border. At the east end is a small terrace where walls are clothed with the strangely variegated pink and green *Actinidia kolomikta* and a vigorous *Clematis montana*. Note the large silvery-green masses of the Chilean *Pittosporum tenuifolium* in this border and elsewhere in the gardens, indicative of the comparative mildness of the garden climate. Other climbers on the walls include a fine rich-blue-flowered *Ceanothus impressus*, honeysuckles, roses, clematis and the vivid orange Trumpet Vine *Campsis (Tecoma) radicans*.

The mixed borders (10) look most colourful in July to September. They are backed by a collection of modern climbing roses growing on pillars and chains. Large, bold clumps of such perennials as *Crambe cordifolia*, *Hosta*, *Euphorbia* and *Ligularia* blend with shrubs and summer planted subjects like sweet-peas, *Canna*, *Cleome* and *Dahlia*. The summer garden (11) is usually used for 'tapestry' displays of half-hardy plants in silver, blue, pink and red using a blend of *Pelargonium* spp., *Salvia patens*, fuchsias, *Lobelia* and the silvery *Helichrysum petiolatum* edged with Cotton Lavenders *Santolina chamaecyparissus*. The rose garden (9). Hybrid roses do not grow too well on these lighter chalky soils. Shrub roses generally do far better. The layout of the beds in this garden is still not satisfactory and may be changed, with the rose collection, in the next few years. Late June is an important month for the gardens and the end of term festivities, and more colour is now added to the rose garden by the inter-planting of groups of newer delphinium varieties, kindly donated by the Delphinium Society of Great Britain. The bright blues, purples and whites of these new hybrids seem to mix very well with the bronze-green foliage of the roses and the reds, pinks and yellows of the majority of the blooms.

The wild garden is an informal area mainly planted with ornamental trees and shrubs in grass, particularly the more vigorous shrub roses and viburnums. The grass is massed with narcissus and some fritillaries in April. Note here, one of the best limes for garden planting, *Tilia petiolaris*, the Weeping Silver Lime, planted in 1954. The hedges around the tennis courts are of the fast-growing Leyland Cypress, × *Cupresso-cyparis leylandii* and most of these are at least 15 years younger than the beech and yew hedges in the formal gardens. The main south-west front of the old Hall and the hostel blocks (not shown on plan) look across a small park to the college farm beyond. On the walls of the Hall are Banksian Roses, *Rosa banksiae* and the dainty-leaved evergreen *Azara microphylla* with tiny chocolate-scented flowers in February. It needs the protection of a warm south or south-west wall. An ancient and splendid plant of the Moutan Peony *Paeonia suffruticosa* grows beside the main windows of the Hall. It has been there ever since anyone in the area can remember. It flowers in May. On the hostel walls is a profusion of climbers, dominated by a vigorous and free-flowering white wistaria *Wisteria floribunda (multijuga)* 'Alba', *Campsis radicans*, *Akebia quinata*, the unusual winter-flowering *Clematis cirrhosa*

inghurst, Kent: the mystery and excitement of its many close-knit enclosures, as seen from central tower, looking south-east across the rondel

field Park, Sussex: the first breath-taking view the visitor normally sees, across the Top Lake, on a fine day in mid-October. The panoramic silhouette of this view (p. 184) names the main s in this vista

Great Dixter, Sussex: the Long Border in mid-summer. The fine oak seat against the yew hedge the far end of the border was specially designed by Edwin Lutyens for this strategic place in the garden

Denmans, Sussex: rich and exotic planting in the Walled Garden effectively creates the qualities a Mediterranean riviera garden, enhanced by the sunshine of the Sussex coast. Outstanding plants here are the steely-blue Eucalyptus, the white cloud of Crambe and a blend of aromatic herbs and half-hardy shrubs growing in gravel chippings

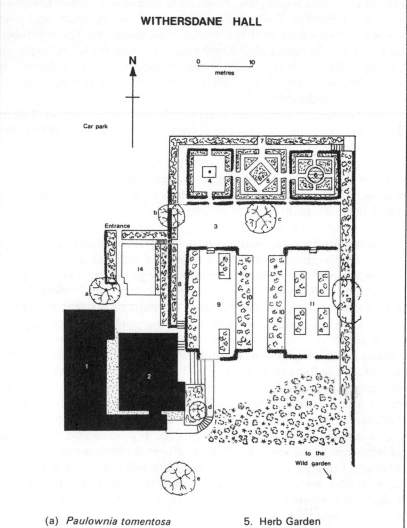

WITHERSDANE HALL

N

0   10
metres

Car park

Entrance

to the
Wild garden

(a) *Paulownia tomentosa*
(b) *Sophora japonica*
(c) Mulberry
(d) Yew
(e) Wellingtonia

1. Withersdane Hall (Part)
2. Centre for European Agricultural
   Studies
3. Lawns
4. Sundial Garden

5. Herb Garden
6. Lily Pond Garden
7. Long Border
8. Peony Border
9. Rose Garden
10. Mixed Borders
11. Summer Garden
12. Grey Border
13. Woodland
14. Kate Barratt Garden

and many attractive shrubs. *Magnolia × soulangiana* 'Alba', *Ceanothus arboreus* 'Trewithen Blue', a double-flowered pomegranate and even an olive survive here in this favourable microclimate. These climbers and wall shrubs once suffered some damage from nocturnal explorers paying unofficial visits to lady friends in the rooms above. Nowadays the curfew is generous, all students have keys, and the planting has improved considerably!

The Mulberry (c) is probably 100–120 years old. Props or bracing are usually essential to keep mulberries from falling apart when they reach this age.

The peat garden is the only artificially created garden of lime-free soil for a collection of lime-hating shrubs such as rhododendrons, azaleas, heathers and other plants. It was planted in the spring of 1974 using a special mixture of fibrous peat and shredded bark about 24 inches deep over the existing soil. Note on the very shaded walls of the north entrance to the main hostel block the unusual self-clinging evergreen *Pileostegia viburnoides*, a relation of the hydrangea. It flowers in late summer and should be more widely grown. In the island here is the hybrid flowering cherry *Prunus* 'Accolade', underplanted with mixed low shrub cover. The plants in the gardens are reasonably well labelled. A short guide is usually available on the open days.

Maintenance presents increasing problems at the present time and changes in the design and planting of the gardens are being affected to meet the reductions in finance and staff available. A staff of four or five men is responsible for the gardens at Withersdane as well as the many other small gardens and quadrangles of the main college building in Wye village and the sports fields and estate woodlands.

For a magnificent bird's-eye view of the Wye area and the expanse of landscape south and west of Wye, it is well worth driving up to the Wye and Crundale Downs National Nature Reserve about 1 mile from Withersdane on the Hastingleigh road. This reserve also protects some of the finest chalk downland flora in east Kent, including a fine variety of wild orchids.

Woolton Farm

TR 192 588 (Sheet 179) East Kent. Bekesbourne, 1 mile N of village.
3½ miles SE Canterbury off A257 Sandwich road. Owner: Mrs J. Mount.
Open several Sunday afternoons in May and June for the N.G.S.

A comparatively recent garden created immediately after the Second
World War, most of the planting being some 25–30 years old. The
late Mr John Mount and his wife created the garden with great energy
and enthusiasm from few existing features apart from a small number
of large and attractive trees such as the copper and green beeches and
the pines near the house. This house is a pleasant brick and tile farmhouse with associated outbuildings and courtyard. The garden of about
5 acres slopes gently to the south-east. The area is one of fairly intensive
fruit growing with some adjacent parkland and farmland. There is
good shelter except from the south and south-east. The area lies some
130 ft above sea level. The soil is a light, acid, sandy loam of the
Thanet Beds series, enabling the successful growth of rhododendrons
and azaleas of which there are many in the garden.

The design is primarily informal, with islands and drifts of shrubs
and ornamental trees, at their most colourful in May and early June.
Autumn colours are produced by some fine Japanese Maples, *Acer
palmatum*, *Hibiscus* and the bright-pink-flowered bulbous plant *Nerine
bowdenii*, as well as many other plants. Many fine, healthy specimens
of foliage trees are strategically placed in the shrub areas and lawns.
Especially note the Blue Atlas Cedar, *Cedrus atlantica glauca*, Red Oak,
Quercus rubra, Fern-leaf Beech, *Fagus sylvatica 'Laciniata (heterophylla)*,
Chinese Foxglove Tree, *Paulownia tomentosa (imperialis)*, and a number
of ornamental cherries and crabs. Also note the newly established rock
and scree bed near the Copper Beech just west of the house. Ground
cover here includes the delightful white-flowered *Viola cucullata* and
many small bulbs, including fritillaries. A fine Dawn Redwood,
Metasequoia glyptostroboides grows here. North of the house one enters
a small enclosed formal garden paved in York stone and an attractive
descending terrace of shallow brick steps. There is some good foliage
planting in this court of paeonies and spurges and the delightful
Clematis macropetala trailing over the walls. Hardy *Cyclamen* flourish at
the foot of the hedges here. Leading off from this is another brick paved
court with a new conservatory along one side, open to visitors and

housing an interesting collection of half-hardy shrubs and camellias, *Carpenteria* and *Passiflora*. There is an effective corner planting in this court of *Acer palmatum, Camellia* × *williamsii* 'Donation' and many creeping thymes.

An interesting, very well-maintained garden unusual in its lime-free soils in a primarily chalk area and displaying a good range of trees and shrubs for such conditions. Note the generous mulching treatment given to the shrub beds.

Supplement

A supplement of other gardens normally open in Kent (mostly for the N.G.S. and G.S.O.).

ANGLEY HOUSE Cranbrook. Large woodland garden and lake. Several open days.

AYLESFORD, THE FRIARS Near Maidstone. Restored Carmelite monastery. Rose garden.

BELMONT PARK 4 miles S Faversham nr Belmont Golf Course. Late eighteenth-century mansion in extensive parkland. Walled garden, orangery, Victorian grotto, small pinetum and enormous, beautifully maintained kitchen gardens.

BRENCHLEY MANOR Brenchley, near Tonbridge. Medium-sized garden. Roses, herbaceous borders.

COBHAM COURT Bekesbourne, near Canterbury. Simple, medium-sized garden. Picnics in meadows.

COLDHAM Little Chart Forstal, near Ashford. Compact enclosed garden with excellent collection of alpines, unusual bulbs and good mixed borders developed over the last 5–6 years.

COLDHARBOUR PARK Hildenborough, NW of Tonbridge. Flowering trees and shrubs and spacious lawns.

CROACH'S Ide Hill, near Sevenoaks. Very pleasant, 4-acre garden on acid soil with woodland, flowering trees and shrubs and fine views across to Ashdown Forest. Parking is rather a problem.

DODDINGTON PLACE 6 miles SE of Sittingbourne. Large garden of considerable variety and recommended especially for very fine woodland planting associates.

DOGHOUSE FARM 3 miles SW of Petham on B2068 (Stone Street) Canterbury to Hythe road. Mr Peter Godden's delightful garden of modest size around a small seventeenth-century farmhouse. Excellent plant collections and associations for chalky soils.

EVERLANDS 7½ miles SW of Sevenoaks. Edwardian terraced garden with fine views from Ide Hill. Good trees, azaleas and rhododendrons.

HALES PLACE Tenterden. Enclosed, walled garden of Tudor origin with interesting terraces, gazebos and the old Tudor mansion. A spring garden and orchard are included.

HORTON PRIORY Sellindge, SE of Ashford. Former medieval priory, now a picturesque residence with simple gardens, pond and rock garden.

LONG BARN Weald, near Sevenoaks. Medium-sized garden created by the late Vita Sackville-West and Harold Nicolson when they lived here 1915–30 before moving to Sissinghurst. Terraced lawns, box hedges and raised flower beds designed by Lutyens who also supervised the conversion of the fourteenth–fifteenth century house.

LYMPNE CASTLE Near Hythe. Fine restored castle with enclosed terraced garden from which one can get superb views of the Romney Marshes.

MERE HOUSE Mereworth. 7 miles W of Maidstone. Medium-sized garden with shrubs, lake and lawns.

MOUNT EPHRAIM 1½ miles N of Boughton, 6 miles SE Faversham. A mainly Edwardian terraced garden to match the imposing brick and stone nineteenth-century mansion. Topiary, a Japanese-style rock garden; herbaceous borders; rose gardens and a small lake are some of the features to be explored in this large garden.

THE OLD RECTORY Aldon, near Offham, W Malling. An old garden noted for its magnificent roses, fine trees, old walks, mixed borders and shrubs.

THE OLD VICARAGE Ide Hill. SW of Sevenoaks. 3-acre woodland with flowering shrubs, rhododendrons, azaleas and camellias, and fine views.

OXEN HOATH Hadlow, near Tonbridge. 12 acres of mature gardens approached by fine cedar avenue. Sloping lawns and a lake.

PORT LYMPNE GARDENS AND WILD LIFE SANCTUARY Lympne, near Hythe. Recently restored terraced gardens created by the Sassoon family this century.

THE POSTERN Tonbridge. 4-acre garden with lawns, flowering shrubs and roses and orchards.

THE RED HOUSE Crockham Hill, Edenbridge. Roses, expansive lawns and fine trees and good collection of flowering shrubs. Good views.

SISSINGHURST COURT Cranbrook. Well planted and designed enclosed garden with good azaleas and rhododendrons, a large rose garden, lily pools and fountains and many other features.

SISSINGHURST PLACE Sissinghurst. 5 acres of mostly lawn and flowering shrubs. Several fine old trees.

SQUERRYS COURT Westerham. 1 mile W of town off A25. For opening see H.H.C. and G. Good historical guide book available. A fine late seventeenth-century William and Mary house with associations with General Wolfe. It has been in the ownership of the Warde family for over 200 years.

The great formal gardens depicted in the Badeslade engraving of 1714 which is normally on view in the house (fig. 10), were much admired by John Evelyn during a visit in 1685. Only a few traces of these gardens can be discovered today in the terraces to the south and west of the house, most of the present grounds being created in the eighteenth and nineteenth centuries, including the lake below the house, the Gazebo (1740) and a number of fine trees, especially veteran Sweet Chestnuts, and the fine Blue Cedar, *Cedrus atlantica* 'Glauca' near the lake. There are fine views from the north elevation of the house.

STONEWALL PARK Near Penshurst. A dramatic wilderness garden in process of restoration by the present owners. A rocky valley is one impressive feature.

STREET END PLACE Street End. S of Canterbury. Walled gardens, lawns, flowering shrubs, naturalized daffodils and Jacob's sheep flocks.

WAYSTRODE MANOR Cowden, near Edenbridge. An excellent 8-acre garden, well-designed and planted including a grey garden, borders, ponds, bulbs, shrub roses and clematis and attractive old house.

WEST FARLEIGH HALL W Farleigh, near Maidstone. Attractive eighteenth-century house with enclosed gardens and a fine collection of old roses.

WOODLANDS MANOR Adisham. 5 miles SE of Canterbury. Recently restored garden around a pleasant Georgian lawn in woodland and parkland. Many features within old walled gardens. Good pleached lime walk well planted for summer display. Pleasant woodland walks and shade gardens.

SWANTON MILL Mersham, near Ashford. Beautifully restored working water-mill on the Little Stour, with pleasant gardens and a riverside setting. A visit is strongly recommended. The Mill and gardens are open most weekends.

The Gardens of
East and West Sussex

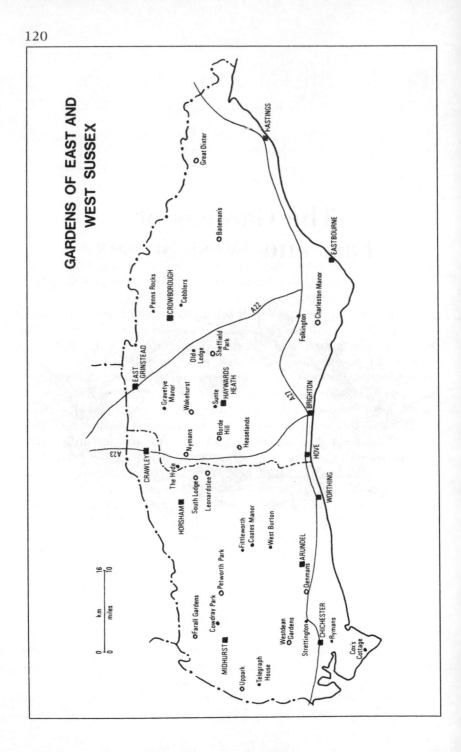

GARDENS OF EAST AND
WEST SUSSEX

Borde Hill Gardens

TQ 324 267 (Sheet 198) West Sussex. 1½ miles NW of Haywards Heath on a minor road to Balcombe. 17 miles N of Brighton. Owner: Mr R.N. Stephenson Clarke. Open late March to late August usually Wednesdays, Saturdays, Sundays, and Bank Holidays. See current H.H.C.G.

Over 300 acres of mainly informal tree and shrub gardens, woodland and parkland developed over the last century on acidic forest loam, and including many rare and exotic trees and shrubs that enjoy the lime-free soils and woodland habitats. Teas and light lunches are available and there is very good car parking. There is a delightful picnic area in the car park.

The name Borde derives from one of the old land-owning families of the Cuckfield district. Sir Stephen Borde built the western section of the present house, using local stone, around the year 1600. The bulk of the present house represents enlargements carried out in the last century using local stone and building in the neo-Elizabethan style. In 1895 Robert Stephenson Clarke CB acquired Borde Hill. He was an enthusiastic horticulturalist and during the next 40 years or so he established the gardens, pinetum and woodland arboretum that largely survive today. Stephenson Clarke was also an ardent subscriber to the plant-hunting expeditions of 1912–30 referred to elsewhere, and he received seed from the Asiatic collections in particular. He was generally less interested in the Australian and South American species.Colonel Sir Ralph Clarke KCB, TD, MP succeeded his father, coming to Borde Hill immediately after the Second World War and concentrating particularly on the trees, forestry and the botanical and commercial sides. In 1970 he established the Borde Hill Garden Trust. He died four years later and was succeeded by his son, the present owner Robert N. Stephenson Clarke, who is now Chairman of the Garden Committee. He takes a keen interest in the general management of the gardens and is particularly interested in *Rhododendron* species.

Borde Hill is another great Sussex garden in the Weald on the extreme southern edge of the former St Leonard's Forest, with generally similar setting and soils to Nymans, South Lodge, Leonardslee and Wakehurst. The soils here are largely acidic, sandy loam of the Hastings Beds, with weald-clay over the main garden area that makes cultivation and management more difficult. The gardens lie on three ridges at a general height of about 275 ft above sea level, running east–west. Rainfall averages 31.5 inches. Sunshine 4.5 hrs. Most of the gardens and woodland lie above the frost pocket zones.

A well-illustrated guide and plan of the gardens is available at the gate on open days and describes the general layout and design of the gardens. The essentially informal woodland glade style of much of the gardens becomes apparent to the visitor. There is some formal design to the south and east of the house, although these areas represent the conversion of former functional walled and kitchen gardens into ornamental features. The wall of the kitchen garden area was built in 1906 and some of the oldest plants on these walls date from the first decade of this century. Unusually fine specimens may be seen of *Magnolia delavayi* planted in 1910; *Cupressus lusitanica*, the Cedar of Goa, planted in 1911 (67 ft × 6 ft in 1968); *Cercis racemosa*, the Chinese Judas Tree; and in the corner, one of the largest examples in Britain of the Chinese shrub *Viburnum cinnamomifolium*, looking like a large *Viburnum davidii*. In the plantation by the south-east corner are more large magnolias – a 58 ft *Magnolia × veitchii* which flowered for the first time in 1937, and *Magnolia campbellii*. Shrubs in the grassy piece below the south wall include the unusual *Rosa roxburghii* with spiny fruits.

The azalea ring lies to the north on top of the ridge and is so named after a collection of deciduous late May-flowering azaleas of the famous Knaphill strain planted by Colonel Stephenson Clarke some 55 years ago. These are exceptionally colourful in late May. More magnolias also grow here and the rare Chinese tree *Emmenopterys henryi* planted in 1928 from seed collected by George Forrest. Many interesting rhododendrons grow on the back path, some only introduced in this century, such as *R. mallotum* and *R. mollyanum*. There are some magnificent trees on the Azalea Ring lawn, outstanding being a huge Turkey Oak, *Quercus cerris*, now 95 ft tall (50 ft in 1932), a fine columnar Californian Red Fir, *Abies magnifica*, at 94 ft (24 ft in 1932) and a very fine Japanese Black Pine, *Pinus thunbergii*, raised from seed brought from Japan by a member of the family in 1890. There is also a very tall Corsican Pine, *Pinus nigra maritima*, here at 102 ft. The old rhododendron garden lies to the west of the azalea ring, nearer the house, and is an informal planting of many different rhododendrons, mostly hybrids of Himalayan species. In 1971–72 a new grassy glade was created at the back of this garden and named Jack Vass walk in honour of the present head gardener. Many new species and varieties of rhododendrons are planted here.

The south lawn provides a fine expansive setting and prospect for the house. It was levelled and made in 1898. The well-placed ha-ha on the south-east side allows uninterrupted views from the house of the Weald landscape. There are some fine magnolias on this lawn and against the house. The large *Magnolia* x *soulangiana* was planted in 1895 and is a magnificent sight in late April. Against the house is a 45-year-old specimen of *Magnolia grandiflora* 'Goliath', the evergreen late summer-flowering species. The long walk, west terrace and old house garden is an Edwardian romantic place with winding paths, shady dells, a terrace and old estate buildings all fairly richly planted with a rather dense and exotic collection of plants. There are fine mature specimens of the purple cut-leaf Japanese Maples, *Acer palmatum* 'Dissectum Atropurpureum', beside the long walk, a cluster of the hardy Chusan Palms, *Trachycarpus fortunei*, in the round dell (they were 16 ft high in 1935) and in the old quarry-like long dell, more large-leaved and early-flowering rhododendrons. In the west terrace and Italian garden is the unusual Californian Nutmeg or Headache Tree, *Umbellularia californica*, now over 50 ft high (25 ft in 1935), and a gnarled Judas Tree, *Cercis siliquastrum*, planted in 1960 and since damaged by wind. The marble statue of the Veiled Lady, called 'The Bride', is by Antonio Tantardini of Milan (compare with that at Husheath in Kent). New planting is in progress in this area to make good the serious drought losses of 1976 and to generally extend the colour effects over a longer period. There is an extensive collection of rare and unusual rhododendrons in the Old House Garden and on the rock bank near the house.

The north park garden was originally part of the park and was included in the planted garden in 1925. The soil here is ideal for rhododendrons and a number of the Kingdon Ward introductions from his 1924–25 expeditions grow here. Immediately opposite the entrance gate is a good specimen of the Tasmanian Tea Bay, *Drimys lanceolata*, raised from seed collected by Comber. There are many other rare and unusual plants here and several fine trees. Look for the magnificent specimen of the Chinese Tulip Tree, *Liriodendron chinense*, now nearly 75 ft high and a gnarled 80 ft Himalayan Pine, *Pinus wallichiana*, that is the same size now as in 1932.

For those who wish to explore the more distant and less frequented parts of Borde Hill, a visit to Warren Wood is recommended in May for the wide variety of rhododendron hybrids, and at any time of the year for the many different conifers. Here one can find the finest Cyprian Cedar, *Cedrus brevifolia*, in the UK at 65 ft, and a similarly outstanding rare Tecate Cypress, *Cupressus guadalupensis*, now 70 ft tall; also many unusual spruce, pine and other trees. Much of Warren Wood was planted from 1905 onwards. Little Bentley Wood and Stephanie's Glade may also be reached from Warren Wood and more exciting unusual trees, for the most part of 40–60 years' maturity, may be found. There is a fine group of hickories *Carya* spp. planted in 1911, and some unusual walnuts. In Stephanie's Glade (named after Colonel Stephenson Clarke's grand-daughter) there is one huge Robel Beech, *Nothofagus obliqua*, measuring 98 ft and some unusual limes, among the many other trees. Gore's Wood is more remote and is accessible only by special appointment.

There is a head gardener, Mr Jack Vass, and three other permanent gardeners, with occasional casual labour. Jack Vass has had a lifetime of experience in gardening, having at one time held the head gardener-ship of Sissinghurst Castle. In 1974 he received the A.J. Waley Award for the most outstanding contribution to rhododendrons by a working gardener. The estate forestry staff has been much reduced since the death of the present owner's father. There is also a part-time gardener manager and the Garden Committee, who formulate policies for the future of the gardens.

Charleston Manor

TV 523 007 (Sheet 199) East Sussex. Between Littlington and West Dean. 7 miles W of Eastbourne, 4 miles S of Wilmington off A27 Lewes–East-bourne, N off A259 Eastbourne–Seaford at Exceat Farm. (The Seven Sisters Country Park and Information Centre at Exceat Farm is also well worth visiting.) Owner: Lady Birley. Open mid-May to late September most days 11–6. Consult current issue of H.H.C.G. and N.G.S. for precise times of opening, admission charges, etc.

A romantic garden of about 10 acres, created in the 1930s in the extensive English cottage-garden style, recommended especially for its fine collection of old-fashioned and shrub roses in a delightful setting of the old manor house with its great tithe barn and the surrounding South Downs.

The site of the house is of considerable antiquity and historical interest. The original Norman manor house is mentioned in Domesday Book under the name 'Cerlestone', probably derived from an early

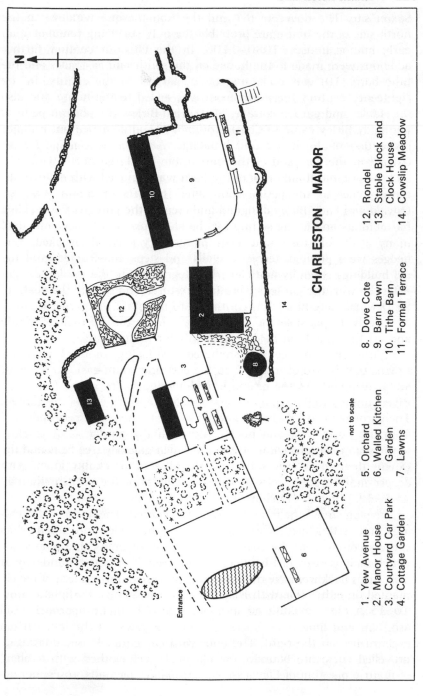

CHARLESTON MANOR

1. Yew Avenue
2. Manor House
3. Courtyard Car Park
4. Cottage Garden
5. Orchard
6. Walled Kitchen
   Garden
7. Lawns
8. Dove Cote
9. Barn Lawn
10. Tithe Barn
11. Formal Terrace
12. Rondel
13. Stable Block and
    Clock House
14. Cowslip Meadow

not to scale

Entrance

N

Saxon site. The dovecote (8) and the Romanesque window on the north side of the house are probably the only surviving remains of an early manor house *c*.1080–1100. In the fifteenth century further additions were made to the house on the south and east sides and the tithe barn (10) was built, one of the largest in the county. In the eighteenth century the north front was added to the house and also the stables and garden cottage. Sir Oswald Birley, the portrait painter, and Lady Birley came to Charleston in 1931 and carried out a major restoration of the house and buildings. A studio was made for Sir Oswald in the east end of the barn (note the large north windows) and the original thatch roof of the barn was replaced with eighteenth-century tiles in the period soon after the Second World War. Sir Oswald and Lady Birley designed and created the gardens to provide a harmonious and fitting setting for the old house and to accommodate many of the old roses and other plants they particularly liked. Yew hedges were planted, terraces, walls and steps constructed, and the old buildings carefully and cleverly integrated into the garden design. After the war, the gardens were fully restored and despite the death of Sir Oswald, Lady Birley has continued to maintain the gardens and to be largely responsible for the annual Charleston Festival of music and art that has been held here in July for many years.

Charleston Manor lies in a sheltered west-facing combe of the South Downs that rise to over 230 ft to the east and south-east. To the west and south-west lies the dramatic meandering valley of the Cuckmere River running to the sea only two miles to the south-east of the garden. The gardens lie at 98–130 ft above sea level. The site is very sheltered from the north-west and north. Although the garden is quite close to the sea, it is protected from the salt-laden gales by tree belts and the Downs themselves. The soil is a light alkaline or chalky loam, with deeper more organic soils in the lower parts of the garden. Rainfall 31.5–32.5 inches. Sunshine 4.8 hrs.

The plan shows the main layout of the garden. The house, old buildings and setting are an essential part of the style, and much of its success comes from the selection and siting of many fine plants, for which Lady Birley must be given great credit. The house stands about 300 yards back from the road and is approached down a long drive (1) planted on either side with Irish Yews, *Taxus baccata* 'Fastigiata', now 10–15 ft high, making an impressive and dramatic approach. Tall ash, elm and lime trees cluster behind the yews on the left. An old orchard lies on the right. The courtyard car park (3) is a charming, gravelled enclosure bounded by old walls well-clothed with a blend of mature planting of *Cotoneaster microphyllus*, clematis, roses, honey-

suckles and the strong foliage of *Mahonia japonica* against the walls.
Two old 'umbrellas' of *Cotoneaster frigidus* and *C.* 'Cornubia' frame the
entrance to this court.

One of the longest and most delightful axial vistas at Charleston
may be seen by standing in the car park and looking west, through
the wrought-iron gate (usually standing open) into the cottage
garden (4) and beyond through another gate into the old orchard (5).
The entrance to the cottage garden from this direction is guarded by
two fine Golden Irish Yews, *Taxus baccata* 'Fastigiata Aureomarginata'.
Roses on the cottage walls provide a tapestry of charming and colourful
varieties including: 'Madame Alfred Carrière' (fragrant blush creamy
white); 'Alberic Barbier' (pink clusters); 'Caroline Testout' (pink
clusters); 'Souvenir de Claudius Denoyel' (deep red) mingling with
jasmine, honeysuckles and clematis. The formal borders in this garden
are planted with a rich and colourful blend of perennials, low-growing
shrubs and some annuals, in themes of gold, red, purple and silver.
In the south corner of the garden stands a fine Medlar tree, *Mespilus
germanica*, planted about 1940 and a Mulberry, *Morus nigra*, grows
in the east corner. A large overhanging ash shades the south-west
corner of this garden.

The orchard (5) leads off from the cottage garden through another charming gate and an inviting brick path runs through the orchard to its far end. Here are old, gnarled apple trees, festooned with climbers, growing in a flowering hay meadow thick with bulbous plants in the spring. This is a cool restful place. A meadow effect is created beneath the trees, the grass being richly naturalized with a succession of bulbs, including snowdrops, crocuses, narcissus, fritillaries, hardy cyclamen, anemones, bluebells and autumn crocus. Grassland herbs are also profuse. A large walled kitchen garden (6) leads off from the orchard. It is well maintained and grows vegetables, soft fruit, glasshouse crops and hardy plants for the gardens for sale. A timeless nostalgic atmosphere hangs about this place.

The dovecote (8) is an area of many interests. at the south-west end is a cool shaded copse of different species of Horse Chestnuts, *Aesculus*, planted by the Birleys about 40 years ago. There is a good specimen of the yellow-flowered Sweet Buckeye, *Aesculus flava*. A fine ash dominates the lawn here. An excellent collection of shrub and old-fashioned roses also grow in this garden, some as specimens trained as 'baskets' in the lawn, others are free-growing shrubs, while the more vigorous climbing varieties are grown on the long, low wall that separates this area from the orchard and cottage gardens. A selection of some of the roses is noted here from a visit in the summer of 1976. Only some were labelled at the time. The following were lawn specimens: *R. brunonii*, the Himalayan Musk Rose, single, creamy-white, very fragrant; 'Souvenir de la Malmaison', fragrant, double cream blush, Bourbon; Hybrid Musks, 'Cornelia' (apricot), 'Buff Beauty', 'Penelope' (pink); 'Cerise Bouquet', raspberry fragrance, deep crimson; 'Fantin Latour', peach-pink, cabbage rose; 'Empress Josephine', rich pink, now called *R. francofurtana*; 'Hippolyte', a deep purple Gallica; 'Gold Bush'; 'Day Break'; 'Capitaine John Ingram', purple/crimson Moss Rose. And the following were wall-trained: 'Cécile Brunner', pale pink miniature blooms; 'New Dawn', pale pink; 'Alberic Barbier'; 'Golden Showers'. A touch which is very appropriate to this area and to the gardens is the casual use of a few plants of an old-fashioned, very sweetly scented strain of sweet-pea planted at the base of the rose baskets in May.

Near the house is a warm, sheltered border alongside the path, brimming over with an aromatic blend of low shrubs and perennials that enjoy the sun and the well-drained chalky soil. On the corner of the house near the Romanesque window is a fine plant of the white climbing rose 'Mme Alfred Carrière', to match the white fantail doves that flutter round the old house. Two fine Italian Cypresses, *Cupressus*

kehurst Place, Sussex: the cool, green remoteness of Westwood Valley where many Asiatic
nts, particularly rhododendrons, thrive in a setting they love

al Horticultural Society's Garden Wisley, Surrey: a colourful border of permanent planting in
spring, an especially rewarding time of year to visit this garden

Northbourne Court, Kent: greys and pinks are the predominant colours in this courtyard planting south of the house. Such carefully blended associations are characteristic of this fine garden

sempervirens, stand beside the dovecote, probably planted 40 years ago and surviving all the cold winters since. The barn lawn (9) – the superb and well-restored tithe barn is the great feature of this area. It overlooks a spacious lawn with perimeter planting and the ground on two sides to create a terraced amphitheatre effect, beyond which lie the cowslip meadow (14) and the wooded foothills of the Downs. More roses grow on the south walls of the barn itself including: 'Etoile d'Hollande'; 'Maigold' (yellow); 'Mme Grégoire Staechelin' (pink); 'Alberic Barbier' (white); 'Danse du Feu' (cherry red) and 'Guinée' (deep velvety red). The narrow borders at the foot of the barn and the walls have been fully exploited with rich and attractive associations of *Euphorbia, Agapanthus*, sages, *Stachys, Santolina, Iris* and everlasting peas. With the roses on the wall grow honeysuckles, clematis and *Ceanothus*.

A formal *parterre* of clipped yews penetrated by fastigiate columns and bounded by a battlemented outer hedge stands on the terrace to the south (11). In the *parterre* are seasonal plantings of foliage beds using Lady Birley's imaginative themes. At the east end of this area one can leave the lawn and enter, through a small gate in the hedge, a mysterious semi-formal hidden garden among the trees.

The rondel (12) is another delightful and intimate enclosure overlooking the eighteenth-century front of the manor. A circular gravel court and a circle of mown grass create a simple space that shows off to good effect the rich planting that enclose all the boundaries. Two fine *Magnolia grandiflora* planted in the 1930s, and two large columns of *Taxus baccata* 'Fastigiata' give maturity and character to the area. The borders are delicately blended with stocks, perennials and some annuals in themes of grey, purple and silver, using the purple-flowered Rugosa rose 'Roseraie de l'Haÿ', purple sage, purple fennel, pink/ purple deadnettle, *Lamium maculatum*, the magenta-flowered *Geranium psilostemon* and contrasting silvers and greys of *Artemisia, Stachys* and *Santolina*. Box edges have been introduced as a piece of traditional design here. Roses, hollyhocks, fuchsias, clematis and other such plants grow profusely beside or over the walls with old-fashioned sweet-peas. The immediate approach to the house has a simple planting treatment of lavender and box. The clock house and stable block (13) (toilets incorporated) – One should enjoy the setting and planting of these charming buildings. The roses on the clock house include 'Ena Harkness' (deep red) and 'Mme Alfred Carrière'.

Two gardeners only manage the total area of something around 20 acres, of which about ten acres constitute the main gardens. The head gardener, Mr Edward Lambert, has had over 30 years of service with

Lady Birley at Charleston Manor. He is a man of infinite knowledge and experience. Maintenance is related to the philosophy of the owner and the kind of garden she enjoys. Herbicides are used only on the drives and paths. All roses are regularly sprayed with fungicides and aphicides.

Coates Manor

SU 997 178 (Sheet 197) West Sussex. Fittleworth 1½ miles to N. 4 miles SE of Petworth, 1 mile W of B2138 Fittleworth–Arundel road. Owner: Mr and Mrs G.H. Thorp. Open usually 3 or 4 days in mid-summer for the N.G.S.

A comparatively new garden, on acidic valley soils, created around a fine small manor house by the present owners. The garden has been carefully and cleverly designed to create a series of pictorial effects from outstanding tree and shrub association.

A small stone-built manor house of the late sixteenth century, now a listed building, it suffered many years of neglect in this century before being bought by Mr and Mrs Thorp in 1960 with about an acre of land. At this time the property and the present garden site were neglected with old pigsties, difficult slopes and no really important trees.

Coates Manor lies in the reasonably sheltered and fertile valley of the River Rother (not the East Sussex Rother) in pleasant, agricultural landscape. The garden is at about 110 ft above sea level and slopes gently to the north-east. The soil is a light sandy loam, about 12 inches in depth, overlying river gravels. The pH is about 6.5. Rainfall probably about 31.5 inches.

The one acre of garden takes the form of a simple rectangle with the house on the south-west side hard up against agricultural land. Mrs Thorp has cleverly divided the garden into three areas, each of which has a distinctive character of style, planting and textures. The front lawn area is the first part of the garden that one enters from the road and the informal car park beside the house. The house stands with a planted terrace as a setting. A brick wall extends from the house right across the garden and is divided by an attractive arched gateway. The wall has been well-clothed with attractive climbers. A Common Walnut, *Juglans regia*, of moderate size stands in front of the house. The unbroken space of smooth lawn offers a splendid foil for rich and lustrous planting associations that characterize the perimeter of the garden.

The main lawn area lies to the north-west of the dividing wall, through the tempting arched gateway. Here is a most effective corner planting feature with the back drop of the stone wall and a glossy purple beech hedge. The weeping flowering cherry in the corner is the unusual variety *Prunus* 'Tsubame' (meaning the swallow), a delicate single pink raised by Captain Collingwood Ingram, with the spreading masses of the golden *Juniperus—media* 'Pfitzerana Aurea' fanning out at its base. Against the wall is a rich blend of *Acanthus*, *Hemerocallis*, *Helleborus*, the strong variegations of *Elaeagnus pungens* 'Dicksonii', the rounded felted leaves of *Senecio reinoldii* (*S. rotundifolius*) contrasted with a feathery purple fennel. On the wall is a good form of *Euonymus fortunei* 'Variegatus'. One emerges into an area of contrasts, a smooth sea of unbroken mown grass as the central space, fringed and broken with curving peninsulars and islands of planting in the north-west area and a raised, curving bed with retaining walls in the south-west. The house is set in a paved terrace, creating a charming cottage style enclosure at this end of the garden. Looking to the south from the house across the lawn lies a most flamboyant and exciting tree and shrub screen, devised as a sweeping curve and backdrop to the lawn and at the same time effectively screening off a somewhat intrusive cottage with a particularly nasty chimney on the adjacent property. The main theme of this screen is silver and gold, the rounded form of the silver-leaved Whitebeam, *Sorbus aria* 'Lutescens', the feathery delicate yellow foliage of *Gleditsia triacanthos* 'Sunburst', the golden lilac *Syringa vulgaris* 'Aurea' and blue sages and other related colour groupings of tree planting in the foreground. One detail noted was some effectively clipped bushes of the glaucous blue-leaved *Hebe carnosula* as a frame to a pathway through an old wall. The variegated red stemmed dogwood *Cornus alba* 'Spaethii' can be found here and in summer, tall lily species including *Lilium henryi* should be in flower. The curved peninsula of close planting of *Bergenia*, *Hosta* and *Phlomis* sweeps back into a bold corner group of *Catalpa bignonioides* 'Aurea', *Ligustrum ovalifolium* 'Argenteum' (a carefully selected form of variegated privet), the silvery mounds of *Ballota pseudodictamnus*, a fine spreading architectural mass of *Picea pungens glauca* and against the silver, grey and gold, massés of blue *Agapanthus* 'Headbourne Hybrids'. A most effective site in the peninsula has been chosen for a Swedish Birch *Betula pendula* 'Dalecarlica', now seven years old and some 32 ft high. A curved island bed also blends into the design here.

Looking north-west from the arch, note the solid green boundary hedge of clipped Lawson Cypress selected seedlings providing a valuable windbreak and enclosure to the garden and attractively broken with a buttressed 'clairvoyée' from which one can see fine views of the Rother Valley and the distant town of Petworth on the rising sandstone hills to the north-west. Tubs at the front of the buttress have been planted with *Rhododendron yakushimanum*. The levelling of the lawn from the original slope has been exploited to create a curving terrace in the west corner, now planted with mostly autumn colouring trees and some shrubs, such as *Ginkgo biloba*, *Malus tschonoskii*, *Sorbus* 'Joseph Rock', *Acer griseum* and a good underplanting of shade tolerant perennials, especially *Hosta* spp. An old apple tree has also been retained here for its character and shade. A narrow raised grass walk offers a pleasing prospect across the full extent of this garden to the inter-locking curved foliage borders on the north-east side already described. In the extreme eastern corner stand three sentinel-like fastigiate specimen shrubs emerging from a sea of grey and silver foliage. Two of these are forms of Lawson Cypress, *Chamaecyparis lawsoniana* 'Lutea' (golden green) and *C. l.* 'Pembury Blue' and the other is the columnar Japanese Cherry, *Prunus* 'Amanogawa', whose rather dull summer appearance is enlivened with a wreath of blue-flowered clematis. On the lawn is a healthy young tree of a specially selected good autumn colouring form of 'Sweet Gum', *Liquidambar styraciflua* 'Worplesdon'. It resembles a maple in general appearance. There is also some good low maquis shrub and conifer planting near the house.

The walled garden is the smallest and most exclusive enclosure at Coates Manor, lying in a warm, sunny, walled courtyard on the south-west corner of the house. Mrs Thorp has fully exploited the existing walls, the concrete floor and the brick terrace that she found here in 1960. Windows look from the house into this pleasant area. Careful choice of contrasting wall planting has yielded very attractive effects. Note the following: *Vitis vinifera* 'Purpurea', *Hedera colchica* 'Dentata Variegata', *Hedera helix* 'Cavendishii', *Clematis × durandii* and *C.* 'Perle d'Azur', and *Schizophragma integrifolium*. The narrow borders at the foot of the walls have been thickly planted with bold and distinctive shrubs to create a pictorial, all year round effect from the house windows. The focal specimen at the end of the courtyard is a beautifully sited Golden Irish Yew, *Taxus baccata* 'Standishii'.

Other shrubs and conifers include *Abies koreana*, *Juniperis sabina tamariscifolia*, *Phlomis chrysophylla*, *Ceanothus* varieties, *Choisya ternata*, *Cotinus coggygria*, *Philadelphus coronarius* 'Variegatus', *Hibiscus syriacus* forms, several varieties of sage, *Salvia officinlis*, and a number of well-placed hardy ferns.

The very high standards achieved in this garden are the result of thoughtful planting in the initial stages. Mrs Thorp is mainly responsible for all the garden maintenance.

Cobblers

TQ 530 296 (Sheet 188) East Sussex. Jarvis Brook, near Crowborough. 8 miles W of Wadhurst. 12 miles SW Tunbridge Wells. Owner: Mr and Mrs M. Furniss. Open several Sunday afternoons throughout the summer for the N.G.S. Visiting arrangements are well-organized, but parking can be a problem.

The garden lies on quite steeply sloping ground to the south-west and west some 420 ft above sea level. There are views to the south-west. It is deceptively sheltered and enclosed from neighbouring residential areas, with excellent examples of tree and shrub foliage and shelter screening. Rainfall about 31 inches. The soils are acidic sands and clays of the Hastings Beds. The garden has been developed by Mr and Mrs Furniss over the last seven to eight years with much thought and ingenuity and a clear knowledge of plants and planting design. They have been quite adept in their design treatment of the contrasting contours of the garden. There is a good collection of plants to be seen with some especially effective planting for the summer months.

The gardens flow easily round a restored attractive Wealden tiled cottage with its associated buildings, its main elevation facing south. There are no major enclosures in the garden, the design concentrating mainly on the plant collections and as a place of relaxation. Good screen and fringe planting to the north in the highest parts of the garden is achieved by reinforcing indigenous hedgerow species with coniferous species like Lawson's Cypress and *Thuja plicata*. There is a good foliage blend in the north-east corner of *Acer pseudoplatanus* 'Brilliantissimum' and *Acer negundo* 'Variegatum', *Prunus cerasifera* 'Atropurpurea' and *Cornus alba* 'Variegata' – cream, silver, yellow and purple. There are few really large trees in the garden. There is one good ash as an important feature, and a small oak provides a shaded habitat for perennials like *Hosta* and *Helleborus*. Narrow brick paths link the areas of flowering informal borders with such features as steps and terraces. An elongated pool and water garden is an important and very successful feature on the south slope of the garden. It resembles a flooded serpentine ha-ha as it runs below the crest of the slope, almost invisible from the top of the garden. It is exceptionally well planted with a good range of marginal and aquatic plants that are well worth studying. Here one can find the spectacular waterside perennials *Ligularia* and *Rodgersia* and a variety of *Astilbe*, *Iris kaempferi*, *Hemerocallis*, Day Lilies, in yellow, orange and apricot; the brilliant red *Lobelia cardinalis* and the purple-blue spikes of the less common hybrid *Lobelia × gerardii*; *Pontederia cordata*; the 'Flowering Rush', *Butomus umbellatus*; Purple Loosestrife, *Lythrum salicaria*, and many more. The water is clear and abounds with ornamental fish. Old apple trees and some shrub roses protect the pool on the north side. Near the house is an attractive stone paved area beside the gravelled drive, well planted with low-growing sun-loving shrubs, rock plants and perennials. Some good plants include *Convolvulus cneorum*, *Genista lydia* and many *Helianthemum* varieties. There are some rhododendrons and 'cool' planting in the shaded area to the south-west of a tall 16 ft beech hedge.

Plants are normally available for sale on open days. A high standard of maintenance is evident.

Cooke's House

SU 000 139 (Sheet 197) West Sussex. West Burton village, 1 mile W off A29 Pulborough–Arundel road at Bury. Owner: Miss J. Courtauld. Open several afternoons in April and June in conjunction with other gardens in the village. For details see N.G.S. publication.

A site of considerable historic interest and importance. The delightful old stone-built manor house was built in 1558 by a member of the Cooke family and the Elizabethan garden of that time was famous in the locality. Cooke's Knot Garden is mentioned and the outline of this feature still survives in part today. The present garden was laid out by a Mr Holland, the uncle of the present owner, in the period 1924–39. He created a small, intimate, formal garden in the Tudor style, probably following some of the lines of the original garden. He built steps and walls, laid the flagstone paths using the local ragstone and York stone, and planted the yew hedges in 1928.

Two important trees existed on the site at that time. One is the fine Cedar of Lebanon, *Cedrus libani*, on the front lawn. This is featured in an article on Cooke's House in *Country Life* of 1909 when it seems to have been 30–40 years old, which would put its age now at about 100 years. The other is the Evergreen or Holm Oak to the north-west, which may be even older. The Tulip Tree, *Liriodendron tulipifera*, was planted in 1928 and has flowered regularly for many years.

Cooke's House lies in a delightful peaceful and completely unspoilt setting in the tiny village of West Burton in pleasant, intimate country-side on the north side of the South Downs. This is dry, well-drained chalk country. The garden lies about 98 ft above sea level on light, chalky loam. The climate is generally sheltered, warm and congenial.

This is quite a small garden and the style is neo-Elizabethan; formal and intimate, Mr Holland's designs mostly exist still today. The de-tailing of the constructed features is extremely good in a range of local materials, cobbles, flint, stone and brick. The small lawn on the west and front side of the house is dominated by the cedar tree. There is a charming flight of steps from the road up to the main garden gate. The enclosed yew-hedged gardens behind the house are mainly planted with foliage perennials to give blends of greys, purples, pinks and yellows for summer effects. California Tree Poppy, *Romneya coulteri*, is used in one enclosure. Urns and statuary are also used effectively. In more recent times the old enclosure of the garden has been broken on the east side to create a more expansive area of garden leading away to more open countryside. Long borders of shrubs and perennials are the features here, and a recently constructed bog garden in a dell near a small wood has been well planted. Among the many interesting and unusual plants in this garden is a fine specimen of the Burr Rose or Chestnut Rose, *Rosa roxburghii*, a viciously armed shrub with pink fragrant flowers and unusual prickly receptacles and flower stalks, like a Sweet Chestnut fruit.

Two gardeners manage this garden extremely well. The droughts of the 1975 and 1976 summers affected the garden very badly indeed.

Cox's Cottage

SU 851 929 (Sheet 197) West Sussex. In West Street, Selsey. Chichester 8 miles N. Owner: Mrs P.C. May. Open usually one weekend in June for the N.G.S. Visits at other times may also be made by previous arrangement with the owner.

A seaside, suburban setting on the flat, windy promontory of Selsey Bill, less than ¼ mile from the sea. Cox's Cottage is a small, picturesque, thatched, flint and stone house with a history that goes back to Domesday. Until 1937 it stood in remote alluvial grazing pastures on the light, neutral shingle and sandy soils of this area. Today it is part of a great residential development that has engulfed much of the Sussex coast. Mrs May has skilfully developed the garden since 1968, incorporating a second adjoining garden into the scheme and creating a deceptively secluded series of sanctuaries and enclosures, with great emphasis placed on shelter and an expert use of planting for floral and foliage effects. Note the skilful siting of the enclosure hedges, particularly a fine hedge of *Escallonia macrantha*, one of the best ever-green seaside hedges, and the retention of old apple trees and other features to create the feel of a peaceful country cottage garden although only ¼ mile from the sea.

The paved garden on the West Street side makes a fascinating feature, a basic surfacing of random paving-stones laid on sand richly planted with many different prostrate herbs, dwarf shrubs and even a few trees. There are in addition charming vistas, and the training of the apple trees to form arches garlanded with old roses is also a pleasant feature. The site is very flat, but to create a feeling of change of level, Mrs May has cleverly added steps here and there into the different gardens. Some good detailing, too, of brick paths, seats and statuary should be noticed. The use of roses of many kinds is a great feature of the gardens, with climbers such as wistaria, honeysuckle and scented and foliage shrubs. New foliage trees are now establishing well, including a fine young copper beech and the glaucous-blue Arizonian Cypress, *Cupressus glabra*. Elms were once important in the landscape here but most of these have died. Mrs May has recently become very interested in alpine plants. There is also a well-stocked vegetable and fruit garden and there is even room for some very healthy-looking chickens.

One part-time man helps Mrs May with the maintenance of this interesting garden which very much reflects the personality of its owner.

Denmans

SU 942 071 (Sheet 197) West Sussex. S off A27 W of Fontwell Racecourse in Denmans Lane. 5 miles Chichester and Arundel. Owner: Mrs J.H. Robinson. Open every Saturday and Sunday throughout the year, usually 2–7. This is a unique and very unusual arrangement offering great opportunities for seasonal visits.

An outstanding collection of trees, shrubs, wall plants and herbaceous plants developed over the last 30 years from a former intensive mixed horticultural holding into a delightful garden. Denmans is recommended to the plantsman and specialist for a visit at any time of year, but especially between April and July. Many rare and unusual plants growing in the gardens are usually on sale from the Denmans plants propagating unit, run in conjunction with the gardens.

The small lodge-type house, the associated buildings and the present gardens were originally the walled gardens and service and staff residential complex of the large early nineteenth-century house, now under separate ownership, on the west side of Denmans Lane. Mrs Robinson's charming cottage was originally the flint and brick bothy, or garden boy's house, dating from about 1820. The stables and coach-house with its turret clock also date from this period. The walled gardens have been retained as a feature of the present property which Mr and Mrs Robinson took over with some adjoining farmland in 1946 and they developed a flourishing commercial unit producing fruit and flowers with an associated Guernsey dairy herd. After the death of her husband, Mrs Robinson gradually converted most of the intensive market garden into a very personal plantsman's garden designed to be managed by herself and one man.

This is another example of a garden in the flat, fertile, alluvial coastal plain some five miles due north of the sea at Bognor Regis. The site lies about 65 ft above sea level. The setting is one of a partially broken up nineteenth-century country estate, but with some of the finest features surviving, such as the mature trees, old buildings and walls which create a secluded atmosphere despite the comparative closeness of the very busy A27 trunk road. The climate is very equable and favourable to plant growth. The proximity of the sea, the high level of sunshine, the comparatively mild winters and the sheltered micro-climate are reflected by the great range of plants that flourish at Denmans. Westerly gales are the most serious factor here at any time of the year and are occasionally salt-laden. Rainfall 27 inches. Sunshine 4.5–5 hrs. The soils are fertile, free-draining loam over deep deposits of alluvial calcareous gravels and flints. The pH is relatively high and the water table at about 2–3 ft deep. The ground rarely waterlogs and is liable to dry out in the summer months. An old shoreline crosses the site, accentuating the gravelly, flinty texture of the soils.

The exotic and secluded character of Denmans derives almost entirely from the clever planting design using bold specimens and informal groupings to furnish the relatively simple walled enclosures. To quote Mrs Robinson, 'the emphasis is on the shape, colour and texture of the whole growing picture, rather than the plants.' The entrance drive is planted with predominantly autumn and winter colouring trees and shrubs. There is a very good silver variegated tree here *Acer negundo* 'Variegatum'. On the south side of the cottage lies the first large and partially walled enclosure with drifts and islands of contrasting trees and shrubs. Beneath the trees and shrub roses, *Helleborus corsicus* seed freely and the scattered groups of *Verbascum* and *Salvia turkestanica* are also self-sown. This area is worth careful, exploration. Most of the young, healthy ornamental trees are about 30 years old. Note in particular the *Cedrus deodara* south of the house, a snake bark maple *Acer pennsylvanicum* and the reddish peeling bark of *Acer griseum*. To the east are two fine outstanding foliage plants, the copper purple *Cotinus coggygria* 'Royal Purple' and the light gold large-leaved *Catalpa bignonioides* 'Aurea'. A fine *Metasequoia glyptostroboides* grows here. It is about 25 years old. The mature shrub groups beyond the maples and cedar should be seen; one of *Rosa rubrifolia* (purple-leaved), *Rubus* 'Tridel' (white-flowered), *Viburnum farreri* (*fragrans*) (winter-flowering) with low growing masses of the sweetly scented *Daphne* 'Somerset' and the strong foliage of *Acanthus*. To the south is another effective group of *Cupressus macrocarpa* (dark green), *Sorbus aria*, Whitebeam, (silvery foliage), the Golden Elder, *Sambucus racemosa* 'Aurea', and the Mexican Orange, *Choisya ternata*.

The paved terrace is well planted with a fine collection of low-growing shrubs and perennials that enjoy the warm sheltered site and the light, gravelly soils – Mediterranean shrubs like *Cistus, Cytisus*, some fine mature dwarf conifers, *Helianthemum* varieties, grey-foliaged herbs, and for late summer bold groups of *Romneya coulteri*, Tree Poppy. A delightful, small courtyard in the corner of the wall to the west of the house provides a sheltered home for a fine specimen of the unusual variegated shrub *Rhamnus alaternus* 'Argenteovariegatus'. Beside this shrub are two fine wall plants, *Trachelospermum jasminiodes*, a scented, early summer flowering evergreen, and the early spring flowering evergreen *Clematis armandii*. Note the important background and shelter screen of the 10 ft 'wall' of Lawson Cypress, *Chamaecyparis lawsoniana*, down the entire west side of this garden. Sea gales from the south-west can be devastating to exposed gardens in this area.

Most of the groups and islands of planting in this garden once grew in mown grass but Mrs Robinson is becoming increasingly pleased with the effect and the low maintenance requirements of gravel. She uses some herbicide on the gravel but in carefully controlled zones so that seeding of many interesting plants is encouraged. The most recent development at Denmans is a small arboretum where Mrs Robinson is again concentrating on foliage contrasts in a simple setting of longer grass and mown paths. Planting has been in progress for the last 8–10 years. To the east of this garden lies another walled garden full of exciting plants and some original groups and planting. The south end of this garden is a highly original gravel, herb and foliage association, the plants growing in a natural manner reminiscent of the steppe or 'garigue' flora of the Mediterranean. Groups of fennel, thyme, ornamental grasses and *Euphorbia* thrive in the gravel layer overlying the deeper soils, and by judicious use of herbicides Mrs Robinson can control and manage the seeding of many plants into the gravel. There is a particularly fine specimen of the Moroccan Broom *Cytisus battandieri*. A huge white mound of Seakale, *Crambe cordifolia* grows close to a steely blue *Eucalyptus*. The north end of this garden has gradually been converted from vegetables. Some more fine wall plants, freestanding 'Peregrine' peaches and an apricot look well in fruit and flower. On the east wall here planting includes a magnificent *Actinidia chinensis*, *Buddleia* and *Ceanothus* and the prolific, attractive leaved *Vitis betulifolia*. A Golden Hop, *Humulus lupulus* 'Aureus', grows in the angle of the north-west facing wall where it colours well. To the east is a fourth walled area with the glasshouses and nursery and plant sales area. The 'conservatory' collection of hardy plants is very diverse and worthy of explorations.

The design and planting, the use of gravel and residual herbicides and the careful attention to selection and planting of plants suitable to the soil and area have created a remarkable collection and a fine garden. This is a highly personal garden and remarkable in that it is entirely maintained by Mrs Robinson and her gardener, who has been with her for over 40 years.

Farall Demonstration Gardens

SU 925 290 (Sheet 186) North-West Sussex. Very close to Surrey border at Blackdown and Roundhurst. 3 miles SE Haslemere. Not easy to find, but the map reference will help and the gardens are usually signposted. Owner: Mr M. Haworth-Booth. Open several Saturdays in early and mid-summer as special days for the N.G.S. The nursery enterprise attached to the gardens and the gardens themselves are usually open most week days.

The 20 acres of garden have been developed by Mr Michael Haworth-Booth since he built the house and planted the garden in 1946. The story of the creation of the gardens is told with great realism and detail in *The Flowering Shrub Garden.** The site is certainly dramatic and challenging being nearly 650 ft above sea level on the south-east of the scenic Blackdown Hills, part of the Lower Greensand ridge, with magnificent views to the south-east and south over Surrey and Sussex. The soils are acidic sandy loams, with reasonable depth on the lower slopes. The natural vegetation is forest and heath. Despite the hill-top site the gardens are remarkably sheltered with rich, enclosing tree and shrub planting, and the south slope microclimate is well above the late spring valley frosts that can bedevil Surrey gardens in April and May. Rainfall 31.5–32.5 inches. Sunshine 4 hrs.

The style is very natural and almost wild, the design rightly allowing the natural character of the site to mould the atmosphere and shape of the gardens. The small cottage-style house stands in a small gravelled circular plateau which is reached after a winding and fairly steep climb by road. The nursery lies opposite the house and the main garden area slopes away below the house. Note the good wall plants on the house, including a particularly fine *Hydrangea integerrima*. The massed planting style favoured by Mr Haworth-Booth is dramatically apparent in the drive up to the house where the narrow curving road passes through great masses of 30-year-old rhododendrons (some

* Michael Haworth-Booth, *The Flowering Shrub Garden*, Farall Publications, Blackdown, 1971.

particularly good red hybrids), *Viburnum, Cornus* and *Hydrangea,* the latter having for many years been a great speciality of Farall. Immediately below the house lies the most exciting and richly planted part of the garden, about ⅓ acre being mass-planted with a maquis of low-growing and specimen shrubs, traversed by narrow winding paths. Note the low carpeting mounds of *Cistus, Halimium,* dwarf rhododendrons and azaleas, and even some trailing and climbing plants. Beyond are taller shrubs and evidence of the warm favourable microclimate at Farall is here in the shape of mature plants of the usually half-hardy *Rhododendron* 'Lady Alice Fitzwilliam', the deep purple-blue *Hebe* 'Alicia Amherst', the leathery-leaved, white-flowered Japanese *Raphiolepis umbellata,* the vivid blue evergreen *Ceanothus* 'Southmead', the Australasian *Telopea truncata,* the Chilean Fire Bush, *Embothrium coccineum lanceolatum,* and many magnolias, including really fine plants of *Magnolia obovata* and *M.* × *watsonii.* The many *Eucalyptus* spp. here were planted in the early 1950s and many are now quite large trees. The 20-year-old *Paulownia tomentosa,* the Foxglove Tree, indicates the favourable growth conditions. There are good evergreen azalea varieties massed here, many of them raised by Mr Haworth-Booth — his cross 'Bengal Beauty' (F.C.C.) is one of his favourites. The general management of this area is sympathetic and realistic; a 'controlled wilderness' approach which allows many other advantages including the regeneration of many unusual seedlings such as *Cornus kousa,* for example. Also trailing plants like the brilliant blue *Lithospermum diffusum* 'Heavenly Blue' are allowed to trail freely over and among the shrubs.

To the west of the main drive lies the woodland garden, rather overgrown and fringed with thickets of the bright green bamboo *Sasa tessallata.* There are fine groups of *Hydrangea paniculata.* In the upper part of the wood there is a canopy of mature pines and some oaks and the leafy paths can be explored by the adventurous who will be rewarded with fine plants of many *Rhododendron* species, notably the blue-mauve *R. augustinii,* the yellow *R. campanulatum,* the fragrant white *R. decorum* and the bright scarlet hybrid 'Tally Ho'. There are also some of the large-leaved species such as *R. macabeanum.* The path drops steeply to a secluded pool, standing in more open scrub away from the woods, fringed with willows and partially fed from a pump that has been installed by the springs in the lower part of the garden. A pleasant place to linger, with matured planting around the pool's margin: Greater Spearwort *Ranunculus lingua,* irises, *Astilbe,* the rampant Water Hawthorn *Aponogeton distachyos* and bamboos. Huge fish swim lazily in the pool and dragonflies flit over its surface. The garden continues to fall away below the pool, with more winding paths and massed shrubs in the open clearings – brooms, magnolias, eucalyptus and more rhododendrons, including a magnificent group of *R. augustinii* just above a very deep narrow valley with a stream flowing far below.

Farall is a garden for those who love unusual and naturally grown plants, a garden to explore and re-visit on several occasions, and above all a garden devised to create the minimum of necessary maintenance, a cultivated ecological garden.

Folkington Gardens

TV 558 039 (Sheet 199) East Sussex. Folkington village. 5 miles NW Eastbourne 1 mile off the A27 Eastbourne–Lewes Road. Owners: various (see text). Open usually one Sunday afternoon in July for the N.G.S.

Folkington (pronounced 'Fowington') is a small detached hamlet of great charm and character in the wooded foothills of the South Downs that rise dramatically to over 490 ft to the south of the village. The soils are mostly alkaline, chalky loams, light, well-drained, with deep deposits. Rainfall average 31.5 inches.

FOLKINGTON PLACE

The home of Mr and Mrs H.J. Voorspuy. This delightful garden is strongly recommended to the plantsman and connoisseur. It has been developed over the last 40 years by Mrs Pearl Voorspuy and her enthusiastic and knowledgeable gardener, Miss Coventry, around the old, mellow brick house, most of the garden being created in the former kitchen garden which has a gentle slope to the south-east of the house. There is a fine sheltering belt of beeches and other trees to the south-west and west, some of which have been included in a woodland garden to one side of the house. There are drifts of shrubs, old roses, clematis, spurges and ornamental grasses and *Allium*, *Eryngium*, many grey-foliage plants, annuals and perennials beside the brick paths and over the old walls. A judicious and delicately balanced maintenance programme with careful hand-weeding (herbicides are totally banned!) allows the natural seeding and regeneration of many fascinating plants, including some British native plants. The main lawn is devoted to a very successful 'natural' chalk pasture still being developed by a special cutting regime. Historic atmosphere is enhanced with the tall old Irish yews on the front lawn and the veteran apple trees from a former orchard.

A unique garden reflecting the personality of its owner, who is willing to show interested visitors round by appointment on other days given suitable notice.

THE OLD RECTORY

Owner: Mrs Ingram. A Gothic-style house of the mid-Victorian period standing amid magnificent beech trees in a very secluded setting. It is in fact the setting and seclusion that are the most attractive features of the garden, much of which has been created from an old chalk quarry and a number of shrubs, old roses, lilacs and viburnums have been introduced. A path winds through the shrubs above the quarry and one can see distant views to the north-east, as far as the old windmill on Summer Hill.

OLD RECTORY COTTAGE

Owner: Mr & Mrs Jennings. This lies nearly a mile from the main hamlet of Folkington in a quiet setting off the chalk and on heavier soil to the north-east nearer the A27 main road. A more extensive arable landscape surrounds the house with the remains of a hedgerow system of elms (mostly diseased now) which replace the beech on the heavier soils. Over the last 10–12 years Mrs Jennings has developed a very pleasant, intimate, one acre garden in keeping with the charming old brick and tile cottage which she has also restored. The garden has been cleverly divided into a series of small enclosed gardens each with its individual character and planting. Emphasis is placed on foliage, texture and the use of many good wall plants. The most open area is the hedged lawn to the south-east where two very good perennial borders should be noted. The garden looks extremely well managed.

Great Dixter

TQ 818 252 (Sheet 199) East Sussex. Close to the village of Northiam on the A28 Tenterden–Hastings Road. Tenterden 8 miles, Hastings 12 miles. Bodiam Castle 4 miles (a fine place for a picnic). Owners: the Lloyd family. Open normally 6 afternoons per week April–October. Full details available in H.H.C.G. The nursery is usually open during normal working hours throughout the year.

An outstanding plantsman's garden of five acres developed early in this century by the Lloyd family from an original design by Sir Edwin Lutyens and now showing fine examples of Christopher Lloyd's mastery of plant associations and unusual groupings, held within Lutyens's formal design. An extended fifteenth-century timbered hall house makes a magnificent central feature to the gardens.

The manor of Dixter is first mentioned in 1220. The oldest part of the present building is the great hall and porch and this dates from the mid-fifteenth century (1450–64). It is a large example of the many hall houses that were built in the Kent and Sussex Weald at this time. It was purchased as a neglected farmhouse in 1910 by Mr Nathaniel Lloyd (father of Christopher Lloyd who lives at Great Dixter today) who collaborated with his friend Edwin Lutyens in the restoration and enlargement of the house and the design of the gardens. Between 1910 and 1914 an ambitious scheme of work was executed and it involved cleverly grafting on to the south side of the original hall house another early sixteenth-century yeoman's hall house which Mr Lloyd had noticed standing derelict at Benenden. Lutyens enjoyed working with local traditional materials such as bricks, tiles and oak timber and he used these skilfully in the surgical operation of joining the two houses together. At the same time he drew up his plan for the design of the garden, taking great care to incorporate as many features as possible from the old farmstead. A signed copy of his original plan, dated July 1911, is in Mr Lloyd's possession. Lutyens restored the old outbuildings, cowsheds and barns, and these make a charming and entirely appropriate setting to the Dixter of today. The group of oasts attached to the barn is particularly fine. They were last used for drying hops in 1939.

The sunken garden with its octagonal pool was designed and constructed by Mr Nathaniel Lloyd in 1923. His original sketches for this garden also survive. He was also responsible for the fine lengths

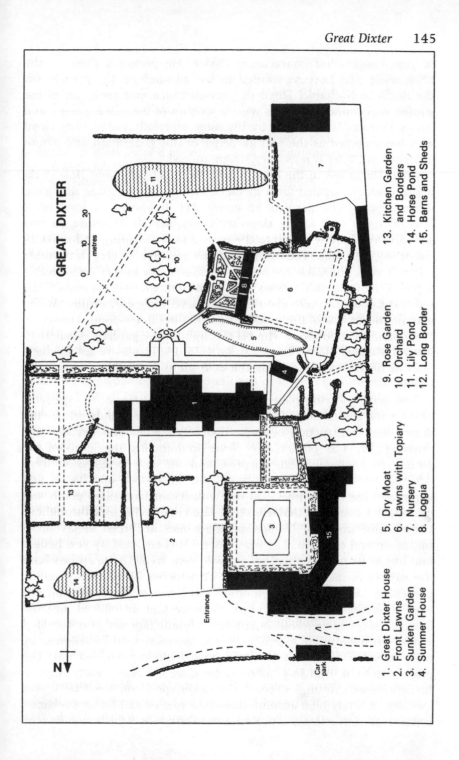

GREAT DIXTER

N

0 10 20
metres

Entrance

Car park

1. Great Dixter House
2. Front Lawns
3. Sunken Garden
4. Summer House
5. Dry Moat
6. Lawns with Topiary
7. Nursery
8. Loggia
9. Rose Garden
10. Orchard
11. Lily Pond
12. Long Border
13. Kitchen Garden and Borders
14. Horse Pond
15. Barns and Sheds

of yew hedges that characterize Dixter. He preferred these to the brick walls that Lutyens wanted to use throughout the garden. On the death of Nathaniel Lloyd the maintenance and evolution of the garden was continued by his wife, a woman of boundless energy and strong personality, and also by his sons, especially Christopher Lloyd who has emerged as the real gardener of this generation and whose influence at Dixter is now very strong indeed.

Great Dixter lies in the high Weald, like Crittenden and Hole Park. It is unusually elevated for a medieval hall house, a hilltop site being the exception. The gardens lie about 210 ft above sea level on a gradual south-west facing slope with considerable exposure on this side. Shelter planting of ash to the west is now maturing and provides essential protection. The walls and hedges give a very favourable microclimate. The soil is essentially Wadhurst clay to very considerable depth. Prolonged cultivations and management have improved the soil texture for the cultivation of many perennials and shrubs. At the extreme north end of the garden, near the old horse-pond, Tunbridge Wells sandstone outcrops. The pH throughout the gardens is generally neutral. Rainfall 30 inches. Sunshine 4.25 hrs. Frosts are less frequent than at nearby valley sites as the cold air rolls off this site into the valleys.

The accompanying plan shows the main features of the gardens. The visitor should look for examples of Lutyens' handwork in the design and construction of steps, doorways, walls and terraces (see drawing). He was particularly clever in handling the levels of the garden to create interest, surprise and an easy progression from differing levels. From the entrance gate and kiosk one has a first glimpse of the low rambling house with its ancient, tilted porch and the long flagstone path that leads to it. The York paving used throughout Dixter came from old London paving-stones discarded in favour of macadam and concrete. The front lawn (2) is enclosed by yew hedges and has as its main feature an old wild pear tree. The lawn has been the subject of many years of what Christopher Lloyd calls meadow gardening. Developed by his mother, the late Mrs Lloyd, the aim has been to create a flowering mead of native and introduced meadow flowers. In the spring both lawns are a bright tapestry of naturalized bulbs, crocuses, narcissi, fritillaries and anemones, to be followed by many meadow flowers in May and June, including wild orchids. The grass is not cut until July, followed by a second cut in early August. In September, Autumn Crocus, *Colchicum* spp., and the true *Crocus speciosus*, a lovely blue autumn-flowering species and hardy cyclamen continue the attractive effects. Beside the north face of the house note the simple and effective use of hardy ferns and *Cotoneaster horizontalis* against the ancient timbered beams. The borders to the south of the house are usually extremely colourful, these being the subject of many interesting planting associations with annuals and perennials that change from year to year. There is a fine example of the variegated Persian Ivy, *Hedera colchica* 'Dentata Variegata', on the kitchen wall. The sunken pool garden (3) lies to the west of the front lawn, with the splendid protection and back-drop of the lawns and oast houses. Its

formality is richly decorated with a profusion of plants. On the walls of the barn one should look for the half hardy and exotic climbers *Schisandra grandiflora rubriflora*, *Abutilon megapotamicum*, a vine and clematis. Three large Brunswick figs grow on one wall. In the borders beside the paths are many fine foliage shrubs including *Olearia macrodonta*, *Ozothamnus rosmarinifolius*, *Skimmia japonica* and others. Note also the striking blue-green pinnate-leaved *Melianthus major*; a hardy Chilean evergreen fern, *Blechnum chilense*, and ornamental grasses and bamboos. In the Italian flower pots near the pool, silvery sprays of *Helichrysum petiolatum* spill on to the stone paving. South of the pool garden is the wall garden, an intimate enclosed garden, it has some good examples of Lutyens's architectural detailing in the steps and archways. There are some good shrubs here too, especially *Viburnum* and *Hydrangea*, and many perennial associations. *Hosta* spp., hardy orchids and more ferns grow in the cool moist soils here and the dainty white or pale blue *Viola cornuta* is everywhere. Note the fine enclosing tall hedge of Evergreen Oak, *Quercus ilex*, to the right as one descends the steps past the 'coffee pots', and the tiled piers of the old cowshed as restored by Lutyens and now wreathed in climbers.

The rose garden (9) is probably the most successful rose garden of all those mentioned in this book. It derives its success, I think, from the setting, intimacy, scale and enclosure, the use of flagstone paths and the delightful and haphazard selection of mostly old or well-proved roses made by Christopher Lloyd himself. These include the old Bourbon roses 'Mme Isaac Pereire' (a superbly scented light crimson-red rose), 'Gruss an Teplitz' (dark crimson and spicy scented), 'Mme Ernest Calvat' (vigorous, pink and raspberry scented), which produce endless successions of fragrant blooms encouraged by the pegging down of the vigorous shoots each year. Also you may find the old hybrid tea rose 'Madam Butterfly', and others chosen for their reliability, clean foliage and long flowering period. Clematis are grown over chestnut poles here, and over the loggia or converted cow-byre that offers such an attractive setting. A deep and regular mulching of lawn-mowings seems to keep this rose garden remarkably free of such disease as black-spot. The nursery (7) lies close at hand. A visit is recommended after touring the garden. Many fine and unusual plants from the garden can usually be found for sale in this small but extremely well run nursery.

The long border (12) is one of the finest features of the gardens at Great Dixter and is the subject of one of Christopher Lloyd's many books. It represents a splendid and rational amalgamation of the traditional herbaceous border and the shrub border and as a result of many years of careful selecting and siting, Christopher Lloyd has reached a refined standard of associations of many plants in this border that can look dramatic and effective at almost any time of the year, but especially between April and November. I find the October colours quite as exciting as those produced in high summer. The border is over 200 ft long and 15 ft deep with a flagged path as a viewing platform and perfect foil to the frontal plants that spill and sprawl over the stone paving. It faces south—south-west and is sunny and fairly exposed. Some of the many plants were labelled during visits in the 1976 season and to illustrate the great range of planting of this border a brief summary is given of four outstanding groups to be found here.

Group 1 by the old oak seat (a Lutyens design) at the far south-east end of the border: *Ilex* × *altaclarensis* 'Golden King' (variegated corner planting); *Gleditsia triacanthos* 'Sunburst' (gold pinnate foliage); *Tamarix pentandra* (pink feathery plumes); *Alchemilla mollis*; *Hosta plantaginea*; *Astrantia maxima* (the last three ground and frontal planting).

Group 2 at the south-east end: *Escallonia* 'Iveyi' (tall, white-flowered evergreen shrub); *Rosa spinosissima* 'William III' (carmine Burnet rose); *Acanthus* (foliage); *Salvia nemorosa* 'Superba' (blue-purple); *Sedum* 'Ruby Glow' (deep red-purple); *Miscanthus sinensis* 'Gracillimus' (ornamental grass); many herbaceous perennials including *Rudbeckia*, *Phlox*, *Hemerocallis* and the silvery *Senecio leucostachys*.

Group 3 at the north-west end: *Heliopsis scabra* 'Golden Plume' (yellow); *Aster* × *frikartii* (violet-blue); *Indigofera gerardiana* (pink); *Eryngium* × *oliverianum* (steely blue); *Sedum* 'Autumn Joy' and *Sedum maximum* 'Atropurpureum' (both autumn, pink and red); *Senecio cineraria* 'White Diamond' (silver).

Group 4 at the north-west end: *Rhamnus alaterna* 'Argenteovariegata' (variegated background shrub); *Miscanthus sinensis* 'Zebrinus' (striped Zebra Grass); *Genista aetnensis* (tall, yellow Mount Etna Broom); *Hydrangea paniculata* 'Praecox'; more perennials including *Hosta*, *Phlox* and *Viola*; *Mahonia* 'Undulata' (metallic-leaved shrub); *Sambucus racemosa* 'Plumosa Aurea' (golden cut-leaved elder).

Look back again from near the Mulberry Tree. Note that one can see virtually no bare soil in this border due to the complex and effective cover planting. Near the Mulberry Tree notice also the intricate circular steps designed by Lutyens and featured in his original plan. On the terrace wall here grow the unusual deliciously scented *Buddleia auriculata*, *Choisya ternata*, jasmine, clematis, fig and an apricot amongst the many other plants.

The kitchen garden areas have gradually been converted from pre-war fruit and vegetable areas to nursery and ornamental flower gardens. The espalier pears still line the paths and have been used to support more clematis. Note the battlemented yews here. Many unusual plants edge the paths, especially *Hebe*, the pink legume *Dorycnium hirsutum*, *Iris innominata*, *Phlox*, *Bergenia*, hardy ferns and many others. Note the vigorous metallic-leaved trailing *Rubus tricolor* scrambling over a pear tree beside this path. The orchards (10) are a great contrast to the enclosed and richly planted gardens. Below the long border, they are treated as hay meadows and are gold with daffodils in the spring. The informal ponds are also a contrast, with good waterside planting and grassy banks. Oaks fringe this area to the north, some of the very few established trees found on the site when the Lloyds bought the property in 1910. The horse pond area (14) — good examples of waterside planting and note the vigorous clumps of white Arum Lily, *Zantedeschia*, hardy here for many years.

Originally the garden had a staff of nine men. Now there are three full-time gardeners under the direction and supervision of Christopher Lloyd and his head gardener, Mr Van de Kaa. Mr Lloyd has no illusions about the labour-intensive nature of some of his gardens at Dixter. He insists on high standards of wall-plant training, staking of borders and trimming of hedges. He generally uses few chemicals, other than herbicides on the paths. He believes in biological control as far as is possible. He mulches all areas with a sawdust-based litter (no weed seeds) plus compound fertilizers. He uses lawn-mowings as a thick mulch on the rose garden. Much of his philosophy of plant and garden management is delightfully described in his book *The Well-Tempered Garden*,* which everyone should read. I have resisted quoting from it, but will end with the following observation from the book which, I think, summarizes simply and effectively his philosophy and approach to gardening:

> In this book I have exploited most of the ingredients which, in my case, combine to make for happy gardening. Sometimes the reader may be incited to exclaim: 'what a lot of trouble!' or 'who wants to go through all that?'. But however labour-saving you make your hobby, you will never get more out of it than you put in. Now and again it seems worth taking that extra bit of trouble that brings in its train some rather exciting result. You feel you have got somewhere. Effort is only troublesome when you are bored.

* Christopher Lloyd, *The Well-Tempered Garden*, Collins, 1970.

Heaselands

TQ 312 228 (Sheet 198) West Sussex. 1½ miles SW Haywards Heath on A273 road to Burgess Hill. 8 miles NW Lewes. Owner: The late Mr Ernest Kleinwort. Open most Wednesdays and Sunday afternoons in May only in aid of various charities including N.G.S. and the World Wildlife Fund.

A popular and comparatively recent large garden of over 20 acres designed by Mr Kleinwort on a bold and spectacular scale with emphasis on massed plantings for late spring and early summer effect. Rhododendrons, azaleas, a series of water gardens and a large rock garden are among the main features. Movement (apart from the flocks of visitors!) also comes from a wildfowl collection and the aviaries near the car park. Teas on the lawn are another feature.

The present impressive stone-built house dates from 1934; a large, solid country house which replaced an old farmhouse on the site. The house is beautifully situated on a south-west slope to command fine views over the garden and the wooded Sussex countryside beyond. The garden was developed from the mid-1930s with the first phase being the large-scale planting of many shelter trees (this is a hilltop site) including pines, red oaks and maples, which are now maturing well and giving character to the gardens. Most of the shrub planting and other areas date from the 1950s onwards.

The house stands strategically on a levelled small terrace on the 200 ft contour with most of the gardens sloping gently away to the south and south-west. Soils are of Wadhurst and wealden-clays, giving medium to heavy acid soils (compare Borde Hill and Sunte House). These soils respond to good cultivation and organic matter. Rainfall 29.5–31.5 inches.

Ernest Kleinwort has exploited the natural features of the site and has created a large, essentially informal, garden embodying with some degree of coherence many of the traditional elements of English gardens of the pre-Second World War era, such as rock garden, rose gardens, sunken gardens, wild, water and woodland gardens. Some mature oak and beech trees have been incorporated into the designs and supplemented with large scale plantings in the 'new' woodland areas and on the eastern flanks (the shelter trees already mentioned).

A plan of the garden is available to visitors (not reproduced here).

Car parking is ample and well-organized, as are the teas, and other visitor attractions. In front of the house, a sunken garden and pools match the style and scale of the house. There is some scope for bright annual bedding here. The Blue Cedar, *Cedrus atlantica glauca*, is a feature of this area. A series of well-constructed, semi-formal gardens lead down the slope below the house, interconnected with steps and gateways. The walled garden is an attractive, well-planted feature fringed with rocks and massed with many good shrub specimens, notably *Eucryphia*, camellias, azaleas, Flowering Dogwoods, *Cornus* spp., and many others. The rose and herbaceous gardens are rather undistinguished. The rock garden bounding the drive and forecourt is mass-planted with dwarf shrubs, especially dwarf rhododendrons (*R. yakushimanum* noted), *Cytisus*, *Helianthemum* and spreading conifers. There are very few herbs or mats of Alpine species. The maintenance is impeccable. The immaculate lawns that slope away to the water and woodland runs are broken up with bold masses of planting, especially rhododendrons and some specimen trees. The woodland and water garden offers scope for exploration and there is good planting of the bog garden with waterside species of *Primula*, *Rodgersia*, *Iris*, etc., and the wild garden with rhododendrons, azaleas and maples. On the way out, note the well-designed and planted retaining walls that line most of the drive – the drive garden.

Heaselands is a well-groomed, highly maintained garden. Six gardeners are employed for the 25–30 acres under the able direction of the head gardener. The lawns are exceptionally well managed.

Horsted Place Gardens

TQ 469 185 (Sheet 198) West Sussex. 1 mile S of Uckfield on A26 Lewes Road. Owner: Lord Rupert Nevill D.L., JP, and Lady Nevill. Open Easter to end of September; Wednesdays, Thursdays, Sundays and Bank Holiday Mondays 2–6. A very helpful detailed guide to the gardens is usually available at the gate. Teas available some days. See H.H.C.G.

Charming restored Victorian-style gardens around the mid-nineteenth-century 'Gothic' mansion, standing in a commanding position overlooking delightful wooded countryside. The soils are acidic and there are many examples of good design and planting features.

The mansion of Horsted Place is immediately impressive to the visitor. It was built in 1851 by George Myers who carried out many of Pugin's plans. An earlier house once stood to the south-east on the site of the Round Garden. The present house is on a shallow terrace on the brow of a gentle south slope some 100 ft above sea level on acidic loams derived from Wadhurst clays. The gardens are screened and protected from the cold north and north-east quarters by an attractive mixed tree belt of Common and Copper Beeches, conifers and flowering trees, which also seems to reduce sound from the A26 trunk road on that side. The gardens are approached down a long drive. Near the car park and entrance stands a magnificent Turkey Oak, *Quercus cerris*. There are pleasant picnic seats around this tree.

There are many pleasing contrasts in this garden. The formal area east of the house has a distinct Victorian style with pleached limes on the southern border (note the effective 'windows' and seats with views away to the South Downs and beautiful countryside), rose-covered arches and roses in painted iron baskets 'floating' across the lawn, inspired by Humphry Repton's plans for the Brighton Pavilion. The many borders and delightful planting features show the combined mastery of an overall design by the landscape architect, Geoffrey Jellicoe, with Lady Rupert Nevill's philosophy of creating scent, rhythm and blended harmony, and for planting to 'feel unrestricted except where there is a specially made framework to contain it'. Away from the more formal areas one can wander through a laburnum arch looking splendid in late May, down a serpentine shrubbery of cool glades with massed effective shrubs against a back-drop of fine trees. A newly planted Round Garden hidden away among the shrubs and trees is already looking effective with cool, shady associations of *Hosta*, *Hemerocallis* or Day Lilies, box, hydrangeas and azaleas. There is some splendid planting of low aromatic shrubs, junipers, pinks, thymes and *Campanula* to mention only a few, on the terraces around the house. The collection of old roses and scented plants is very comprehensive and appropriate to this garden.

The maintenance is sensitive and in keeping with the different styles of the garden areas. This applies particularly to the grass maintenance. To quote Lady Nevill: 'The rough and smooth grass makes pleasing patterns and natural currents which guide one's progress through the garden.' A visit is strongly recommended to this garden which has only been opened to the public in the last few years.

The Hyde

SU 247 303 (Sheet 187) West Sussex. 1½ miles W of Handcross off the A270 Handcross–Lower Beeding road, 7 miles S of Crawley, 7 miles E Horsham. Good parking and access. Owner: Mrs Raymond Warren. Open several Sunday afternoons in May, late June and October, usually for the N.G.S.

A pleasant large garden of good mature trees and shrubs on acid soils and a delightful lakeside setting. A visit in May is especially recommended.

A garden of about 9 acres in an extensive wooded estate with a farming enterprise attached. There are long, scenic drives from the main road through delightful bluebell woods (in late May), the south approach crossing the head of one of several small lakes that are an attractive feature of the garden. The solid, stone Victorian house stands on higher ground in the north-west corner of the garden. The style is a blend of formal and informal, the formality near the house giving way to a shrub and woodland garden with the lakes as a special feature.

The Hyde lies in the south-eastern part of the ancient St Leonard's Forest. Soils are of the wealden Lower Greensand in the Tunbridge Wells sand zone. The garden lies at about 325 ft above sea level and slopes to small valley streams and lakes to the south-east. It is reasonably sheltered and enclosed with woodland to the east and south. Rainfall and microclimate similar to Nymans.

Formal garden east of house – the central feature here is a formal pool of 1930s vintage with fountain and axial vistas between blocks of shrubs and formal herbaceous borders and beds of roses and lavender. There is an impressive glade of mature Japanese Maples for autumn colour. To the south of the formal area is sloping land towards the lake. Massed groups of Japanese Cherries, flowering crabs, rhododendrons and other mature specimens make a colourful sight in May and early June. There is a fine group of two *Eucryphia × nymansensis* 'Nymansay' (August flowering) at 33 ft and a free-flowering form of the Chilean Fire Bush *Embothrium coccineum*, a spectacular sight in late May. Note also fine specimens of *Pieris floribunda*; *Rosa Moyesii*; a good Judas Tree, *Cercis siliquastrum*; *Exochorda racemosa*; and fine thickets of mixed *Olearia macrodonta*, azaleas, heathers and many different *Cotoneaster* species. A series of several small lakes and pools have been created from small dams providing a lakeside setting and planting of bold groups of evergreen Japanese azaleas and Japanese Maples provide pictorial effects and reflections in May and June. The large specimens of *Aralia elata* 'Variegata' (*Aralia chinensis* 'Albo-marginata') look particularly splendid on the water's edge. There are also many shrub roses; *Rubus* 'Tridel'; two fine groups of the flowering Dogwoods *Cornus florida rubra* and *C. nuttallii*; and the bold waterside perennial *Gunnera manicata* and the Bog Arum, *Lysichitum americanum*. There is a horseshoe shaped lawn as a fine setting for the house on the south side, flanked by massed groups of rhododendron hybrids and the wooded fringes. These provide a fine back-cloth to such specimen flowering trees as Snowdrop Tree *Halesia carolina*, *Styrax japonica* and the autumn colouring *Parrotia persica*. Note the small, intricate rose garden to the east of the lawn behind a wistaria-clad pergola with a bower effect of honeysuckles, enclosing shrubs and flowering cherries. The stone-paved terrace along the south side of the house is planted with low-growing, grey foliage plants such as lavender, and *Artemisia*. On the house itself are fine specimens of Banksian Roses, *Ceanothus* and wistaria.

The maintenance of the nine acres of gardens is in the hands of the head gardener, Mr H.G. Worsfold, and three staff. The standard of upkeep is traditional and impeccable. An unusually well-groomed garden.

Leonardslee

SU 224 259 (Sheet 187) West Sussex. Lower Beeding, just E off A281 Horsham–Shoreham road, 4½ miles SE of Horsham. Owner: Sir Giles and Lady Loder. Open Wednesdays, Thursdays, Saturdays and Sundays from late April to early June and weekends in mid-October. Full details in H.H.C.G. Excellent access, parking and visitor arrangements. Teas/coffee available.

A large and spectacular woodland and water garden of about 80 acres on acid soils, developed over the last 90 years by the Loder family, the emphasis being on the great collections of rhododendron species, cultivars and hybrids. These, with many other interesting and unusual trees and shrubs, are at their most colourful during late April and May. There are also fine autumn colours in October.

These important gardens lie on the southern edge of the former great tract of wealden woodland known as St Leonard's Forest. The name of the gardens is derived from the forest and remnants of these woodlands provide a magnificent setting and structure to the garden. This area was formerly important for iron smelting and the lakes are derived from former hammer ponds. The sturdy mansion was built of local stone in the Georgian style in 1855, being superbly sited on a natural terrace some 290 ft above sea level with fine panoramic views across the gardens and estate and away to the south-east to the South Downs some 10–15 miles distant. In 1887, Sir Edmund Loder, Bt., the grandfather of the present owner, began planting the garden, and for the next 30 years he created the great layout and planting collections that are reaching their maturity today. He exploited with great skill and flourish the natural features of valleys, streams, lakes and rock outcrops and embodied many fine native forest trees into his schemes, with some introduced North American conifers like Redwoods and Wellingtonias planted by an ancestor owner soon after the house was built. Some of these are now over 100 ft high. Rhododendrons were Sir Edmund Loder's greatest passion and he was responsible for raising many fine hybrids, of which probably the most magnificent for general planting are the 'Loderi' crosses of which there are many fine mature examples at Leonardslee. He was also very interested in camellias and many other Asiatic trees and shrubs. The gardens continued to flourish and develop under the succeeding Loder generations and today Sir Giles and Lady Loder and their sons are enthusiastic, devoted and very hard working in their determination to maintain the gardens and great plant collections and to enable the public to enjoy them at seasons of the year when they are at their finest. Their approach to the management and education of the many visitors is enlightened and professional. Many plants in the gardens are very well labelled.

The setting, microclimate and soils are comparable to the other fine gardens in the St Leonard's Forest area. The great oak, beech and other forest trees provide the ideal light shade and high canopy for the introduced Asiatic plants, and the other important factor is that of the soils, which are light, acidic forest loams derived from the Tunbridge Wells sandstone of the Lower Greensand. These soils are also well watered with springs and streams flowing down to the series of lakes. Rainfall 35–36 inches. Sunshine 4–4.25 hrs. Spring frosts are not serious on these slopes but can occur as frost pockets in the lower valley and lakeside areas.

The plan gives some idea of the informal and almost wild character of the 82 acres of garden, and a full day or more is needed to explore all the remote parts, preferably with visits at different seasons to appreciate the diversity of plants and effects at Leonardslee. The style is large scale, informal 'amenity' woodland and trees in scale with the dramatic landfall, the stature of the woodlands and the range of plants the Loders have chosen to grow. There are smaller more intimate areas in the rock garden, and associated with the buildings, and, more recently, in the half-hardy collection in the new display of glasshouses near the car parks. Note the policy of block or group plantings, the skilful exploitation of views and the layout of the many winding paths that thread through the garden, offering a series of varied experiences and contrasts. A detailed and well-illustrated guide is available on open days and visitors are recommended to buy one of these before touring the gardens. A summary of the main features follows:

Entrance drive and house area (1) — Massed shrubberies of many rhododendron hybrids with *Magnolia liliflora* 'Nigra'; *Viburnum plicatum* 'Mariesii'; flowering cherries, and a particularly good group of *Acer griseum* whose peeling bark glows mahogany brown in winter. Near the publication kiosk there stands an 80 ft tall specimen of the Incense Cedar *Calocedrus* (*Libocedrus*) *decurrens*. Nearer the house are massed beds of Japanese evergreen Kurume Azaleas and an unusual form of Japanese Cedar, *Cryptomeria japonica* 'Araucarioides' (this was planted in 1935 and is now nearly 65 ft high), also Douglas Fir, *Pseudotsuga menziesii*, and Wellingtonia, *Sequoiadendron giganteum*, both nearly 115 ft high. There are also good mature cedar trees, magnolias and Japanese Maples opposite the house.

The rock garden (21) is a period feature of massive construction of local sandstone, now largely concealed by mature planting of mostly shrubs and conifers rather than alpine or rock plants. Note the great colourful hummocks of Kurume Azaleas and dwarf rhododendrons such as the vivid scarlet 'Jenny' ('Creeping Jenny') and 'Elizabeth', the deep green of 40–50-year-old specimens of dwarf Norway Spruce, *Picea abies*, cultivars and many other shrubs. The wishing well is a whimsical touch and no doubt a good source of funds for the charity it helps to support!

The house lawn gives splendid views of the main extent of the gardens lying below. Here is one of the largest Tulip Trees, *Liriodendron tulipifera*, in the country, a lofty single trunk with a high canopy over 115 ft high. It flowers in May and June. On the west side is a large tree of *Magnolia campbellii mollicomata* and some large old specimens of *Camellia japonica* flowering very freely in April. The Camellia Walk (19) leads off from the south-west corner of the lawn and was one of the first parts of the garden to be made, many of the great camellias being over 50 years old and over 20 ft tall. They are interspersed with hardy palms *Chamaerops humilis* and more rhododendrons. Near here is the original plant of the Leonardslee form of *Rhododendron 'Luscombei'* with large pink clusters of flowers in May. The fine Japanese Maples *Acer palmatum* which are everywhere at Leonardslee, and particularly in this part of the garden, were mostly grown from a special consignment of seedlings imported from Japan many years ago.

The house walls – on the south-east face of the house one can see all four forms of the delightful rose species, *Rosa banksiae*, first introduced into this country from China in 1807; the type species, also known as *R. banksiae* 'Alboplena', double white, thornless and delicately scented; *R. b.* 'Lutea', the Yellow Banksian Rose with double rosette-like flowers and some thorns; *R. b. lutescens*, single yellow and very sweetly scented; while *R. b. normalis* is the wild form with single, creamy-white, sweetly scented flowers. All these forms flower in May and early June. Note also the wistaria and the Trumpet Vine *Campsis radicans*. At the east end of the terrace steps is one of the oldest and largest camellias at Leonardslee, *C.japonica* 'Variegata', thought to be over 100 years old and with a circumference of about 65 ft. In the *Gardener's Chronicle* of 1907 this was photographed as an unusually large specimen! On the bank in front of the house are many low-growing and dwarf rhododendrons. There is also an excellent collection of dwarf conifers and ericaceous shrubs on the east-facing bank beside the path leading to the Rotunda. Note on the stable block walls here the large *Camellia reticulata* 'Captain Rawes' dating from 1900, now a huge specimen that grows here without frost protection. The exploration of the rest of the garden is best left to the visitor to discover for himself with the aid of the guide. One can gradually descend by a series of paths through different areas of woodland planting to reach the lakesides eventually. Some of the finest views of the garden can be had from the Rotunda path (see plan opposite) which tracks in a north-west direction to end at the Rotunda itself (18) where the view is superb. The planting is especially rich and mature along this walk, including *Magnolia campbellii mollicomata*, the unusual white-flowered form of *Paulownia tomentosa*, more magnificent Leonardslee rhododendron crosses of the Loderi and other groups, many fine Asiatic foliage rhododendrons like *R. fulvum* (brown 'fur' or indumentum on the undersides of the leaves) and *R. grande* with huge leaves and silvery indumentum, and the free-flowering *Camellia × williamsii* 'Donation'.

Cox's Walk (15) is yet another exciting experience to ensnare one on the way down to the lake. Here the sheer size of the native trees,

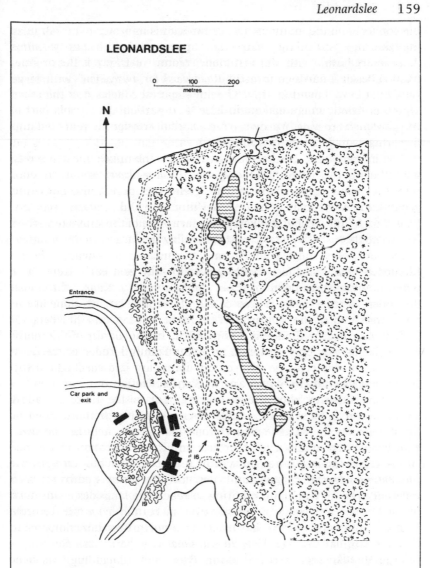

LEONARDSLEE

N

Entrance

Car park and exit

1. Leonardslee House
2. Daffodil Lawn &
   Dwarf Conifers
3. 'Loderi' Garden
4. Middle Walk
5. The Dell
6. *Magnolia campbellii*
7. Memorial Table
8. Cross Paths
9. Rustic Bridge
10. Top Garden
11. Coronation Garden
12. Mossy Ghyl
13. Rhododendron Walks
14. Waterfall
15. Cox's Walk
16. Terraces
17. Camellia Grove
18. Rotunda
19. Camellia Walk
20. Lower Drive
21. Rock Garden
22. Tea Room
23. Conservatory

⟵ Good Views

the conifers and the many introduced species is impressive. Do not miss the unusual, spreading, pink-edged purple beech *Fagus sylvatica* 'Roseomarginata', with the fastigiate column of Dawyck Beech contrasting beside it and a good fastigiate oak not far away. The Coronation Garden (11) was planted in 1953 with a special collection of the more vigorous Asiatic magnolias including *M. campbellii, M. c. mollicomata, M. sargentiana robusta, M. sprengeri diva,* all now over 20 years old and flowering usually in early spring with large pink flag-like flowers on the bare branches. The Mossy Ghyll (12) is planted almost entirely with the richly-scented yellow azalea *Rhododendron luteum,* its cool primrose-yellow flowers beneath the great oaks here being especially delightful in May. Near here are the Hungarian Oak, *Quercus frainetto,* nearly 82 ft high, and an exceptionally large tree of the snake-branched Norway Spruce, *Picea abies* 'Virgata', possibly the largest in the country. Across the lakes, more planting and explorations lie ahead with the Rhododendron Walks (13), and on a hill to the east is a collection of pines, many of these being of great size and quality. Nearer the house the Loderi Garden (3) is another feature to explore on this slope at the north-west end of the Rotunda Walk. Here in May one can become quite intoxicated by the scent and overpowering glamour of the many fine *R.*'Loderi' varieties raised here by Sir Edmund Loder at the very beginning of this century. The parent for many fine seedlings is the superb but not fully hardy species *R. griffithianum.*

The Dell (5) is another remote and lush part of the garden. Massed azaleas cover both sides of a small stream and in the moist bowl of the dell grows the huge-leaved rhubarb-like plant *Gunnera manicata,* with bluebells, primulas and other late spring flowers carpeted around. At the top of the Dell is a good specimen of the Snowdrop Tree *Halesia carolina,* and note the vigour and height of the young Redwoods, and especially the Dawn Redwood *Metasequoia glyptostroboides.* This was planted in the 1950s and is already over 50 ft tall. The white, sweetly scented, summer-flowered *Magnolia × watsonii* grows here, alongside its large tree-like relative *Magnolia virginiana*; a 130 ft tall Redwood; a large Handkerchief Tree; Mexican *Pinus montezumae* with its five-needled tassels of grey and green silvery foliage; Macedonian Oak, *Quercus macedonica (Q. trojana)* and flame-coloured forms of Mollis Azaleas, ablaze with colour in May.

Naturalists will notice the bird and insect life in this great garden sanctuary, particularly near the lakes, and for the botanists the moist, acidic flora gives carpets of bluebells, many ferns, mosses and patches of foxgloves, harebells and wild orchids.

The conservatory and glasshouses (23) – a new and interesting feature near the car park is a very functional and educational large aluminium glasshouse which is fully automated for ventilation and irrigation and has a good collection of well-labelled, half-hardy and tender shrubs and coolhouse conservatory plants. There are two other glasshouses close by, both being entirely filled with camellias representing collections from many parts of the world, including many of the new large-flowered varieties and hybrids from America, Australia and New Zealand. In recent years several gold medals have been won by the Loders with exhibits of these camellias at the RHS shows in London.

A staff of several gardeners manage Leonardslee with direction and some help from the Loder family. Standards are commendably high, particularly near the house and in the glasshouses. Note the widespread use of bracken compost for mulching. Labelling is comprehensive, there are very good clear notices and direction signs and the printed guide is well written and produced.

Mill House

SU 009 184 (Sheet 197) West Sussex. Fittleworth, 3 miles SE Petworth off A283 Petworth–Pulborough Road on the B2138 at Lower Fittleworth. Owner: Sir Geoffrey and Lady Hardy Roberts. Open usually several Sunday afternoons in May and June in collaboration with several other Fittleworth gardens.

A pleasant riverside garden designed by the late Percy Cane in the early 1950s. An historic, picturesque setting, beside the River Rother. A mill has existed on the site since monastic times, and the present early-seventeenth-century mill building makes an attractive picture from the old roadbridge that crosses the Rother just to the east of the gardens.

The present house in the comfortable, neo-Elizabethan country house style was built in the 1920s and embodies the former eighteenth-century mill-owner's house that stood on the site until the early part of this century. The present owners acquired the property during the Second War War and in 1945 called in the garden architect Percy Cane to advise on the garden design. Between 1945 and 1955 he and Lady Hardy Roberts created the present layout which shows a number of typical features of his design style at that time. His main theme was to create a spacious terraced garden on the sloping site, using the natural river terraces beside and below the house and incorporating very effectively his favourite elements of wide flights of stone steps, bold retaining walls, pergolas, flagged stone walks, urns and statuary. He created a wide, flat terrace of unbroken mown grass beside the river.

The soils are light, sandy, acidic loams on the terrace with heavier alluvial clays nearer the river. Flooding is now a rare occurrence after recent improvements to the whole drainage of the Rother Valley. In the mill zone one may occasionally see a few sea trout moving up the river to spawn in the upper reaches. The garden is very well sheltered, with good tree cover and the valley site as protection.

A few particular features to note on the terraces are the shaded *Camellia* and *Hosta* associations on the top terrace; the effective use of sculptural or foliage conifers and shrubs on the terraces, especially fastigiate yews, cypresses and two very fine sentinel-like *Chamaecyparis lawsoniana* 'Columnaris' flanking the steps leading to the river lawn; good massed planting of foliage and scented shrubs on the terraces, with a strategically placed *Magnolia* × *soulangiana* at the west of the main terrace; well-planted urns on the patio around the house; and the retention of the ancient yew incorporated into the retaining wall near the house. On the main river terrace lawn an old cowshed has been restored as a charming garden-house, with a well-placed silver birch behind it. Herbaceous perennials and foliage plants grow in the borders near here. Good examples of silver foliage can be seen in the two *Pyrus salicifolia* 'Pendula' framing the entrance to the front drive. Note the fine group of mature ash and oak in the grassy little dell over the river on the island beside the old mill itself. The two areas of garden are now well managed by one full-time gardener and some part-time help. A policy of using plenty of organic matter in the rather hungry sandy soils is evident in the excellent growth and quality of the plants.

Nymans

TQ 266 295 (Sheet 198) West Sussex. Handcross on B2114 close to A23 London–Brighton trunk road. 1 mile SE of Handcross, 5 miles S of Crawley. London 35 miles. Owner: The National Trust (under the direction of the Earl and Countess of Rosse). Open normally several days a week April–October including Sundays and Bank Holidays (see H.H.C.G. and National Trust literature).

One of the outstanding National Trust gardens in the South of England. It was established at the beginning of the century by the Messel family and there is an exceptional collection of rare and unusual trees and shrubs, many of them half-hardy and enjoying lime-free soils. Parking is excellent and other facilities for visitors are well-organized, as with so many National Trust properties. Tea is available.

A regency house stood on the site of the present structure and several of the great trees on the lawns today date from this period. One wing was incorporated into an enlarged, pretentious stone-built Victorian house dating from the 1870s. Mr Ludwig Messel acquired Nymans in 1890 and immediately began to develop the garden. At the time there was apparently very little designed garden at Nymans. The park-like grounds and groves of native beech and oaks would have been there as well as the walled garden with the rows of apple trees, and the fine views to the south-east and south. Messel's work began in the orchards and walled garden where he began his first plantings (see plan p. 167). Here he laid out his famous summer border (14), with advice from William Robinson on the planting design (Gertrude Jekyll also visited Nymans at this time). He then made the sunken garden (4) and created one of the first heather gardens (8) in this country. He developed a natural hill into the Mount, with its weeping Camperdown Elm, *Ulmus glabra* 'Camperdownii', and nearby created a Japanese garden in the current fashion of the turn of the century. The stone lanterns were genuine imports from Japan and the great stone wistaria-clad pergola is very redolent of this period. Ludwig Messel then moved to the pinetum area (1a), planting the bulk of the area with a fine collection of conifers but leaving a great expanse of grass to accentuate the massed groups and profiles of these collections. He gave a very special place to a small temple in the classical style (2) designed by his architect brother Alfred Messel. Ludwig Messel also created the lime avenue which leads to a balustraded prospect (3) from which one can enjoy superb views to the east and south-east across the wooded ridges of the Weald with the distant South Downs visible on a good day. He exploited the existing laurel walk of over ¼ mile in length to serve as a boundary feature. The implementation of these pioneering schemes was shared by his head gardener James Comber. During the first decade of this century a large and rare collection of plants was established.

Ludwig Messel died in 1916 and was succeeded by his son, Colonel Leonard Messel, who quickly took to gardening and rapidly acquired a skill and plant knowledge that enabled him to continue and expand the work of his father. He sponsored plant collections, and his gardener's son, Harold Comber, undertook several expeditions to South America and Australasia. Colonel and Mrs Messel also entirely re-built the Victorian house in the style of a stone-built West Country Jacobean mansion, importing genuine Somerset stone. The stone loggia (4) in the Italian Renaissance style was built at this time by the Messels with the Byzantine urn as a focal feature. Unfortunately most of this picturesque house was destroyed in a disastrous fire in 1947, together with Colonel Messel's priceless horticultural library. One wing of the

house has subsequently been refurbished as a home for the Earl and Countess of Rosse when they are at Nymans. The remainder of the shell of the house stands as a romantic climber-clad ruin among the gardens.

Colonel Messel died in 1953 and bequeathed the garden to the National Trust, who took it over in 1954 with Colonel Messel's daughter, the Countess of Rosse, as director. James Comber, the head gardener, also died at this time and his place was taken by the second gardener, Mr Cecil Nice, who is now head gardener. The Earl and Countess of Rosse, with the energetic Cecil Nice, have been steadily renovating and replanting the gardens over the last 20 years.

Nymans lies on the southern edge of St Leonard's Forest on Lower Greensand soils, acidic, fertile, sandy loams which when well-managed will produce magnificent growth of native and exotic trees and many shrubs and garden plants. The oaks and beeches are very fine specimens here. The gardens lie at about 390 ft above sea level at their highest point on the sandstone ridge, sloping gently to the south and south-west and abruptly to the north and east. A sheltered microclimate is conferred on the innermost parts of the garden by the native tree belts and the rich plantings of the last 70–80 years. The climate is relatively cool and moist for West Sussex. Rainfall averages 39 inches per year. Radiation frosts are not usually common with a hilltop garden site like this, the cold air flowing away into the valleys.

There are two important aspects to look for at Nymans: first, the basic design features of the original garden laid out by Ludwig Messel 70–80 years ago (see plan), and the rare plants imported by him from 1896 onwards, and secondly the great collections of rare and half-hardy plants imported by Colonel Messel and James Comber in the 1920s, which have been greatly augmented during the last 20 years by the Earl and Countess of Rosse. Except to the knowledgeable or informed plantsmen, these introductions, now large mature specimens, are not immediately obvious to the visitor and reference is therefore made to the approximate location of the most outstanding on the plan which is based on the one printed in the detailed guide written by the Countess of Rosse and available at the shop on open days. Reference to this guide is recommended. The summary which follows cannot hope to do full justice to this garden.

Pinetum (1a) – The entrance is from the car park. Glades of massive pine, oak and Sweet Chestnut are underplanted with large-leaved Asiatic rhododendrons. Note particularly *RR. macabeanum, sinogrande* and *magnificum*. The fringe of mature 70 year-old conifers includes many cultivars of *Chamaecyparis lawsoniana*, Lawson Cypress, especially the unusual 'Wissellii'; the largest *Cryptomeria japonica* 'Spiralis' Japanese Cedar in the UK; many cedars and junipers; and a fringe of the handsome North American Western Hemlock, *Tsuga heterophylla*, interplanted with the famous Nymans introduction *Eucryphia* × *nymansensis* 'Nymansay', a July and August-flowering shrub raised at Nymans in 1915 by Ludwig Messel and James Comber. There are other fine specimens of this shrub now over 30 ft tall in the gardens. Here also are hydrangeas (a splendid blue colour on these acid soils) and more Asiatic *Rhododendron* collections of George Forrest and Kingdon Ward, especially *R. cerasinum* and *R. crassum*. From Alfred Messel's temple (2) there is a fine view across the grass meadow to the valley below and the Weald beyond. In March and April this meadow is spangled with narcissi, including the wild daffodil *Narcissus pseudonarcissus*.

The Sunken Garden (4) – A circular sunken garden with the main architectural features being the Italian loggia, the Byzantine urn and the formal beds of spring and summer displays presided over by the four sentinel-like specimens of *Chamaecyparis lawsoniana* 'Grayswood Pillar' and surrounded by a collection of modern camellia cultivars introduced by the Rosses. Note the excellent back-drop of trees and evergreen shrubs to the east and north-east, making this a warm sheltered garden. There are two fine specimens of *Magnolia denudata* and *Magnolia sargentiana* here.

The heather garden and rock garden (7 and 8) were created by Ludwig Messel. They are protected from cold winds by a fine mixed hedge of *Escallonia* 'Langleyensis' and *Elaeagnus macrophylla*. Here one can find veteran masses of tree heaths, notably *E. arborea* and *E. terminalis*, as well as masses of the Cornish Heath, *E. vagans*, and a rich and colourful maquis of dwarf rhododendrons, and dwarf shrub roses. In the rock garden, outstanding are *Pieris formosa forrestii*, *Pieris floribunda* and a magnificent silvery mass of the unusual Tasmanian shrub *Hakea acicularis* (*H. sericea*). *Embothrium coccineum lanceolatum* in the background in one area has a foreground planting of low-growing heaths, *Sarcococca* and dwarf Kurume azaleas.

The pergola and Japanese garden (9) – The pergola is a massive construction of stone pillars dating from the 1890s and clad with specially selected seedlings of *Wisteria floribunda* 'Macrobotrys' (*W. multijuga*) imported from Japan. This pergola lies on the western boundary of the garden close to the extremely busy Handcross to Haywards Heath road and traffic noise is fortunately deadened to a certain extent by thick evergreen and other planting on the roadside. More new camellias can be found here.

The lawns and house (11) – the fine mature specimens dating from

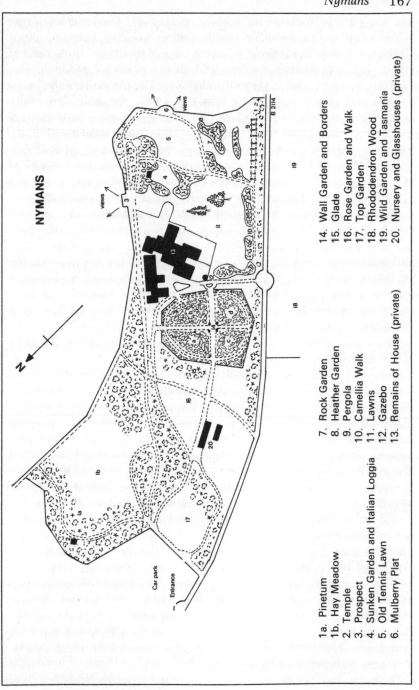

NYMANS

N

1a. Pinetum
1b. Hay Meadow
2. Temple
3. Prospect
4. Sunken Garden and Italian Loggia
5. Old Tennis Lawn
6. Mulberry Plat

7. Rock Garden
8. Heather Garden
9. Pergola
10. Camellia Walk
11. Lawns
12. Gazebo
13. Remains of House (private)

14. Wall Garden and Borders
15. Glade
16. Rose Garden and Walk
17. Top Garden
18. Rhododendron Wood
19. Wild Garden and Tasmania
20. Nursery and Glasshouses (private)

Car park

Entrance

B 2114

views

views

the last century have already been referred to: *Cedrus libani*, *Fagus sylvatica heterophylla* Fern-leaf Beech, Copper Beeches, oaks and pines. To the south note the striking foliage border of *Phormium*, New Zealand Flax; *Cistus*; columnar conifers and dwarf pines. A group of Bird Cherries, *Prunus padus*, is very effective here. The old ruins of the house provide a romantic and almost folly-like setting for many fine plants that mantle the skeleton walls and house windows. The more outstanding of these wall plants include: *Magnolia grandiflora* 'Goliath', (the only original plant remaining from before the fire), yellow *Rosa banksiae*, *Wisteria venusta*, *Chimonanthus praecox* and a delightful blend of climbers such as clematis, *Campsis*, jasmine and roses, all planted in recent years by the Countess of Rosse. The terraces at the foot of the walls and the borders here are massed with aromatic and summer-flowering plants, shrubby *Salvia* spp., roses, peonies, catmint and others. Box and yew sculptural topiary echoes the architecture of the house, and the charming Somerset stone dovecote is a much photographed feature of the garden. The outer walls of the sanctuary garden (now used as a private garden by the Rosse family) are massed with great specimens of *Camellia japonica* 'Adolphe Audusson' and the fine white *Rhododendron yunnanense*.

The wall gardens and borders (14) – this was one of the first areas to be laid out by Ludwig Messel over 80 years ago on the site of an old orchard, some trees of which remain to this day. There are many rare and unusual plants in this area which pass almost unnoticed by the casual visitor since so much of the planting is in a naturalistic, almost woodland style. The plan shows the approximate quadrant design of the garden. The centrepiece is a fine Italian fountain encircled by four globular, clipped yews trained in an original crown-like form. The two famous Robinson borders run the full length of the garden and are really colourful in July and August. The four sections of this garden each have a quite distinct character. They are numbered 14 a, b, c and d on the plan for convenience of description. 14d is shaded and semi-woodland in character, dominated by tall magnolias and other fine flowering trees; *Magnolia campbellii*, the fine Himalayan Pink Tulip Tree that flowers very early in the year in February and March; and the superb hybrid from *M. campbellii*, 'Charles Raffill', deeper pink in colour; *Magnolia macrophylla* with large leaves and flowers; *Cladrastis lutea*, the Yellow Wood, and *Staphylea colchica*, the Bladder Nut, with white flowers in May. Beneath the trees in spring there is a rich carpet of herbs and bulbous plants, snowdrops, tulips, *Erythronium*, fritillaries, anemones and many more. The woodland flora is encouraged by sensitive management. Area 14c is more open in character, with outstanding specimens of unusual trees: two *Nothofagus*, Southern Beeches, from New Zealand reach over 45 ft in height here; *N. cliffortioides*, the Mountain Beech with small, curled-edged leaves; and *N. fusca*, the Red Beech with deep coppery-red leaves in April. There is also a coppice of old apple trees and more *Eucryphia × nymansensis* 'Nymansay', and *Magnolia campbellii*. Note also the Kentucky Coffee Tree, *Gymnocladus dioicus*, with distinctive pale grey winter twigs and vivid pinkish unfolding leaves. There are also *Stewartia*, *Styrax* and several large *Rhododendron* hybrids. Area 14a faces south-west and its very sheltered enclosed microclimate has proved to be ideal for an extraordinary range of very half-hardy or unusually tender shrubs from New Zealand, South America and California. Look for the collection of *Leptospermum* species from New Zealand; the Headache Tree or Californian Bay, *Umbellularia californica*, with very aromatic, evergreen leaves (so aromatic that excessive inhalation can cause headaches!); the striking holly-like *Desfontainea spinosa* from Chile with tubular gold and scarlet flowers in late summer; more enormous *Eucryphia* with buttress-like trunks; camellias; magnolias; and a rich ground flora of herbs and perennials. Area 14b is rather mixed with more diverse tree planting: Black Mulberry, *Morus nigra*; the Handkerchief Tree, *Davidia involucrata*; magnolias; the New Zealand shrub *Hoheria* with white flowers in July; and a particularly fine Chinese *Styrax hemsleyana* with white racemes of flowers in June.

A fine belt of beeches and pines lies to the north of the wall garden, giving shelter and background. Note the deep blue colour of the many groups and scattered specimens of hydrangeas in this woodland and elsewhere at Nymans – a good indication of the lime-free soils. Lady Rosse's old rose garden (16) – designed and planted in the 1960s and incorporating some of Mrs Messell's original roses. The top garden (17) became an overflow area for the great flood of imported plants that Comber and the Messels were bringing to the gardens in the 1920s and 1930s. Nymans subscribed to many plant-collecting expeditions at this time. Introductions came also from Harold Comber's own tours to the Antipodes, particularly Tasmania, Australia and New Zealand, and to South America. This explains the fine collections of plants from these regions, the *Nothofagus* (New Zealand and South America), *Eucryphia* (Chile), *Embothrium* (Chile) and many evergreen South American *Berberis*. The old quarry with its moist habitat is planted with *Gunnera manicata* (like great rhubarb), the Chusan Palm *Trachycarpus fortunei*, and a nearby *Nothofagus* group of *N.menziesii*, *obliqua* and *solandri*. There are also bold and effective masses of species and hybrids of *Camellia*, *Deutzia*, *Syringa*, *Weigela* and *Hydrangea*. The rare small

Chinese trees *Meliosma veitchiorum*, with large pinnate leaves and white fragrant flowers in May, and *Tetracentron sinense*, red-tinted young leaves and long catkin-like flowers, grow here – both introduced very early this century. There is also the Chinese Honey Locust, *Gleditsia sinense*, with branched spines and fern-like foliage. Magnolias grow to a great size in this area, particularly *M.·× veitchii* (65 ft), *M. kobus* (32 ft) and *M. campbellii mollicomata* (32 ft). Lord and Lady Rosse added a fine border of peonies, delphiniums, roses and day lilies along one side with more 'cosmopolitans' that love the microclimate and soils of Nymans; *Lindera megaphylla* (west China), *Abelia schumannii* (China); *Buddleia colvilei* (Himalayas); *Kalmia latifolia* (North America); *Embothrium coccineum* and *Eucryphia cordifolia* (South America); *Eucryphia moorei* (New Zealand); *Genista aetnensis* (Sicily); and *Cytisus battandieri* (Morocco).

The rhododendron wood and wild garden (18 and 19) – To accommodate at Nymans even more of the great plant collections that were built up in the expansion period, in the 1920s a further area was taken into the gardens on the south-west side of the main road and a nursery, rhododendron wood and a wild garden were gradually established there. After seeing the main gardens the visitor can explore this remote and quiet place and discover many fine collections of unusual plants from Asia and especially Tasmania. One area is even called Tasmania after the collections of species from the island planted there. A collection of Asiatic rhododendrons has recently been identified and catalogued by Mr John Clarke of the Royal Botanic Gardens, Edinburgh, assisted by Mr Alan Hardy of Sandling Park and the head gardener, Cecil Nice.

A small team of gardeners under the present head gardener, Cecil Nice, and the direction of the Earl and Countess of Rosse, achieve very effective maintenance of these large and complex gardens.

Penns in the Rocks

TQ 524 347 (Sheet 188) East Sussex. Motts Mill, 3 miles S of Groombridge E off B2188. 7 miles SW of Tunbridge Wells. Owner: Lord and Lady Gibson. Open two or three afternoons in spring and summer for the N.G.S. and other charities.

A dramatic garden incorporating a charming part-eighteenth-century house and formal gardens and an impressive outcrop of Tunbridge Wells stone used to create a wild garden with spring bulbs and flowering shrubs. There is also a lake and parkland.

Penns in the Rocks at Penns Rocks summarizes the two most important historical associations of this fascinating place. The estate and adjoining Rocks Farm came into the hands of the Penn family in the seventeenth century and William Penn, founder of Pennsylvania, was the owner for some time. It was his grandson who enlarged the farmhouse in the more impressive Georgian style in 1737. The middle and north blocks were added later in the 1830s and 1850s respectively. The Rocks are a spectacular outcrop of Tunbridge Wells sandstone to the south of the house, offering a striking contrast to the formality and order of the house and gardens there. The haunting beauty and atmosphere of the place attracted a subsequent owner in this century, the poetess Dorothy Wellesley (Lady Gerald Wellesley), who bought the house in 1925 from the Rhys Pryce family who had owned it since 1852. She built the Temple of Friendship that stands today at the top of the glade to the south of the house – with the sculptural rocks flanking it on one side – as a shrine to fellow-writers of the time, W.B. Yeats, Walter de la Mare, Ruth Pitter, Vita Sackville-West and others. These names, an ode to poets by Thomas Nash (1593) and some of Dorothy Wellesley's own poetry are inscribed on stone slabs in the building. The present owners, Lord and Lady Gibson, bought Penns in the Rocks in 1957 and have carried out an extensive programme of restoration to the house and garden.

Penns lies in the scenic hilly East Sussex and West Kent Weald countryside that typifies the settings of Scotney Castle and Groombridge also. The Tunbridge Wells outcrops of pale coloured sandstone are very characteristic in this area, giving rise to light, well-drained, acidic soils. Woodland around the gardens gives shelter and seclusion. The gardens lie about 250 ft above sea level. Climate similar to Scotney.

The house and gardens are approached down a long winding drive through attractive woodland, yellow with daffodils in April. The house seems perched on a raised terrace with the formal gardens to the north side. Through wrought-iron gates one can enter the walled garden, with fine walls of local stone enclosing a well-designed and planted garden of old roses, perennials and many climbers. Note the massive wistaria on the garden building in the south-east corner. The swimming pool garden has well-kept lawns, some fine *Magnolia stellata* and a number of flowering trees, especially Flowering Crabs and *Sorbus*. A good specimen of the 'Kiftsgate' rose covers an old tree here. A shrub area is thick with daffodils in the spring. The 'tea pot' rock area is approached over a small rustic bridge, and many interesting trees have been planted here since 1957 by Lord and Lady Gibson, including fine looking Southern Beeches, *Malus* and *Sorbus*. There are also conical dark green groups of Stone Pine, *Pinus pinea*. From the Temple of Friendship one gets a fine romantic view of the house. The true Lent Lily or wild daffodil *Narcissus pseudonarcissus* has been naturalized here and is a delightful carpet in April in many parts of the garden. On the lawns near the house are two fine specimen conifers, a massive *Cedrus libani* and a Wellingtonia. There is a small, attractive lily pool garden and an azalea garden in addition to rock outcrops and the glades amongst them. The lake below the approach drive is less than 12 years old. Pastures and grazing cattle add to the peaceful atmosphere. The standards of maintenance are sensitive and effective for the styles of garden to be found here.

Petworth House

SU 975 220 (Sheet 197) West Sussex. Petworth, main entrance being in the town itself. 5½ miles E of Midhurst. Owner: The National Trust. Open: The park is open daily to the public all year. Car parks and pedestrian access to the park are marked on the plan (8). House and pleasure grounds usually open April–mid-October, Wednesdays, Thursdays, Saturdays, Sundays and Bank Holidays 2–6.

One of the finest surviving Capability Brown landscape parks in the country, in a very beautiful part of Sussex. The splendid mansion is especially noted for the fine collection of pictures.

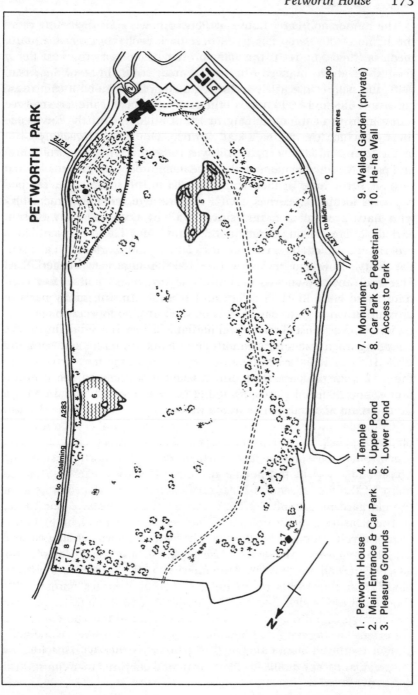

PETWORTH PARK

1. Petworth House
2. Main Entrance & Car Park
3. Pleasure Grounds
4. Temple
5. Upper Pond
6. Lower Pond
7. Monument
8. Car Park & Pedestrian Access to Park
9. Walled Garden (private)
10. Ha-ha Wall

The manor and early house at Petworth were for over 300 years the home of the Percy family. A deer park probably existed in early medieval times. In 1670 the sole surviving heiress to the vast Percy estates, Elizabeth, married Charles Seymour, sixth Duke of Somerset. With the help of his wife's fortune, he completely re-built the house between 1688 and 1693, adding the great west façade that one can see today in front of the older patchwork of buildings on the town side through which the visitor usually enters. He built surprisingly close to the town and later a high wall was to be thrown round the house and park. No trace remains of the seventeenth-century gardens known to have been made at this time. The pleasure grounds (3) were laid out as a formal 'wilderness' with a pattern of straight-edged walks with narrow winding paths between. Charles Wyndham, the third Earl of Egremont, succeeded to the estate and began an ambitious programme of enlargement of the house and park. He called in Capability Brown to re-design the park. A contract between Lord Egremont and Brown was drawn up in May 1753 and further contracts were made in 1754, 1755 and 1756 for the lakes and pleasure ground. Brown's great design can be seen in plan form on page 173. He swept away most of the formal baroque design in front of the house, regrading the terraces into smooth grass banks. A ha-ha and retaining wall (10) was built down the entire west side of the house separating the park from the pleasure grounds laid out to the north-west of the house. The main lake or upper pond (5) was created by damming a small stream and collecting surface water, and a second, more distant, lower pond (6) was made in the same way. Large numbers of trees were planted as belts — groups and specimens of sweet chestnut, oak, beech, pine and some cedars, particularly to the north-west of the house and away in the middle distance. The third earl also placed many of the fine seventeenth-century carved urns on pedestals from the old gardens around the park and on the parapets of the house.

The pleasure grounds (formal 'wilderness') to the north of the house were scarcely modified by Brown. The perimeter was re-shaped and a ha-ha made to link them to the park. He also added temples for adornment and meditation. The internal paths and planting were modified in the 1850s to create a Victorian pleasure garden with rhododendrons added later this century. A vast 14-mile stone wall was thrown round the estate, which then included the 730-acre park, the extensive stag park and beyond this to the north-west, woodlands known as the Pheasant Copse. The painter Turner was inspired by the great landscape qualities of Petworth and captured them on several fine canvasses.

The era of the third Lord Egremont (1757–1837) was the golden age of Petworth. He was a remarkable man, humane, cultured and distinguished as a patron of the arts and as a progressive agriculturalist. As early as 1780 he cleared the great stag park and established a model farm 'designed for experimental agriculture'. The buildings of this 'modern' unit still remain intact today (not open to the public). The title of Egremont became extinct in the nineteenth century, a nephew inheriting who was created Baron Leconsfield in 1859. During the Victorian and early part of this century more pleasure gardens were added to the south-west of the house adjoining the great complex of walled and kitchen gardens (9) and glasshouses (also not open). For the first half of this century the head gardener was the late Fred Streeter, who was still broadcasting practical gardening talks in 1976 at well over 90. At one time he had a staff of 40 gardeners. In 1947 the third Lord Leconsfield conveyed Petworth, with a large endowment, to the National Trust. His nephew John Wyndham was created Lord Egremont in 1963 and his eldest son, the present Lord Egremont, still lives in the house.

Petworth Park lies in a particularly beautiful part of West Sussex on the Lower Greensand ridge which provides a scenic corridor from Kent through much of Sussex into Hampshire. The Park reaches its highest point at the northern end of the pleasure ground, some 240 ft above sea level, from where one can enjoy fine views into the valley north of Petworth town. The ridge rises even higher westward (425 ft) where a distant monument (7) can be seen. The soils are generally acidic, sandy loams overlying clays. Trees grow especially well here, reaching a great age and size. There is abundant shelter planting to the north-west and also to a lesser extent on the south side of the house, the microclimate of the pleasure grounds being especially sheltered and secluded. Rainfall 30–33 inches.

The preceding historical section and the plan outline the essential character of Petworth Park. Lancelot Brown's grand design of over 200 years ago is still largely intact, particularly in the park where the great house looks across an unbroken sward of grazed grass that flows right to the very windows of the house. The deer that are largely responsible for grazing this parkland can wander unrestricted up to these windows, as was precisely the intention in the eighteenth century. Note the apparently casual, but in reality carefully planned, disposition of the trees in the park, as specimens, groups, clumps and belts, and particularly the great age of many of them. Those being felled at present are part of a long-term renewal plan referred to under the management section on p. 177. Sweet chestnut, *Castanea sativa*, is a dominant species at Petworth, with lime, beech, oak and Horse Chestnut.

Apart from the skilful modelling of the land to fit the natural 'capabilities' of the site, the other outstanding element in Brown's design is the large lake in the middle distance, known as the upper pond (5), covering about 13½ acres and curving like a broad river in Brown's characteristic manner. The more distant lower pond (6) covers 7½ acres and glimpses of it between tree planting invite exploration. Away to the west and north-west are woodlands and tree belts, with the monument (7) rising up out of the trees and attracting the eye due west of the house. The pleasure grounds and courtyard approaches to the house will be of greater interest to the horticulturist and gardener. The entrance court (1) is normally crossed to get to the house, gardens and park and it lies just inside the high wall at the grand entrance from Petworth town. A stone arched gateway leads out into the pleasure grounds (3). Note the two well-placed Fastigiate Hornbeam, *Carpinus betulus* 'Fastigiata' ('Pyramidalis') flanking this archway. On the walls of this court are roses and other climbers and there are also good specimens of *Magnolia grandiflora*, *Magnolia* × *soulangiana* and a reasonably young Black Mulberry *Morus nigra*. Young camellias are establishing on the shady walls of the house.

The pleasure grounds are approached across well-mown lawns with fine limes, Horse Chestnuts and Sweet Chestnuts gradually thickening into fairly dense ⌐hrubberies and fine trees threaded by wide bridle tracks and gravel paths. Rhododendrons grow well here, including forms of *R. arboreum*, *R. decorum*, *R. desquamatum*, *R. falconeri*, *R.* 'Loderi' and many deciduous azaleas. There are also a number of good specimens of Japanese Maples, *Acer palmatum* (note one with mistletoe on it), and a range of other shrubs and smaller trees including *Cornus nuttallii*, *Parrotia persica*, *Fagus englerana*, *Enkianthus perulatus*, *Acer griseum* and *Cercidiphyllum japonicum*. This area is especially fine in the autumn. Outstanding trees here include probably the tallest Cedar of Lebanon in the UK at over 130 ft, near the rotunda temple (4); *Abies grandis* 135 ft (planted in 1908); *Picea polita*, the Tigertail Spruce (77 ft); *Castanea sativa*, the Sweet Chestnut (115 ft); *Aesculus hippocastanum*, Horse Chestnut (125 ft); *Liriodendron tulipifera*, Tulip Tree (95 ft); *Quercus velutina*, the Black Oak (98 ft); and in the car park *Quercus acutissima* (68 ft) and *Nothofagus dombeyi* (77 ft). There are also good pines, yews and bamboo thickets. The woodland character of this pleasant, informal place is enriched by the carpets of bluebells, red campion, primroses, bugle and Creeping Jenny, *Lysimachia nummularia*. It was the pleasure grounds in particular that were seriously threatened in 1976 by a proposed Petworth bypass, a much needed relief road for the badly congested town. The route most favoured by the planning authority, faced with a series of equally unpopular alternatives, was by a part-tunnel/part-cutting in the north-east corner of the park, the tunnel passing under the park just in front of the house. However, this threat now appears to have receded and alternative routes are again being looked into. The working areas of Petworth Park, the walled gardens and kitchen garden (9) already referred to, are not usually open to the public, and part of these have been converted as private gardens for the present Lord Egremont.

Management – The National Trust owns a total of about 730 acres, including the pleasure grounds. The latter and the private walled gardens and areas round the house are maintained by a team of four gardeners (there used to be 40 in the great days), but the main park areas and the trees and woodlands are managed by the estate woods department under a head forester. Virtually the entire 700 acres of grassland in the park are maintained as attractive grazed pasture for a herd of about 700 deer, managed on a commercial basis. There are also flocks of sheep. The management of the trees has been the subject of a recent long-term plan, since many of the oldest trees planted over 200 years ago are now well past their prime. Under the expert direction and guidance of the National Trust's Woodlands Adviser, Mr John Workman, the existing trees in the park have been classified into three categories: (a) for immediate felling; (b) for felling in the next few years; (c) for felling in the middle-term and future. A replanting programme is in operation at the same time.

Rymans

SU 843 033 (Sheet 197) West Sussex. 1½ miles SW of Chichester at Apuldram ½ mile W off A286 Chichester–West Wittering road. Owner: The Hon. Claud and Mrs Phillimore. Open several Sunday afternoons throughout the summer for the N.G.S.

An intriguing medieval house and romantic enclosed garden in an isolated setting on the flat saltings of the Chichester harbour area. The main core of this ancient and fascinating house was built in 1402 by William Ryman, a wealthy merchant and lawyer who had an ambition to build a large fortified castle on the site. However, the planning authority of that time under Henry Bolingbroke thought otherwise and refused him permission to crenellate or build a fortified house, planning consent for such privileges being given only to knights and nobles. Ryman's confidence in getting permission had been such that he had already amassed large quantities of stone for his castle from such faraway places as Caen (Normandy) and Ventnor (Isle of Wight). He therefore used some of this to build a smaller, modest house with central towerlike features and the remainder he gave away apparently to Chichester Cathedral to build the bell tower. The site of the house is close to the navigable arm of the Chichester Channel.

For many centuries the house was used as a farmstead with a large estate of flat fertile marshland grazing. In 1910 it was bought with about 80 acres of land by an antique dealer. He was responsible for the main design features of the present garden, the enclosing walls, and the shelter planting. He also carefully restored the house and farm buildings, adding some extensions. The Phillimores bought Rymans in 1949 and have since created a charming garden of considerable character.

The garden is virtually at sea level. Shelter is quite essential and this is well provided by good tree and shrub plantings of the last 100 years using pine, elm, evergreen oaks and other salt and wind tolerant species. The soils are derived from London clay and alluvial loams, deep, fertile, neutral in pH and tending to be wet or poorly drained. This region of Sussex is one of brilliant light intensity, good growing climate and lack of frosts. Rainfall 27.5 inches. Sunshine 5 hrs.

Rymans is a series of rectangular gardens, possibly on the ancient walls of the medieval settlement, having today a very definite atmosphere blending monastic with French and romantic English styles. The short approach drive leads one to the more recent wing of the house, the circular drive being well enclosed with a thick belt of Holm Oaks, *Quercus ilex*, and other trees. A large *Hoheria lyallii* flowering in late July indicates the mildness of the area. Beyond the oaks to the east the ancient church can be seen. Through a gate in the enclosing high wall one enters the main garden; a delightful blend of old roses, shrubs and climbers, flagged stone paths, old steps and occasional well-placed statuary. Apple trees have been left to give character and some shade and there are some mature flowering cherries over which honeysuckles and old roses grow. A small, clear pool lies in a tiny courtyard at the foot of the stone tower of the house. On the old house walls and over the attractive French-style cowsheds grow a wealth of climbers, including *Solanum crispum, Clematis armandii* and *Vitis coignetiae.* Beyond the walled garden to the south-west of the house stands a massive Holm Oak thought to be over 200 years old. Its base is thickly naturalized with hardy cyclamen and other bulbous species. A small orchard nearby is managed as a meadow habitat with more spring bulbs including hybrid *Narcissus* and fritillaries. To the north lies a very large walled kitchen garden now used partially for vegetables and also for more interesting perennials and shrubs. Half-hardy genera like *Pittosporum, Eucalyptus* and *Cestrum* grow well here, and other more exotic plants. Mrs Phillimore is related to the famous Smith family of Trescoe on the Isles of Scilly and she is constantly introducing unusual and exotic planting to Rymans.

The gardens are mostly maintained by the owners in that quite acceptable manner described as 'controlled untidiness' by Vita Sackville-West who used the same philosophy at Sissinghurst in her day.

St Roche's Arboretum

SU 873 113 (Sheet 197) West Sussex. Close to St Roche's Hill and just NW of Goodwood Park Racecourse. 2 miles SE West Dean, 5 miles N Chichester. Turn off A286 Chichester–Midhurst road just W of Singleton, then 1 mile on to Goodwood. Owner: Mr Edward F.W. James. Open one or two weeks in May and June and for a day or two in October. See N.G.S. and G.S.O. publications.

An extensive and quite isolated arboretum of many different species of trees on the south-west slopes of the Downs above West Dean. The soils are generally chalky or clay with flints. The site is rather exposed to south-westerly gales and damage can be severe in late spring and summer when trees are heavy with foliage. Rainfall 31.5–32.5 inches.

The arboretum was apparently first planted in the early part of the sixteenth century by Lord Selsey who then owned the estate, although most of the existing trees are between 100 and 200 years old, with more recent plantings. There are 42 acres of arboretum situated in and on either side of a dry valley leading in a north-westerly direction off the chalk, the setting being high up in the South Downs, close to St Roche's Hill (675 ft). A series of paths and tracks traverse the arboretum, which really takes the form of dense to open woodland with some native oak and beech, richly interplanted with an extensive collection of exotic species, particularly conifers which have reached a surprising size and stature on this windy, chalky site. A sketch map and guide to the main trees is usually available to visitors. Outstanding conifers here, many of which were measured in 1971, include the Douglas Firs, *Pseudotsuga menziesii*, grown from the original importation of seed sent back by David Douglas in 1828, the tallest now measuring 153 ft; Incense Cedars, *Calocedrus decurrens*, at 98 ft; the tallest recorded Lawson's Cypress variety in the UK, *Chamaecyparis lawsoniana* 'Erecta', at nearly 94 ft; very fine specimen of Western Red Cedar, *Thuja plicata*, at 124 ft; and good examples of Californian Redwoods, *Sequoia sempervirens*, and Wellingtonias *Sequoiadendron giganteum*. There is a Norway Spruce, *Picea abies*, at 117 ft, and an impressive Bishop Pine, *Pinus muricata*, at 85 ft in 1971. There are also good specimens of Turkey Oak, *Quercus cerris*; Hungarian Oak, *Quercus frainetto*; Willow Oak, *Quercus phellos*; and an exceptionally fine specimen of the Lucombe˜Oak, *Quercus × hispanica* 'Lucombeana', at 124 ft possibly the tallest in the UK. The soils are also sufficiently acid for some of the American oaks and there is a fine tree of the Red Oak, *Quercus rubra*, at 108 ft. A Norway Maple, *Acer platanoides*, at 86 ft is one of the tallest in Britain.

An extensive programme of re-planting is now under way with a staff of three foresters under the general manager of West Dean Gardens, Mr Ivan Hicks.

Sheffield Park

TQ 415 245 (Sheet 198) East Sussex. 5 miles W of Uckfield, 7 miles E of Haywards Heath, 1 mile E of A275 East Grinstead–Lewes Road. The Sheffield Park railway station of the Blue Bell line is only ¾ mile to the S. Owner: The National Trust. Open most days of the week April–October, but consult the National Trust information booklet or the H.H.C.G. for current details. There is an excellent National Trust shop at the gate. A cafeteria under private ownership is normally open near the car park.

One of the most outstanding large gardens in the country. A great landscaped arboretum dating from the eighteenth, nineteenth and

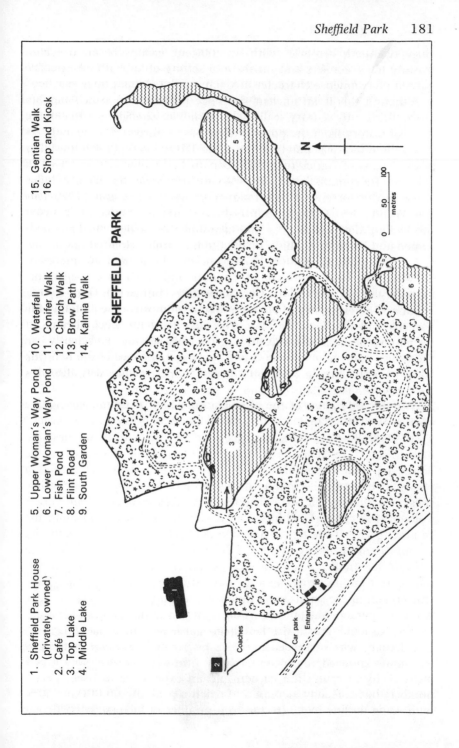

SHEFFIELD PARK

1. Sheffield Park House
   (privately owned)
2. Café
3. Top Lake
4. Middle Lake
5. Upper Woman's Way Pond
6. Lower Woman's Way Pond
7. Fish Pond
8. Flint Road
9. South Garden
10. Waterfall
11. Conifer Walk
12. Church Walk
13. Brow Path
14. Kalmia Walk
15. Gentian Walk
16. Shop and Kiosk

0   50   100
      metres

Coaches

Car park

Entrance

early twentieth centuries with magnificent groups of mature contrasting trees, conifers and shrubs in a setting of four large lakes. The garden has immense character any time of the opening season.

Although this is an ancient site once held by Simon de Montfort in the thirteenth century (called the manor of Sheffield at that time), the real history from the point of view of the garden, begins in 1769 when the estate was purchased by John Baker Holroyd, MP, President of the Board of Agriculture and soon to be created the first Earl of Sheffield. He commissioned James Wyatt to re-style the existing Tudor house in the current Gothick manner between 1775 and 1778. This was Wyatt's first Gothick country-house, and it occupies a strategic site looking down across the top lake and the garden. It is privately owned and has recently been opened to the public. Holroyd also called in Capability Brown around 1775 to design the garden. No record of his work survives but it is thought that he may have been responsible for enlarging or creating the two lower lakes, but not the entire park. In June 1789 Humphry Repton was asked to improve the design of the gardens, but again no Red Book or records of his work survive. It seems possible that he concentrated on embellishing the entrance to the house and the garden in this area, and any improvements of the lakes he may have carried out merges imperceptibly with Brown's earlier work. Years later he said, 'I often regret that Sheffield Park is almost the only place of consequence on which I did not deliver my opinions in a Red Book.'

In 1909 Sheffield Park was acquired by Mr Arthur Soames and over the next 25 years he transformed the original gardens and the landscape around the lakes by building up a magnificent collection of exotic trees, conifers and shrubs suited to the favourable acidic soils and climate. He extended the top lakes and called in Messrs Pulham, the creators of the great Wisley Rock Garden, to build the cataract between the top and second lake (10). This is 25 ft high and one of the most massive stones is delicately balanced on a very small pivot! After the Second World War, Captain Granville Soames undertook a restoration programme of the garden, but in 1954 the estate was broken up, the house and much of the land being sold separately, while the garden was purchased outright through an appeal for funds by the National Trust. The first head gardener under the Trust, Mr F.A. Dench, was succeeded in 1971 by Mr A.V. Skinner, a man of enormous knowledge, experience and enthusiasm with whom it is a pleasure to go round the garden and an experience in itself. Visitor numbers have steadily increased to reach a peak of 165,000 in 1975, with some decline in 1976 due to a number of factors, in particular the prolonged drought and heat-wave of that remarkable summer.

The setting, microclimate and soils are most important aspects of these gardens. Sheffield Park lies on the south-west edge of the high Weald, a well-wooded, undulating landscape which is the setting for many of the fine gardens of Sussex and west Kent. Ashdown Forest stretches away to the north. Many fine oaks and some beeches of the former Sheffield Forest survive, and they form a fine setting and important shelter and enclosure for the garden. The gardens themselves lie in a shallow valley that slopes gently to the east and away from the house. They are some 145 ft above sea level at the highest point (top lake, falling to 98 ft along the third and fourth lakes). The soils are deep acidic Wadhurst clays in the lower parts of the garden with lighter Tunbridge Wells sands nearer the house. Rainfall 30–35 inches. Sunshine 4.25 hrs. The combination of fairly high rainfall, cool moist lime-free soils, very sheltered conditions and the location in Sussex with an average of over 275 growing days in the year, favours the growth and longevity of many introduced species, particularly the conifers and North American trees and the Japanese Maples.

The garden has, justifiably, such fame and publicity, and the guide books available at the gate are so informative, that I am intentionally limiting my description to a summary of some of the outstanding specimens and groups that I feel help to determine the character of Sheffield Park Garden. There are essentially two rather different parts of the gardens. First, the lakeside area and plantings – the lakes may be considered as great mirror-surfaced clearings in the exotic woodland or parkland across whose flat, liquid expanses can be viewed especially contrived groups of dramatic plants, with an exciting mirror-reflection effect on still fine days. Arthur Soames fully exploited the effects of his lakeside plantings so that shape, outline, texture and colour can be viewed in a panoramic fashion from a considerable distance, against the rich dark backcloths of pine, oak and beech. Two outstanding examples of this lakeside planting are illustrated in colour and line silhouettes taken from the west and east edges of the top lake.

A key to the silhouettes assists the visitor in identifying the main specimens, if he stands approximately on the spots indicated on the plan of the gardens. Remember that the time of day and angle of the sun are critical factors, particularly in October for the autumn colours. Remember also that no planting schemes are finite, and in a few years' time some of these trees may have died or been replaced.

Another great panoramic spectacle can be seen by standing on the stone bridge above the waterfall and looking east down to the far end of the second or middle lake. Note the golden column of *Juniperus*

VIEW 1

1. *Pinus radiata*, Monterey Pine
2. *Acer palmatum* 'Atropurpureum'
3. *Cortaderia selloana*, Pampas Grass
4. *Rhododendron* Hybrid
5. *Taxodium distichum*, Swamp Cypress

6. *Betula pendula* 'Dalecarlica' Swedish Birch
7. *Pinus pinaster*
8. Silver Birch
9. *Thuya plicata*, Western Red Cedar

VIEW 2

1. House
2. *Cedrus atlantica glauca*, Blue Cedar
3. *Pinus radiata*, Monterey Pine
4. *Taxodium distichum*, Swamp Cypress

5. *Rhododendron* Hybrids
6. *Acer palmatum*
7. *Fagus sylvatica* Beech
8. *Chamaecyparis lawsoniana* 'Lutea'
9. *Chamaecyparis lawsoniana* 'Wisselii'

chinensis 'Aurea' against the great rugged mass of the glossy green *Pinus radiata* (*P. insignis*), the Monterey Pine, and the rounded masses of the forest beyond. A good collection of water lilies grows in the second lake, giving rafts of soft colours in June and July.

The second, more remote and complex part of the gardens, is the area away from the lake which takes the form of somewhat random arboretum plantings of single specimens and groups connected or crossed by numerous grassy or surfaced paths. It is in this area that one should see the many specimens of *Nyssa sylvatica*, the Tupelo Tree, in their brilliant autumn colours. No other garden in England has such a collection of these trees. There are also many fine Japanese Maples and many other trees. The present policy of opening up more glades and open spaces, particularly on the north-west side, is wise in this respect since it can relieve a feeling of slight claustrophobia induced by the maturing growth of 70-year-old specimens of a great variety of conifers and trees.

Guided by the Gardens Advisory Staff of the Trust, the 100 acres of gardens are maintained by four full-time staff (including Mr Skinner) and one part-time person for about 15 days per month, a remarkable feat. Any tree work 'well off the ground' is done by a specialist contractor. Mr Skinner's energies and drive are already obvious in the appearance of the gardens. He believes in a regular policy of mulching all trees and shrubs with leaves or compost collected from the grass and paths. A number of the plants are labelled. The biggest operation in recent years was the dredging of the third and fourth lakes (5 and 6) in 1972–73. Thirteen acres of water were involved and the lakes had become blocked with silt and mud over the years until the water was scarcely 18 inches deep in places. A major public relations exercise was undertaken before operations began, including consultations with the water authorities, local angling clubs (100,000 fish were taken from the lakes and returned afterwards), the Nature Conservancy and many others. An average of six feet of mud and silt were dredged from the lakes and spread over a 40-acre piece of woodland nearby. The whole operation was completed in less than two years.

South Lodge

TQ 219 254 (Sheet 198) West Sussex. 5 miles SE Horsham in Lower Beeding, 2 miles from Cowfold. Owner: Miss E. Godman. Open several Saturdays and Sundays in April and May in aid of the N.G.S. and other charities. See 'Yellow Book' and H.H.C.G.

A large and extremely interesting garden, on acid forest soils, in the late-Victorian woodland and informal style with particularly fine collections of large mature exotic trees, shrubs, rhododendrons, a fascinating rock garden, extensive lawns, cool glades and a romantic water garden. It is very effective in late spring and early summer.

The present large and imposing house was built by Miss Godman's father in 1883 using Horsham stone and building in the fashionable neo-Jacobean style of many Sussex country houses of the period – ponderous, gabled and with later many additions. Note the clever, secluded siting of the house on a warm levelled terrace on a gentle south slope with fine views to the south and south-west across the Weald and protected from the north and north-west by mature woodland with many superb beeches. The garden was developed in the late 1880s using clearings in this woodland setting and exploiting the other advantages of the site. Mr F.D. Godman was a great plantsman and collector. He was also a keen and authoritative naturalist and scientist. Some of his great collections in the garden at South Lodge include over 360 species; also hybrid rhododendrons planted from 1883 onwards, with a special collection of large-leaved species, and many seedlings from the Wilson, Kingdon Ward and other collections of the early twentieth century. His surviving daughter, Miss E. Godman now manages the gardens and is extremely knowledgeable and very active for her age.

South Lodge lies on the extreme southern edge of St Leonard's Forest on the Lower Greensand, acidic sandy loam and forest soils. The gardens are 195–230 ft above sea level and are generally well sheltered and secluded. Rainfall 35 inches. Sunshine 4–4.25 hrs. A relatively cool microclimate for Sussex.

One of the main features to note in this garden is the fine collection of native trees of beech and oak, many up to 80 ft or more in height, particularly to the south-west and west of the garden, and probably between 120–150 years old. There are also plant collections to be looked for in various parts of the garden, and a good collection of seven different species of *Nothofagus* from the first introductions by Colonel Balfour of Dawyck. Look for the large 65 ft high specimens of N. *betuloides* and also for mature trees of N. *procera*, N. *antarctica* and N. *dombeyi*. There are some particularly magnificent 80-year-old specimens of the Handkerchief Tree *Davidia involucrata* which are usually at their best in May. There is too a good collection of magnolias, also of veteran size and superb in flower. The naturalized masses of bulbs are at their best in early spring, showdrops followed by wild daffodils and bluebells, and then glades of purple and white from autumn cyclamen and colchicums.

The mixed border sweeps on the north-west side of the entrance drive to the rock garden and is backed by trees and shrubs. Here are *Cornus florida*, *Syringa* species, Tree Peonies, *Hibiscus*, a good form of *Prunus padus* and a rich mixture of perennials. In the woodland behind this border is the collection of large-leaved rhododendrons. Note the particularly large specimen of the red flowered *Rhododendron arboreum* hybrid opposite the house, thought to be over 100 years old. Ninety-six rooted layers were taken off the plant a few years ago. In the rock garden many of the original specimens of shrubs and dwarf conifers date from the early 1900s and are fine mature features, particularly the azaleas, Japanese maples and the conifers. Problems of maintenance have allowed the regeneration of an intriguing range of herbaceous and alpine plants. These include a rich 'ecological' mixture of *Narcissus bulbocodium*, *Cyclamen*, *Camassia*, gentians and many more. The Kurume azaleas were a selection of pale-coloured seedlings planted 70 years ago. Note also the good hermaphrodite form of *Skimmia japonica*, the *Podocarpus salignus*, the fine *Eucryphia glutinosa* (*pinnatifolia*), many large heathers and a *Ginkgo biloba*. One can also find the rare South American dwarf shrub *Philesia magellanica* and, in the pool, the Candle Plant *Orontium aquaticum*.

The west wood – Beneath a splendid high canopy of beeches and oaks a rich flamboyant association of many fine shrubs flourishes, most now in a state of maturity. The great billowing scented masses of 'Loderi' *rhododendrons* include 'Helen' (white), 'Loders White' (blush in bud) raised at South Lodge, 'Sir Edmund' (blush-white). Others include 'Ascot Brilliant', 'Luscombei' (deep pink), 'Red Luscombe', 'Princess of Wales', and a large 16 ft plant of the large-leaved Chinese species *R.calophytum*. Here also is the *Nothofagus* collection, large specimens of *Davidia*, good autumn colouring *Parrotia persica* and *Enkianthus*, effective groups of spectacular proportions and associations of *Cornus kousa chinensis*, *Embothrium coccineum lanceolatum* and *Pieris floribunda* 'Variegata', and another even more impressive and outstanding planting of two huge *Rhododendron* 'Helen' with *Pieris formosa forrestii* and *Fothergilla monticola*, great rounded domes of pale pink, scarlet and cream.

In the south-west wild garden area one can move through cool, grassy glades beneath the towering 100 ft high beeches, the grass thick with bluebells in May and broken by more great groups of planting, especially rhododendrons. There are some of the Hoo collection of seedlings, 'Cornish Cross', *R. decorum*, the creamy yellow *Magnolia cordata*, *Nothofagus dombeyi* and *N. betuloides*, two large *Eucryphia* × *nymansensis* 'Nymansay', *Nyssa sylvatica* and fine groups of *Viburnum tomentosum* 'Mariesii'. The autumn colours in this area must be quite spectacular.

The garden slopes away to the extreme south-west where the soil is heavier and more moist and the beeches give way to open glades of scattered oaks where the spring-line breaks out and forms four pools following the contours of a shallow valley. This is a fascinating, remote, wild area of the garden. Dragonflies flick across the water, butterflies are everywhere and wildfowl and birds love the sanctuary of shrubs and water. There are semi-wild associations of many good shrubs here: *Cornus nuttallii*, *Cornus florida*, *Cytisus* spp., *Berberis*, *Osmanthus delavayii*, *Dipelta floribunda*, massive clumps of evergreen azaleas, *Rhododendron amoenum*, and a particularly unusual arching specimen of the Bamboo Oak, *Quercus myrsinifolia*, near the path. The back-drop of the lower pool is an impressive blend of English Oak and green and Blue Cedars. In the grass grow bluebells, fritillaries, wild orchids and many meadow flowers. Masses of the late-June-flowering Ghent azaleas and *Rhododendron occidentale* (*Azalea occidentalis*) grow by the lower pool. The middle pool has an exotic blend of the waterside foliage perennials *Gunnera manicata*; *Lysichitum*, Bog Arum; *Spiraea palmata* (*Filipendula purpurea*) and *Iris sibirica*. The upper pools have something of a Japanese quality, fine old specimens of evergreen azaleas and Japanese Maples fringing the margins and casting colourful reflections in the still waters.

The south terrace below the house is a broad, sunlit, expansive walk of grass, gravel and stone, offering a spacious setting to the house and overlooking the countryside to the south. The ha-ha confines physically but not visually the sophisticated splendour of South Lodge with the pastoral simplicity of the woods and fields beyond. In the far distance can be seen the long ridge of the South Downs. Interesting planting on the terrace and in front of the house is worth studying. Dominant are a huge 80-year-old *Wisteria floribunda* 'Macrobotrys' (*W. multijuga*) and large masses of *Camellia japonica* cultivars (the large C. 'Donckelarii' is older than the house and two others may be over 100 years old). Wreathing the façade of the stone house are *Akebia quinata, Jasminum officinale, Clematis armandii, Passiflora caerulea, Rosa banksiae,* the unusual *Erythrina crista-galli, Itea ilicifolia, Fremontodendron californicum* and *Campsis grandiflora.* In the borders below the terrace is a very favourable microclimate and here, among many attractive dwarf shrubs and perennials, is the quite extraordinary exotic Mexican yucca-like plant *Beschorneria yuccoides* with grey-green sword-like leaves and great arching spikes of coral-red and pink inflorescences with green bells hanging from these coloured bracts.

There are at present four gardeners, two of whom are part-time, under the leadership of Mr J. Collins who has had 30 years' service at South Lodge. His knowledge of, and pride in, the gardens is quite prodigious. The maintenance is traditional and effective.

Sunte House

TQ 334 256 (Sheet 198) West Sussex. Haywards Heath and Gander Hill, ½ mile N of town centre. Owner: Mr Geoffrey Gorer. Open usually a few Sunday afternoons in May and June for the N.G.S. Private visits by interested groups or individuals are possible by previous arrangement with the owner.

A fine garden of about five acres on acid clay loams, created in the last 20–25 years around a superb William and Mary period house. The owner is an enthusiastic and authoritative plantsman and there are fine collections of camellias, rhododendrons and many other shrubs, the garden looking especially beautiful in late spring and early summer.

'Sunte' may be a Saxon word for ridge, since the house and garden stand on a pronounced brow of a hill just north of Haywards Heath. The fine house was originally built as a dower house for the Hamlyn family of Ardingly and is an excellent example of the late-seventeenth-century William and Mary period, built of pale local stone, red brick and slate: it is *not* open to the public. Mr Gorer bought the house in 1949 and, apart from the mature trees, the remains of a pond, and the walled gardens, there was little designed garden when he moved in. He has developed the garden since then.

The house and garden lie some 245 ft above sea level on a somewhat exposed ridge in what would at one time have been open Wealden countryside. In the last 25 years, the rapid expansion of Haywards Heath has sprawled housing estates around the periphery of the town and some of these now lie quite close to Sunte on the south-east side. Mr Gorer saw the need for shelter from winds and seclusion and screening from the 'brave new world', so he has retained and thickened the massive holly hedges he found at Sunte with a scattering of good mature native trees on the exposed flanks of the garden. More tree and shrub planting since has created sheltered microclimates within the garden. The soils are of the Hastings Beds series and are mostly of Wadhust clay, a stiff acidic clay loam with a pH of about 5.0 but responding well to good cultivation and the addition of plentiful organic matter and supporting excellent growth of many trees and shrubs (see also Borde Hill p. 121).

Sunte is a mostly informal, plantsman's garden of great contrasts and strong design features, offering the visitor a series of experiences and surprises that is the hallmark of a well-designed garden. Spatial divisions range from large expansive lawns to secret enclosures rich with exciting plants. Mr Gorer has also deliberately created a choice of walks round the garden and at the division of any pathways where a choice of route is made possible, he likes to place a special feature plant to make the visitor linger and deliberate on the best route to follow while admiring the plant. The planting of the whole garden is highly individual and personal.

The front entrance drive and lawn — The circular gravel drive encircles a bed of colourful seasonal planting, usually selected colours of polyanthus in spring (no blues) followed by dwarf dahlias in summer. The young magnolias in the lawn are now over 25 years old and are of varieties of *Magnolia × soulangiana* and the unusual hybrid *M. × proctoriana*. Two low borders in front of the house are planted with contrasting groups of the double pink *Camellia* 'Donation' and the free-flowering dwarf *Rhododendron* 'Yellow Hammer' and *R.*'Sapphire' (bright blue). Behind this are more exotic and colourful shrubs, especially Bottle Brushes, *Callistemon* spp., from Australia, and the Californian Tree Poppy *Romneya coulteri*. For late summer colour there are many perennials and bulbous plants, including the South African Wand Flowers, *Dierama*, the brilliant scarlet Californian *Zauschneria* and the exotic sun-loving *Tigridia* or Mexican Tiger Flower.

The house walls have been fully exploited as planting habitats for many unusual and attractive plants. The south walls provide warmth and shelter for *Hebe hulkeana*, *Cestrum* 'Newellii', and the magnificent large semi-double red-flowered *Camellia reticulata* 'Captain Rawes'. The narrow, dry and sun-baked border at the front of the house on the south side provides an ideal habitat for such late-flowered bulbous species as *Nerine bowdenii* and *Amaryllis belladonna*. On the west walls one can find the normally very half-hardy and deliciously scented rhododendrons 'Fragrantissimum' and 'Princess Alice' and several others, an achievement indeed to grow these so successfully outdoors. Also note the rose 'Meg', *Solanum crispum* 'Glasnevin' ('Autumnale') and *Magnolia grandiflora* 'Goliath'. The east walls are on the side of the main windows of the house, facing out across the main garden. Roses and magnolias are the main plants here. The roses include 'Mermaid' (cream), 'Etoile de Hollande' (deep red), 'Mme Grégoire Staechelin' (pink), 'Wedding Day' (white), 'Climbing Crimson Glory', and 'Golden Showers'. The magnolias include the early summer-flowering *M. sinensis* and the later *M. grandiflora*.

The main front lawn and gardens – The wide grass terrace and circular pool and fountain are a perfect setting to the house and there are well-planned paved stone paths and steps leading down the terrace to the lawn. The lawn slopes gently down to a large ornamental pond or small lake with a well-planted boundary back-drop to the garden behind it of tall forest trees and ornamental conifers. The few specimen trees on the lawn include *Metasequoia glyptostroboides* and *Amelanchier asiatica*. The pond is almost ¼ acre in area and up to 3 ft deep and may have been an old clay pit. A winding path round the edges of the water enables one to admire the fine waterside planting, with some effective placing of plants for reflection – *Acer palmatum* 'Heptalobum Osakazuki' being one of these, elegant in habit and brilliantly coloured in autumn, matched by two magnificent specimens of the prostrate golden *Juniperus × media* 'Pfitzeriana Aurea'. Slow-growing rhododendrons are on slightly drier sites away from the pool's edge, while close to the water is a splendid blend of Bog Arum *Lysichitum americanum* and forms of *Astilbe*, *Iris* and *Hosta*. Look for the dainty pink-flowered North American Shooting Stars, *Dodecatheon* sp. Large rafts of water lilies of many varieties in pink, yellow, red and white are at their best in mid-summer. Behind the pond against the dark background of the boundary trees are more flowering trees and shrubs. There is a good *Davidia involucrata* now reaching flowering size, *Eucryphia*, rhododendrons and the cascading, scented, white-flowered *Rosa filipes* growing over large laurels.

A vigorous, attractive young Deodar Cedar, *Cedrus deodara*, is a fine feature at one end of the pool.

Two walled gardens lie close to the house. The smallest of these lies behind a gate and is a luxuriant sanctuary of old roses, clematis, buddleias for high summer effect, with early colour from tulips, columbines, stocks, and many more cottage-garden plants. There is a magnificent plant of the deep mahogany red *Camellia japonica* 'Kouron-jura' on the north-facing wall. Through a door at the far end lies a small, charming, intimate rose garden near the house. Fine wall plants should be noted here: the large-leaved, vigorous, bright blue *Ceanothus arboreus* 'Trewithen Blue', *Azara serrata* and *Carpenteria californica*. There is also a rhododendron plantation to the north-west of the house in the shade of the tall boundary trees, including many of Mr Gorer's own seedlings and hybrids. Note also a good selection of camellias to the south on the lee of the tall holly hedges. An old orchard has been largely replanted with ornamental trees for winter bark and autumn colour effects, including some good species of *Betula* (birch). In the kitchen garden are two temperate glasshouses used to grow more of Mr Gorer's rare plants that are too tender to be planted outside. Scented and exotic rhododendrons are here and seedlings of new crosses being investigated. On the walls of the garden notice the superb, rich purple hybrid *Abutilon × suntense*, raised by the owner. It should be cut back hard every year, like most of the genus, to maintain longevity.

The 5 acres are extremely well-maintained by one full-time gardener, one part-time and Mr Gorer, who closely directs all the detailed work.

Telegraph House

SU 784 148 (Sheet 197) West Sussex. 2 miles E of village of Compton off B2146 Chichester–Petersfield road, 8 miles SE of Petersfield (Hants), 9 miles NW of Chichester. Owner: Mr and Mrs D. Gault. Open one or two days over a weekend in June for the N.G.S. There is also a pleasant circular woodland walk through the yew and beech woods with fine views of the South Downs scenery.

The house is named after the hill on which it is built, where a Royal Navy semaphore keeper's cottage stood in the nineteenth century as one of a chain of hill-top stations as a means of communication. The hill is about 525 ft above sea level and is one of many such dramatic rounded hills in the chalk formation of the South Downs. The present house is of interesting design and construction, being built in the early part of this century on the lines of a small French-style country house. It was occupied in the 1930s by the philosopher and writer Bertrand Russell who ran a school there for some years. Mr and Mrs Gault have created the present one-acre garden over the last 8–9 years and there is an estate of 150 acres of woodlands to the south-west of the house, much of this being almost pure stands of ancient yews, *Taxus baccata*, rather like the famous yew woods at Kingley Vale National Nature Reserve about four miles south-east of here. The setting for the Telegraph Hill garden is in fact quite wooded despite the elevated site. The house is approached by a dramatic mile-long curving avenue of purple beeches planted about 60 years ago and now creating quite an impact.

Soils are light alkaline loams, with sufficient depth and with generous dressing of organic matter to create a fertile growing-medium for many good shrubs. Climate similar to West Dean (see p. 201).

An interesting, well-designed garden composed of a series of terraces and enclosures adapted to the steep contours of the site. There is good detailing and finish to the walls and steps, and also the siting and maintenance of a number of good hedges. These enclosures create important shelter. Note the unusual treatment of a triple-tier colour hedge south of the house composed of *Santolina chamaecyparissus*, Cotton Lavender (first tier); *Symphoricarpus orbiculatus* 'Variegatus' (second tier); and yew as the main uppermost tier in the hedge. The small terrace below the house is a luxuriant sheltered sanctuary of shrubs adapted to a chalky soil and selected for foliage contrast, colour and scent. Some good roses here include 'Buff Beauty', 'Celestial', *R. rugosa* 'Alba', *R. rubrifolia*, 'Cerise Bouquet', 'Highdownensis' and 'Marguerite Hilling', with shrubs like blue-flowered *Ceanothus* varieties, *Cotinus coggygria*, the deliciously scented Moroccan Broom *Cytisus battandieri*, and many more. This is an excellent example of how to create an attractive enclosure with naturally grown shrubs. Further down the terraced garden, near the swimming pool, note the fine informal hedge of *Cotoneaster lacteus*, one of the best species for a hedge. There is effective, low-maintenance planting on the drive bank to the west of the house and some good associations of shrubs: *Genista aetnensis*, *Cytisus nigricans*, the silver variegated *Cornus alba* 'Elegantissima' and blue clematis, with more shrub roses and a maquis of Mediterranean-type low shrubs.

The garden is maintained by one full-time man who, with the

owners, achieves a high standard of effective and intelligent maintenance. They believe in using an abundance of leafmould and manure on the light soils.

Uppark

SU 780 175 (Sheet 197) West Sussex. 5 miles SE of Petersfield on B2146, 1½ miles S of South Harting. Owner: The National Trust. Open usually April–September, Wednesdays, Thursdays, Sundays and Bank Holiday Monday 2–6.

A superb eighteenth-century house with unique contents of that period standing in grounds and parkland laid out by Humphry Repton and largely unaltered since. The setting is magnificent, but the horticultural and planting interest is rather limited.

A gentleman's house and a deer park stood on this broad, downland site in Elizabethan times and much of the masonry in the basement of the present house is probably sixteenth century. Sir Edward Ford, whose family had owned Uppark for at least two centuries, invented in the mid-seventeenth century the first effective water-pumps for raising water to hill-top sites such as that at Uppark, and this must have been an important factor in the development of houses on such elevated sites. His grandson, who became Earl of Tankerville after an eventful social and political early life, built the present beautiful house between 1685 and 1690. In 1747 the estate was bought by Sir Matthew Fetherstonhaugh, an immensely wealthy man who spent at least ten years re-decorating and embellishing the house and adding ancillary buildings. He was succeeded by his son, Sir Henry Fetherstonhaugh, who made Uppark a gay and fashionable rendezvous for the courts, including the Prince Regent. Like his father he kept meticulous records of his accounts at Uppark. Later in life he became a great friend of Humphry Repton the landscape gardener and a considerable correspondence between them in the period 1810–13 survives on proposed alterations to the house and park. The north portico and other changes to the house were made and Repton laid down a new approach drive from Harting, taking it through plantations of trees spilling down the hillside in his characteristic manner. He also designed and built a small dairy near the stables, and created pleasure gardens to the north of the house. On Sir Henry's death at the age of 92 the house and estate passed to his wife's family and was eventually left to the Trust in 1954, largely unaltered, by Admiral the Hon. Sir Herbert Meade-Fetherstonhaugh. The guide book gives an excellent account of the house and its contents, and some notes on the gardens.

Undoubtedly the loftiest downland setting of all the houses and parks in this book. Uppark lies about 555 ft above sea level on an exposed hillside facing south-west in the broad uplands of the South Downs, with magnificent panoramic views to the south-east, south-west and west. Shelter from Repton's planting lies mainly behind the house to the north-west and north. The southern side is very exposed in open parkland with few trees. Soils are alkaline loams over the chalk. Rainfall 31.5−33.5 inches.

Kip shows an engraving of Uppark in Lord Tankerville's time with elaborate formal gardens and a round pond in the front of the house. Nothing is recorded or survives of this garden and the style has remained largely that of a simple, unadorned eighteenth-century park flowing right up to the house. The great trees, mostly beeches, which approach the house on three sides, without affecting the bold views to the south, must include some planted by Lord Tankerville in the late seventeenth century. Many are well past their splendid maturity and recent gales have taken their toll. A replanting programme is in hand. Repton must have created the pleasure gardens behind the house. Here one can find two mounts, on one of which stands a little Gothic summerhouse, a great vase on the other. The lawns here contain a number of fine trees notably, a Deodar Cedar, *Cedrus deodara*; Tulip Tree, *Liriodendron tulipifera*; West Himalayan Spruce, *Picea smithiana*; and some maples. The game larders which lie beyond the kitchen were built by Repton and the pebbled path leading from there into the garden is decorated with a pattern of deer bones. The elegant little dairy at the end of the west terrace should also be seen.

In some ways Uppark is a disappointment for the garden-minded visitor, but the composition of house, park and landscape more than compensates for the paucity of planting, allowing one to see an un-cluttered establishment that has survived into the late twentieth century with its essential eighteenth-century characteristics. The maintenance is simple and effective.

Wakehurst Place

TQ 338 315 (Sheet 187) West Sussex. 2 miles N of Ardingly off B2028 Turners Hill–Haywards Heath Road, 6 miles N of Haywards Heath, 10 miles SE of Crawley and A23 London–Brighton road. Owner: The Royal Botanic Gardens, Kew (Ministry of Agriculture, Fisheries and Food) leased from the National Trust. Open every day except Christmas Day and New Year's Day, usually 10–dusk. Full details in current issue of H.H.C.G. Admission charge is modest; excellent printed guides and garden trails are usually available at the shop. In a few years this great garden will rival Kew in its educational and horticultural qualities. Visitors number leapt dramatically from 77,000 in 1975 to over 95,000 in 1976.

This great garden is part of a 500-acre estate and is sited on fertile, acid, forest soils. It was largely created in the first 30 years of this century using the dramatic site of woodlands, rocky valleys, streams and lakes to house a fine collection of rare and unusual trees and shrubs. There is a spectacular display of rhododendrons and azaleas in May and early June.

The site has ancient associations, a Roman road crossing the estate at one point. In the fifteenth century it was owned by the Culpeper family and in 1590 Sir Edward Culpeper built the present house. The date and his initials are carved above the main porch. In the mid-eighteenth century an estate of 3,000 acres was attached to the house. The house must have been vary large at this time with two wings which were eventually removed in 1848. In 1903 the house and estate were purchased by Gerald W.E. Loder who later became Lord Wakehurst. He began planting the garden and landscaping the estate from 1903 until its sale in 1936, by which time the present fine garden had largely been created. His head gardener, Alfred Coates, helped substantially with the great programme of garden making; he died in 1963. The new purchaser of Wakehurst, Sir Henry Price, spent many thousands of pounds restoring the mansion and continuing the development of the gardens and estate. He died in 1963, bequeathing

Wakehurst completes the quartet of great West Sussex gardens that 1 January 1965 it was leased by the Trust for 99 years to the Royal Botanic Garden, Kew. They are developing scientific, research, conservation and educational programmes. A major restoration programme is under way in the garden.

Wakehurst completes the quartet of great west Sussex gardens that lie on the southern edge of the once extensive St Leonard's Forest. The great ridge of the Hastings Beds rocks rises to nearly 460 ft above sea level here, giving sandy, acidic, fertile forest loams in the upper parts of the garden, and heavier acidic weald-clays in the valleys. The garden is generally well sheltered by abundant planting, and the microclimate in the wooded valleys is very favourable indeed to the growth of a wider range of exotic plants. Frost pockets exist in the hollows. Rainfall 34.5 inches. Sunshine 4.25 hrs.

Visitors are strongly recommended to buy a copy of the new guide to the gardens and also one of the excellent garden trails booklets which are instructive, well-written and illustrated, and ideal as a means of learning more about the gardens and the great plant collections to be explored. A summary only is given here, with a plan showing the main features to be described. The style of Wakehurst gardens is for the most part large-scale, informal, amenity woodland related to the naturalistic qualities of the site and the existing features. There is, however, a transition of styles from the intensive formal near the house to the extensive informal in the arboretum and more remote natural woodland areas.

The house area (1) – Wakehurst is now clearly marked on the B2028 and one approaches the gardens down a short drive to arrive at a well-designed and extensive new car park planned to cope with the increasing numbers of visitors. It should be noted that only the garden is normally open to visitors, the house, with the exception of exhibition rooms and restaurant, being used for administrative and research staff. The exhibition rooms are well worth a visit and show the histories of Kew and Wakehurst as well as other exhibits including the natural history of Wakehurst.

The enclosed gardens south-west of the house (9) – The old walled gardens have been redesigned as ornamental features. In 1974 one area was opened as the Sir Henry Price Memorial Garden which the guide book summarizes nicely as a 'modern cottage garden'. This is indeed a focal point for visitors and 'it was not intended that the garden should be fettered by being confined to any set period; it is a garden of foliar textures and predominantly pastel-coloured flowers, a warm sheltered place to sit and rest.' The adjoining enclosure is a charming, intimate, quite small garden enclosed by solid yew hedges. They date from the late-Victorian era when this place was called 'the pleasance'. The warmth and shelter here allow the growth of many special plants from South America, two of special interest being *Berberidopsis corallina*, the Coral Plant, and *Crinodendron* (*Tricuspidaria*) *hookeranum*, both with brilliant red pendant flowers. On the very

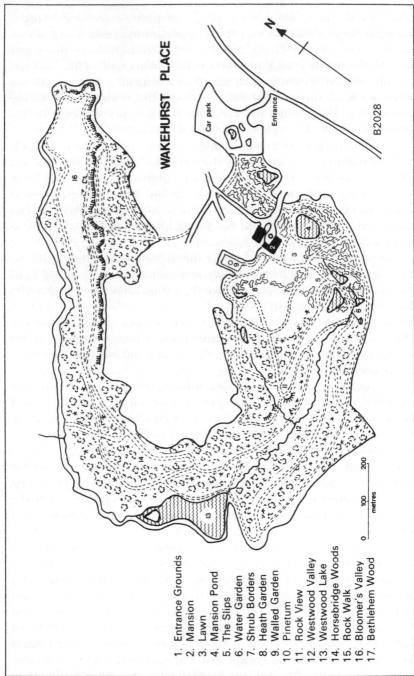

WAKEHURST PLACE

1. Entrance Grounds
2. Mansion
3. Lawn
4. Mansion Pond
5. The Slips
6. Water Garden
7. Shrub Borders
8. Heath Garden
9. Walled Garden
10. Pinetum
11. Rock View
12. Westwood Valley
13. Westwood Lake
14. Horsebridge Woods
15. Rock Walk
16. Bloomer's Valley
17. Bethlehem Wood

sunny south side, a raised terrace allows the growth of the Australian Bottle Brushes *Callistemon* and many Mediterranean sun-loving plants.

The heath garden (8) — This area was originally meadowland laid out and planted by Lord Wakehurst with winding paths and drifts and irregular blocks of many different species of heaths and an existing range of exotic, unusual shrubs. The north end is almost unchanged with some of the original introductions still growing there as mature specimens. Look for *Leptospermum flavescens, Embothrium coccineum lanceolatum, Telopea truncata, Grevillea sulphurea*, and many others — evidence of the extreme mildness of the climate in this area. The heathers are gradually being re-planted and there are also many dwarf and slow-growing conifers, dwarf rhododendrons and azaleas, Japanese Maples and particularly the superb *Pieris formosa forrestii* 'Wakehurst', a beautiful shrub with brilliant red young foliage and white lily-of-the-valley flowers in May.

The slips (5) is a delightful small valley, leading south-west off the main lawn, with a winding stream and rich moist soils. It has been thickly planted with spring-flowering magnolias, foliage maples *Acer* spp., flowering dogwoods (a fine *Cornus florida rubra*), and on the western side a fine specimen of the Golden Larch *Pseudolarix amabilis*. The valley widens into a bog and water garden. Note the sundial erected in memory of Lord Wakehurst and his head gardener, Alfred Coates.

The mansion pond and rock garden (4) — The rock garden includes some 40–50-year-old dwarf conifers which are now relative giants in their mature state. The *Chamaecyparis lawsoniana* 'Ellwoodii', for example, is one of the oldest and largest in the country. There are some effective late-summer-flowering ground cover associations over the constructed rock outcrops. The remarkable Chilean perennial *Fascicularia pitcairniifolia* flourishes here, one of the few half-hardy Bromeliads for warmer southern climates. The pond is a fine reflection feature for the many exotic plants flourishing around its edges, a splendid place for contemplation.

The Wakehurst 'outback' (12–17) — I have used this term to inspire those who wish to experience something of that remote, wild and wooded atmosphere of the Himalayan foothills and the cool, Asiatic forests and glades which are the natural homes of so many of the introduced plants at Wakehurst. One can wander along a 1½-mile track and circular walk through the deep wooded ravine of Westwood Valley (12) down to the stillness and lush swamp-like greenery of Westwood Lake (13) — a heron flapped lazily away across the lake during my visit — then onwards beneath the great canopy of magni-

ficent trees in Horsebridge Woods (14), thick with bluebells in May, and then on to a very exciting ¾-mile rocky walk along a great ledge of Tunbridge Wells sandstone outcrop, where every now and then great clasping, gnarled roots of yew, beech and oak form fantastic sculptural shapes on the rocky crevices in which they miraculously appear to grow. Finally one emerges up out of the valley into the more open glades of the Bethlehem Wood (17) and Bloomer's Valley (16), bright with early spring daffodils in April. During this dramatic walk look out for the following plants among the many which cannot possibly be described in so short a space:

Westwood valley (12) — the large and remarkable *Rhododendron* collection, now being re-planted in more logical grouping according to the botanical classification; *Magnolia campbellii*, one of the largest in the UK, over 65 ft; its huge pink flowers are at their best in late March and early April; *Davidia involucrata vilmoriniana* (seed introduced by E.H. Wilson 1889–1902), the Handkerchief Tree; *Tsuga heterophylla*, the Western Hemlock, and many other fine conifers as well as superb English oaks and beeches.

Westwood Lake (13) — *Gunnera manicata* thrives here, also many good native waterside plants. Waterfowl enjoy the peace and habitat of the lake.

Horsebridge Woods (14) — Many fine specimens of American and Asiatic conifers: *Abies bracteata*, *Sequoia sempervirens*, *Sequoiadendron giganteum*, *Picea omorika*, some good *Pinus sylvestris*, as well as fine oaks and the carpets of bluebells.

Bloomer's valley (16) – More good specimens of conifers *Pinus radiata*; *Araucaria araucana*, the Monkey Puzzle, cedars and others. Bethlehem Wood (17) is an attractive spring woodland with a young but very good collection of *Betula* species and also of North American trees, especially *Carya* spp., the Hickories.

The rock view and pinetum (11) – A fine panoramic view of the 'outback' can be had from the great rock outcrop on the northern edge of Westwood Valley. Another good place for meditation before plunging into the pinetum (10) lies to the north-west, along the hillside. There are 20 acres of almost entirely conifers, including some rare and unusual species. Note particularly the Umbrella Pine and the long, silky, grey-green needles of the Mexican Pine *Pinus patula*. There are also some fine Brewer's Weeping Spruce, *Picea breweriana*, and the rare Himalaya Larch *Larix griffithiana*.

There are some 500 acres of estate and gardens here, managed by a labour force of nearly 40 dedicated staff under the able and dynamic leadership of Mr Tony Schilling, a Deputy Curator of Kew. A comprehensive programme of clearance and re-planting is under way. The maintenance section has its own specialist team of expert woodsmen and tree surgeons and a wide and comprehensive range of horticultural and agricultural machinery for maintenance. There is also a nursery (not open to the public) which produces much of the hardy stock for the gardens, mostly from wild collections throughout the temperate regions of the world. Future plans include the opening of a forest park to illustrate the natural history and conservation importance of natural and semi-natural deciduous woodland. This will encircle part of the new Ardingly reservoir, at present under construction.

West Dean Gardens

SU 864 127 (Sheet 197) West Sussex. West Dean, 6 miles N of Chichester, 3 miles W of Goodwood on A286 Midhurst–Chichester Road. Owner: The Edward James Foundation (gardens only). Open between Easter and mid-September every Sunday and all Bank Holidays, partly in aid of the N.G.S. and G.S.O.

A large informal park-like garden in the late-nineteenth-century arboretum style matching the quality of the flint and stone mansion.

There are some particularly fine trees and the whole setting is extremely pleasant. The massive house is in the Gothic style and is a fine example of the work of the architect James Wyatt and his son; building started in 1804. The house is one of the largest flint-faced houses in the south and it is said that so much flint was required that local supplies were inadequate and additional flint had to be imported from Norfolk. Some of the oldest trees in the park pre-date the house. The American James family acquired the property in 1893, a Mr William James embarking on an ambitious programme of planting and landscaping the grounds. His son Edward James continued his father's work and being a wealthy philanthropist, began to develop an educational interest at West Dean. In 1964 Mr James donated the house, the grounds and a 6,500-acre estate to a charitable educational trust called the Edward James Foundation. In doing this he was able to promote his great interest in the survival of rural crafts and arts by turning part of the house into a training college for students of all ages. Courses in a wide range of crafts are now run at the college. Other activities of the foundation include the provision of the site of the now famous Weald and Downland Open Air Museum close to West Dean (a visit is strongly recommended), an extensive farming enterprise and the management of 1,850 acres of woodlands.

A dramatic, scenic, valley setting in the heart of the South Downs. The well-wooded grounds lie in the valley of the River Lavant which is really an intermittent chalk stream or 'winter bourne' that only flows at times of high water tables in the chalk. The Downs rise up to 550–650 ft around West Dean and the estate lands sweep up to the east to Trundle Hill (St Roche's Hill, 675 ft) on whose western flank lies St Roche's Arboretum. West Dean Gardens lie about 165–195 ft above sea level. The soils are alkaline, medium loams, moisture retentive and fertile, promoting fine growth of trees of which there are some outstanding specimens in the college grounds. Rainfall 32–33 inches. Sunshine 4.5 hrs.

Informal, extensive and nineteenth-century in atmosphere and planting, the gardens very much reflect the style and scale of the house. The outstanding features are the trees, many of which date from the last century and even earlier. For example, the two Cedars of Lebanon, *Cedrus libani*, on either side of the approach drive to the house are known to be over 200 years old. One was planted in 1746 and was measured by J.C. Loudon in 1838 when it was 63 ft high with a girth of 12 ft 6 inches and a 90-foot spread. The *Abies nordmanniana* Caucasian Fir at the entrance gates is over 90 ft high and is an exceptionally tall specimen for the dry chalky south of England. There is one of the largest specimens of the Japanese *Thujopsis dolobrata* known in Britain standing on the lawn beside the pergola, while on the west lawn beyond the house is a huge Horse Chestnut, *Aesculus hippocastanum*, thought to be one of the largest in Britain. Away to the south in the wild garden are two of the tallest Trees of Heaven, *Ailanthus vilmoriniana*, measured in the south-east of England. King Edward VII planted a number of the younger trees in the gardens during his visit in 1905, in particular the Blue Cedar, *Cedrus atlantica glauca*, on the west lawn near the big Horse Chestnut, and some of the cedars in the approach drive area. The garden historian will detect the period features of the earlier decades of this century in parts of the garden, such as the rather ponderous pergola (designed by Harold Peto) leading to a neo-gothic gazebo with its extraordinary floor of knapped flints and horse's molars; the 'Pumice' lined bridge crossing the bed of the River Lavant (usually dry these days) in the wild garden, with relics of a 'grotto'; the great clumps of bamboo; the scattered statuary and massed evergreens, all with a strong flavour of the romantic revival gardens of 70–80 years ago. There has recently been new planting and restoration of some parts of the grounds, and some good modern shrub planting may be seen on the rather unusual timber banks of the new pentagon-shaped car park.

The future of the 30 acres of gardens seems assured. The young and enthusiastic gardens manager, Mr Ivan Hicks, has a staff of five under him and an impressive programme of tree maintenance and tree replacement is now under way, still closely supervised by Mr Edward James himself. One of Mr James's ideas for perpetuating the bulky boles of trees that had to be felled from disease and old age is to have the standing timber professionally 'encapsulated' in fibreglass resin by the noted sculptor, Ralph Burton. The statuesque tree trunks near the wild garden were treated in this way in 1972 and 1974.

Supplement

A supplement of other gardens normally open in East and West Sussex (mostly for the N.G.S.).

ANSTYE PLACE Near Haywards Heath. 13 acres of garden and grounds including woods, a lake, and fine views.

BANKS FARM 4 miles N of Lewes. $7\frac{1}{2}$ acres of shrubs, roses, ponds and water gardens.

BATEMANS ½ mile S of Burwash off A265. National Trust. Rudyard Kipling's house and garden. Fine house; pleasant, simple garden and recently restored water-mill in attractive setting.

BATTLE ABBEY Battle. Picturesque grounds to this historic complex of monastic buildings (now girls' school).

BEECHES FARM Uckfield. Old farmhouse with sunken old-world cottage gardens.

BEECHWOOD Duncton. 4 miles S of Petworth. Refined cottage garden in fine parkland setting. Unusual plants.

BIGNOR PARK Pulborough. Medium-sized gardens, walled herbaceous gardens and roses.

BOWHILL West Stoke, near Chichester. Percy Cane garden of medium size.

CHELWORTH HOUSE 3½ miles S of Forest Row. Informal woodland gardens, forestry plantations, picnic areas.

CHELWOOD VACHERY Near Forest Row. Over 100 acres of lawns, gardens and delightful woodland, owned by the British–American Tobacco Company. The gardens created some 40 years ago are maintained to a very high standard.

CHIDMERE Chidham. W of Chichester. Interesting garden, yew and hornbeam hedges, bulbs, rock garden and flowering shrubs bounded by a large, private nature reserve. A visit is recommended.

CISSBURY Findon. 4 miles N of Worthing. Large garden with views of Downs and parkland. Spring bulbs and shrubs.

COKE'S COTTAGE West Burton. Next door to Cooke's House. Very attractive small cottage garden, old roses, mixed borders. Small herb and vegetable garden.

COLLIERS FARM Fernhurst. 4 miles S Haslemere. Medium-size garden made in last 4 years. S slope setting for shrubs, mixed borders; also a woodland walk with streams and pond.

COW BEECH FARM 4 miles N Hailsham. Many interesting features. Ponds, bog garden, roses and wild garden.

CUCKFIELD PARK Cuckfield. Historic Tudor house and impressive gate-house. S of the town, approached by fine avenue. Formal gardens around the house lead to two lakes with good examples of trees and shrubs. Weekly openings throughout summer.

DAMEREL North Chailey. 6 miles E Haywards Heath. 10 acres open landscape, labour-saving woodland garden.

GOODWOOD HOUSE 3½ miles NE Chichester. The home of the Earl and Countess of March.

GOREHILL HOUSE Near Petworth. Dramatic Norman Shaw house on

hill-top; informal shrub and woodland gardens. Open regularly.
THE HAZELS Fittleworth. 3 miles SE Petworth. Small well-stocked
plantsman's garden. Open with other gardens in the village.
HIGHDOWN Goring by Sea. 3 miles W Worthing. The former garden
of Sir Frederick and Lady Stern who created a fine garden in a large
chalk pit from 1910 onwards. A large collection of unusual trees,
shrubs and perennials, including *Eremurus* and many examples of
Lilium, was built up until Sir Frederick's death a few years ago. Lady
Stern maintained an interest in the garden which has now been taken
over by the Worthing Corporation. Outstanding trees to be noted are
Cornus capitata, Magnolia delavayi and *Cupressus goveniana*, usually
found in very mild areas.
HOLTS Bosham. 3 miles W Chichester. Medium-size garden, 8 years old,
created by owner with good trees, shrubs and roses. Harbour village is
very picturesque.
IVORYS Cowfold, near Horsham. Medium-size garden; azaleas, roses,
shrubs and woodland.
THE MANOR OF DEAN Tillington, near Petworth. Flowering shrubs,
specimen trees and bulbs. Frequent openings in May and June.
MILL COTTAGE and OLD PLACE ½ mile N Pulborough. Open together.
Small garden with interesting features, including mill-stream bog area.
NEWTIMBER PLACE Near Hassocks. Attractive medium-size garden around
old moated house.
OLD LODGE Nutley. 5 miles SW Crowborough. Extensive gardens in
beautiful wooded Ashdown Forest setting.
OLD RECTORY Sutton. 5 miles S Petworth. Medium-sized garden of old
trees, roses and herbaceous borders.
OLD WOLDRINGFOLD Lower Beeding, Horsham. A delightful garden of
many good plant associations and design features from flowering
shrubs and roses to an informal woodland garden with rhododendrons
and azaleas. Autumn colours are good. A visit is strongly recommended.
PARHAM PARK 4 miles SE Pulborough. 4 acres of walled gardens plus
fine pleasure grounds and a lake. Magnificent Elizabethan mansion,
open regularly to the public.
PAXTONS 3½ miles N of Chichester. An attractive small village garden.
SLAUGHAM PARK Handcross. Splendid views. Unusual shrubs in pleasant
setting and a kitchen garden.
STANSTED PARK Rowlands Castle. NE of Havant. Large garden with
vistas, trees, shrubs and historic chapel.
STRETTINGTON GARDENS Strettington, near Chichester. Several gardens

open together, providing interesting contrasts in styles and planting.
SUTTON END Sutton. 4 miles S Petworth. Woodland, water and perennial
gardens.

TOWER HOUSE Crawley Down. 4½ miles W of East Grinstead. 1½ acres
of informal landscape garden looked after entirely by the owner,
garden writer Diana Clegg. Old-fashioned roses and foliage plants.

UPPER HOUSE West Burton. Medium-sized garden, summer flowers and
shrubs.

WESTBOURNE GARDENS 1 mile N of Emsworth. Two attractive village
gardens with roses, shrubs and border plants.

WEST BURTON HOUSE West Burton. Old walled garden, spring bulbs,
roses, herbaceous borders.

WEST CHILTINGTON GARDENS 4 miles E of Pulborough. 4 contrasting
gardens in the village, open early June.

The Gardens of Surrey

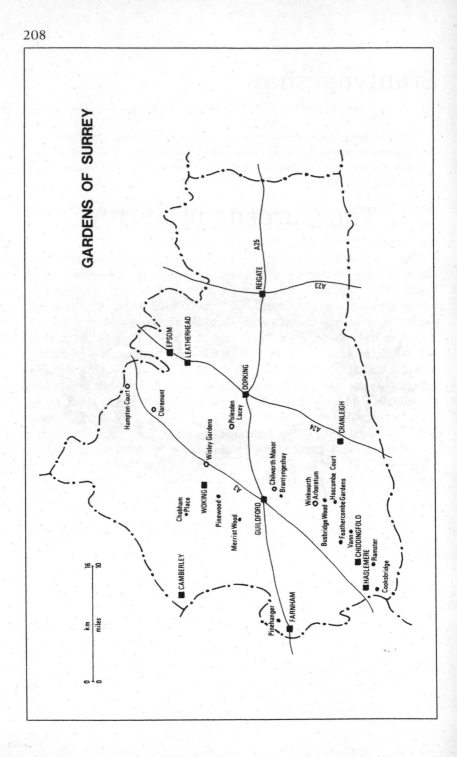

GARDENS OF SURREY

Brantyngeshay

SU 034 466 (Sheet 186) 1 mile SE of Chilworth village. Cross the level crossing in the village on a minor road up a steep hill. Guildford 4 miles NW. Owner: Mrs G. Kimmins. Open several Sundays in May for the N.G.S. Parking very limited.

An extensive woodland garden on acid soils, combining a colourful collection of rhododendrons with a commercial nursery producing rhododendrons and other shrubs for the wholesale market.

This is a property of some 27 acres, providing a secluded setting for the large, late-Victorian country house. The site is well-wooded with mature pine, oak and some Sweet Chestnut. It is adjacent to Blackheath, some of which is owned by the National Trust. The informal garden is on sandy loams of the Bagshot series, growing a limited collection of rhododendrons, and azaleas. During a period of neglect before the present ownership, *Rhododendron ponticum* in particular overran the site. As this shrub is in great demand by the nursery industry as an understock for grafting named rhododendrons, Mrs Kimmins is exploiting the ideal site and soil by producing seedlings of these in considerable quantity. She enriches the light, hungry soils with abundant leafmould dressings made in the garden in large compost pits. This garden is a pleasant place to visit in May when camellias, rhododendrons, azaleas and some other shrubs are very colourful in a natural setting beneath the great pines and other trees. In late May there are masses of the sweetly scented yellow azalea *Rhododendron luteum* in full flower.

The production unit is impressive, resembling an intensively cropped Dutch shrub nursery in a woodland setting.

Busbridge Wood

SU 987 414 (Sheet 186) Hascombe. 2 miles S of Godalming on B2130. Garden entrance is nearly opposite main entrance to Winkworth Arboretum. Owner: Sir George and Mr J. Erskine. Open usually two weekends in April and May for the N.G.S.

A large garden of the pre-Second World War era, on acid sandy soils, part designed by Percy Cane. There are well-managed glasshouses and a kitchen garden on view on open days. The contemporary looking house in brick and stone was built in 1935 and stands in 20 acres of gardens and grounds developed from remnants of the former Busbridge Woods. Much of the scrub and dense tree growth was cleared, leaving groups and specimens of the largest beech, pine and birch. The owner at that time was a racehorse trainer, Mr Ferguson, who called in Percy Cane to assist with the layout of part of the garden. In 1946 he created the paved rose garden and the herbaceous borders and probably also planted the impressive Lawson Cypress hedges that screen the kitchen garden, and the Blue Cedars on the lawns. The soils are of the Lower Greensand, as at Winkworth and Hascombe Court, the ridge here being about 425 ft above sea level. Away to the south-west towards Hindhead one can see the 250 acres of coniferous woodlands that are part of this estate.

The garden is of limited interest to plantsmen, but for those who like to detect styles of garden design, Busbridge has some of Percy Cane's architectural and formal features in a very well-groomed setting, and the glasshouses and vegetable gardens were beautifully stocked and maintained when I visited during 1976. Note the exceptionally precise and skilled maintenance of the long Lawson Cypress hedge beside the drive. Mr Darell, the present head gardener, and one part-time man maintain very high standards indeed.

Chilworth Manor

SU 025 475 (Sheet 186) Chilworth. ½ mile N off A248 Shalford–Dorking road up Blacksmiths Lane. 4 miles SE Guildford, 10 miles W of Dorking. Owner: Sir Lionel and Lady Heald. Open a number of Saturdays and Sundays throughout spring and summer for the N.G.S. and other charitable organizations. There are good car parking and picnicking facilities and teas are provided on some open days. Flower arrangement displays by local societies are also on view. Details in the 'Yellow Book'. Visits on other occasions can be arranged.

A delightful blend of formal and natural woodland garden around the historic old manor, set in beautiful countryside on the south slope of St Martha Hill. Soils here are acid and excellent for gardens.

The attractive old house evolved in three stages. The first and oldest parts of the present house were built of local stone in the mid-seventeenth century by Vincent Randyll, a famous gunpowder maker whose mills were at one time part of an important industry in the Tillingbourne valley near here. A formal enclosed garden was created to the north-west of the house where the ground slopes up St Martha Hill. This meant excavating quite massive terraces and walls, and the great brick piers and mellowed walls have survived largely intact from this period. There was also an area of parkland around the house. John Evelyn, the diarist and tree planter, may have advised on the gardens at Chilworth. His family were gunpowder-makers in this part of Surrey. Rainfall 30 inches. The gardens generally lie above the frost pockets in the valley. Sunshine 4–4.25 hrs.

Sir Lionel Heald points out seven distinct levels to the gardens from north to south across the natural slope. The uppermost three levels are the historic and interesting great terraced walled gardens of the seventeenth and eighteenth centuries which, when constructed, cleverly exploited the natural fall of the land to create a series of three raised promenades and wide terraces. The massive brick piers and walls rise to over 23 ft in height west of the house. The highest level or former kitchen garden referred to in the historical notes has an intriguing 'clairvoyée' in the wall for views of the parkland and St Martha Hill to the north-west. Note the ornate brick columns here. All these terraced gardens are turfed and have attractive old fruit trees along the terrace walls. There are pairs of massive Irish Yews near the steps on the top terrace, also colourful flower borders and

good use of trailing wall plants. The brick walls are possibly the oldest parts of the garden, while the stone walls of the north-east and west sides could be of the period when the Duchess of Marlborough owned the house for a time. A number of new climbing plants have recently been introduced on the walls here.

There is a good mixed border on the west side of the walled gardens outside the great wall, where fine climbers cover the full 25 ft height. *Clematis* 'The President' and *C.tangutica* blend with old roses here. A ha-ha to the west is really more of a raised wall, with pleasant views across pastures to the distant woodlands. The house stands on the fourth level, an expanse of mown lawn and some good specimen trees looking away to the west across the park. Between the old and the newer houses is a small, intimate, paved court, well-furnished with climbers – roses, *Ceanothus* and vines on the retaining walls – and plant tubs and seats. Spring lines break out on the fifth level where one can find the two ancient ponds, considered to be monastic in origin and lined with massive stonework architecture possibly of the same period. This level was embellished in the last century or so with an ornamental rock bank and rockery, now rather more of a pleasant wild garden. There are more trees here, particularly some massive Turkey and English Oaks, a good Californian Redwood *Sequoia sempervirens* and a very ancient *Magnolia grandiflora*. There is also a large Mexican Orange, *Choisya ternata*. The sixth and seventh levels are made up of informal woodland and wild garden with native trees, some rhododendrons and azaleas, and a bog garden fed by a small stream, growing Asiatic *Primula* spp. and other waterside perennials.

Some 10 acres of formal gardens around the house in a total estate of 50 acres are cared for by one full-time gardener with additional help from family and friends.

Chobham Place

SU 965 635 (Sheet 186). Chobham. 2 miles NW of village. W off A383 on Sunningdale road. 6 miles NW Woking. Owner: Sir William and Lady Atkins. Open one or two Sundays in early summer for garden charities.

The impressive house of the early nineteenth century, mainly in the Georgian style, stands on the brow of a small hill some 145 ft above sea level on the acidic sandy loams of the Bagshot series, with some overlying clay. The setting is spacious and dignified, benefiting from the wooded attractive landscape of Chobham Common that spreads away to the north and north-east. Climate, see Merrist Wood.

There are about ten acres of essentially informal garden around the house, composed of mixed tree and shrub plantings of various ages. The lime avenue that flanks the main drive was planted in 1902, but there are remains of an ancient row of Sweet Chestnuts south-west of the house that may be over 300 years old and possibly part of a formal design associated with a house of that period. There are a number of good specimen trees to be found, including a Red Oak *Quercus rubra*, a Tulip Tree *Liriodendron tulipifera* and a very fine Umbrella Tree *Magnolia tripetala*. Island beds of massed shrubs of impressive age and quality include heaths, bamboos, rhododendrons (the bed of *Rhododendron arboreum* is said to be 100 years old), a large *Hamamelis* with 32 ft spread, *Styrax japonica* and *Embothrium*. There is a well-sited ha-ha on the southern edge of the main lawn, beyond which parkland falls away into the middle distance; there are good views south from here. Note the fine *Magnolia grandiflora* 'Goliath' on the front of the house.

There is clearly a restoration programme in progress in the gardens. The 36 acres of parkland associated with the house are of a high quality.

Cooksbridge

SU 895 274 (Sheet 186). 1 mile S Fernhurst on a rather dangerous bend of the A286 Haslemere (4 miles to N)–Chichester Road. Owner: Miss B.E. Van Moppes. Open usually several Wednesday afternoons in midsummer for the N.G.S.

An interesting and popular garden of medium size (six acres) with no outstanding historical, planting or design merit but having the feeling of a large, friendly cottage garden in an attractive setting in the Surrey hills.

The house was formerly two farm cottages attached to a now separate farming enterprise. These were converted in 1950 into one attractive house and the garden laid out at that time. The site is on a gentle west slope looking down a small valley with streams and pleasant countryside views. The soils are light acidic loams of the Lower Greensand. The entrance is through a small intimate approach courtyard, a walled enclosure entered through wrought-iron gates and having a central feature of a well-planted central pool in brick and stone paving. There is good use of a selection of ivies here, particularly *Hedera helix* 'Sagittifolia' and the large-leaved variegated forms of *Hedera canariensis* and *H.colchica*. Shrub planting for foliage contrasts includes goldenleaved *Cornus alba* 'Spaethii', *Vinca major* 'Variegata', *Vitis vinifera* 'Brandt' and an effective blend of *Daphne odora* 'Aureomarginata' and the yellow-flowering *Genista lydia*.

The front garden has a simple lawn and thick-textured, colourful, tall shrub planting and screening which to some extent muffle and soften the sight and sound of the busy trunk road nearby. *Viburnum* species, flowering crabs and other plants grow here. The house is mantled with jasmines, honeysuckles and the Boston Ivy *Parthenocissus tricuspidata* 'Veitchii'. The main garden to the north of the house offers more active entertainment on open days – the swimming pool and tea garden; a glasshouse positively bursting with interesting plants, including orchids; an enclosed reserve of wildfowl in a small pond formed from the stream; and, in the stream valley, an excellent and prolific vegetable garden. Woodland to the north-east provides a solid background to the garden, as well as important shelter.

A well-organized and well-maintained garden managed by the owner and one other gardener.

Feathercombe Gardens

SU 971 395 (Sheet 186). 1 mile N of Hambledon on a minor road to Godalming, 4 miles to N. Owner: Mrs Wieler and Miss Parker. Open usually every Sunday from 1 March–1 November. Details in H.H.C.G.

A medium-sized garden around a comfortable, neo-Elizabethan style brick and stone country house, dating from about 1912, built by the author, Eric Parker, to a design by the architect Eric Newton who was a pupil of Norman Shaw. The site is in that attractive pastoral Surrey countryside so beloved by many visitors and gardeners like Eric Parker and Gertrude Jekyll. These gardens lie on the south-west slopes of Hydon Heath, a thickly-wooded hill (owned by the National Trust) on whose north-west side lie Winkworth Arboretum and Miss Jekyll's former house at Munstead Wood (not open to the public).

Feathercombe Garden lies at 295 ft above sea level and is well protected from the north and east with shelter belts of trees. The soils are light, acidic, sandy loam of the Lower Greensands. Rainfall about 29.5 inches.

The whole of the garden was planned and planted by Eric Parker with the help of one gardener from 1912 onwards. Eric Parker was fortunate in marrying a daughter of Ludwig Messel of Nymans, and as a result many good trees and shrubs came to these gardens from Nymans, noticeably the fine specimens of *Eucryphia* × *nymansensis* planted in the early 1920s. On Mr Parker's death in 1955 the management of the gardens was continued by his daughters and grandson. Problems of maintenance and renewal have obviously arisen with fewer staff available to maintain the extensive arrays of formal and informal gardens. A plant nursery was started in 1972, which is an additional attraction for visitors.

The style of Feathercombe gardens is a blend of formal and informal characteristic of so many gardens in Surrey and Sussex that came into being in the first 30 years of this century. The influence of Gertrude Jekyll and others is apparent. Note the good mature shrub areas behind the house and flanking the drives, the rock garden and terraces near the house, with well-designed steps and stonework. There is a representative collection of mature acid-soil shrubs such as rhododendrons, magnolias and heathers.

Hampton Court Palace Garden

TQ 156 685 (Sheet 176) Hampton Court. 1 mile SW Kingston upon
Thames, 7 miles SW central London on A308. Owner: Dept of the
Environment. Open mostly throughout the year on certain days. See
H.H.C.G. or other guidebooks.

The world famous palace and garden are only briefly summarized here
since there is an abundance of current literature on them and, lying
virtually in the London area, they are on the extreme boundary of the
regions covered in this book. The Tudor palace and some of the
garden spaces of the period survive today, and one can also see the
more expansive baroque and later styles of the late-seventeenth and
early-eighteenth centuries reaching out into the surrounding parkland.

Hampton Court Park and nearby Bushy Park form an extensive
green area of historic parkland in this great sprawling suburban zone
along the Thames valley. The level river terrace site of alluvial gravels
and loams favours the growth of fine trees and the great Horse
Chestnut avenue and the more recent lime avenues at Hampton and
Bushy are splendid evidence of this.

The original Tudor gardens of Cardinal Wolsey's palace were
acquired by him in 1525 and subsequently appropriated by Henry VIII
who enlarged them and planted a flower garden, kitchen garden
and orchards. One of his tiltyards survives on the north side of the
house, also the covered tennis court for 'real' tennis. The Mount of
'10,000 cu. yds. of soil' was levelled in the late seventeenth century. Elizabeth I's knot gardens on the south side of the old palace were enlarged
at that time. Charles I enclosed the great deer parks of Bushy and
Hampton and Charles II, on his restoration, created a Versailles-like
layout (though with limited means) on the east side by building the
long water canal and planting the three great avenues of lime trees
radiating out in the form of the typically baroque goose-foot or *Patte
D'oie*. William and Mary carried out an ambitious programme of
enlargement of the palace and gardens, employing Sir Christopher
Wren to rebuild the east front and Henry Wise to make extensive
alterations in the gardens. He laid out the Great Fountain Garden and
the *parterre* Privy Garden to the south. A 'wilderness' was planned
and eventually became the famous Maze on the north side. Queen
Anne asked Henry Wise to lay this out towards the end of her reign

and it still exists today. The succeeding Hanoverians made few alterations to the garden. When Capability Brown took on the management
of the gardens as 'surveyor' under George III, he only made minor
alterations. He also planted the famous vine in 1768 from a cutting of
the Black Hamburgh vine from an Essex garden. It is now a world
famous plant, producing 500–600 bunches of grapes a year.

In 1878 Queen Victoria opened Hampton Court and Bushy to the
public. Today the visitor can see the blurred outlines of the previous
formal periods and styles of gardening, particularly from the William
and Mary period and from the early twentieth-century styles – for
example, the great herbaceous border influenced by William Robinson
and the shrub and rose garden in the tiltyard area. The legacy of fine
trees adds to the stately and historic ambience of the place, now
surrounded by the frenzy of metropolitan life. Tourists flock to the
palace and gardens in thousands. The maintenance and quality of the
gardens are commendable under the Department of the Environment.

Hascombe Court

SU 993 400 (Sheet 186) S off B2130 Godalming–Hascombe Road 1½
miles S of Winkworth Arboretum. 5 miles from Godalming, 1 mile from
Hascombe. Owner: Mrs C.C. Jacobs. Open for a number of days in spring
and summer for the N.G.S.

A fine mature example of a house and garden of the early-twentieth
century 'Surrey school' of gardening; the house designed by Lutyens
and the garden originally designed by Gertrude Jekyll to combine the
formal and the informal in a delightful setting, on acid soils, with fine
views across the Surrey hills.

The house was designed and built by Sir Edwin Lutyens in 1906, in
local stone with fine detailing in tile and brick and with oak timber
framed gables and attractive loggias. Gertrude Jekyll advised on the
design of the gardens at this time. In 1920 Sir J. Jarvis extended the
gardens and Percy Cane assisted with the planning of these. A plan
by him, dated 1925, is in Mrs Jacob's possession. Mr and Mrs Jacobs
came to Hascombe in 1950. Mr Jacobs died in the early 1970s and
since then his wife has continued the management of the house and
gardens.

Hascombe Court lies in a secluded, idyllic setting high up in the wooded hills just south-east of Godalming. The house is some 360 ft above sea level and stands on a ridge of Lower Greensand soils. To the north-east the gardens fall away steeply, giving delightful views from the house terraces across a wooded and pastoral countryside. The soils are light sandy loams. Rainfall (see Winkworth Arboretum). There is good shelter from mature tree and shrub planting.

The house lies well away from a minor road approach hidden by good tree belts, now 50 years old or more, of conifers and broad leaf trees. The house stands at the centre of a long north–south axis that passes through the house to extend in both directions as two boldly conceived herbaceous borders. The border on the north side lies beyond the approach drive and is flanked by yew hedges with a distant timbered garden house seen as a focal feature from the main door of the house. A kitchen garden also lies behind a hedge here and a line of double pink cherries and two columnar cypresses are probably additions by Percy Cane. On the south side of the house is a great lawn with some fine oaks as specimen features. Well-laid stone terraces are a feature around the house, and from the windows of the main sitting-room one can look south to the second great border backed by hedges.

For the plantsman and the explorer of the rare and remote, the gardens below the house at the north-east side are well worth a visit.

Note the fine and almost flamboyant stone-work for terraces, steps, balustrades and walls that have been used in the design of the formal gardens on this side. A curved arch in the wall below the house has the typical lion-head fountain with basin beneath.

Planting is good here, with fine mature *Acer palmatum* 'Dissectum' specimens on the steps, and many climbing and trailing plants. One can take a long terrace-type walk through a woodland and shrubbery of exotic plants, including magnolias, several good *Cornus nuttallii*, rhododendrons, *Pieris*, and many other shrubs now well-matured, and in some cases over-mature. A natural wood lies to the north-west, and below is a near jungle of shrubbery beyond which one can see the green fields of open country outside the garden boundary. One can find winding paths leading down to a rather neglected Japanese-style water and rock garden of the 1920–30 period. A thatched lean-to shelter here that must have offered a delightful, secluded place for meditation is now sadly decayed. Splendid Japanese Maples, bamboo clumps and other plants of this period flourish in the damp, acid soils, and in the shrubberies in this area are good specimens of such plants as *Embothrium*, *Eucalyptus*, *Desfontainea* and *Nothofagus*. There are also a number of *Rhododendron* species and cultivars, azaleas, camellias and others. A variety of conifers in the informal areas enjoy these soils and there is a particularly good specimen of the unusual Grannies Ringlets form of Japanese Cedar *Cryptomeria japonica* 'Spiralis'. The mildness of the climate here is shown by the size of the *Acacia dealbata* Mimosa on the house terrace.

There are 20 acres of garden maintained by a staff of three or four gardeners. Problems obviously exist in keeping up the standards needed for a detailed garden of this kind.

Merrist Wood Agricultural College

SU 963 535 (Sheet 186) Worplesdon. SW off A322 Guildford–Bagshot road. 3½ miles NW Guildford. Owner: Merrist Wood Agricultural College, Surrey County Council. Open: The Merrist Wood Estate is not usually open to the public. The gardens, however, are open on selected occasions for the N.G.S. and Red Cross.

A county college of agriculture and horticulture developed from the previous Surrey Farm Institute. Merrist Wood is a modern, well-equipped centre for education and training in land-based industries for men and women students. The courses show an increasing emphasis on landscape construction, planting and countryside management. There are now excellent teaching and demonstration gardens of many different designs, well-labelled plant collections and many other features of interest to gardeners and lovers of the countryside.

In the centre of a new complex of buildings may be found the original Merrist Wood Hall, built in 1877 by Norman Shaw, an impressive high-Victorian house, half timbered, tiled and strongly built with local bargate stone. The house was then owned by the Shrubb family and had its own estate of woodlands and timbered park-like grounds. Many of the fine trees around the buildings date from this period; note especially the Wellingtonia near the newer hostels and the oaks, cedars and Copper Beeches on the sloping south-west lawns.

The soils are generally acidic, silty Bagshot sands, inclined to compaction and puddling in wet weather. There is reasonable shelter for the gardens from the woodlands. Rainfall average 26 inches.

Visitors can see well-labelled examples of modern plant associations around the new building complexes and within the very attractive setting of the Victorian grounds. The model gardens made by students as part of their training are well worth seeing. There is also a large hardy-plant nursery. The fine oak woodlands are also being managed with enlightened objectives as part of new courses in countryside management now being developed by the college. It is an important policy of the college to keep the grounds in a rural setting with the main ornamental areas near the buildings. The total estate, including some land at Whipley to the south, amounts to 699 acres. This comprises 484 acres of farm enterprise, 193 acres of woodland, 14.8 acres of commercial nursery and 7.2 acres of amenity areas, sports fields and gardens. Three full-time staff manage the latter, with student help, and a commendable standard is achieved. Labelling is excellent.

Pinehanger

SU 873 464 (Sheet 186) Compton Way. 3 miles E of Farnham approached from B3001 Milford–Farnham road, take signs to Moor Park College. Owner: Mr and Mrs H.V. Farmer. Open several Sundays in May for the N.G.S.

A comparatively small one-acre specialist's garden on light, acid, sandy loams, devoted mainly to a collection of rhododendrons and other interesting shrubs built up by the owner over the last 25 years.

The Compton Way Estate was begun in 1936 when 180 acres were offered for sale as 1 or 2-acre plots. The area was then pine and birch woodland with heath scrub of heather, bilberry and bracken lying some 425 ft above sea level. The soils are on sandy Lower Greensand Ridge loams of forest origin, liable to excessive drying out. In 1976 the drought here was very severe indeed. The site is very sheltered and lies on a warm south slope. Rainfall 31–32 inches.

Mr and Mrs Farmer bought the present house with 1 acre of land in 1937 but did not begin the garden until 1949. The sloping site has been retained and enlivened with a rock garden on the east side and a shrub bank below the house terrace, where a collection of over 40 different varieties of heaths grew at one time. Noteworthy plants among the many in this garden, some now nearly 30 years old, include *Podocarpus salignus*, *Cotinus obovatus* (*Rhus cotinoides*) and *Fothergilla monticola* as a fine group near the rock garden; a splendid Snowdrop Tree, *Halesia carolina*, planted in 1948, now 23 ft high; and some impressive great mounds of *Juniperus × media* 'Pfitzeriana' as a conifer bank, planted in 1938. Note the effective golden-leaved *Thuja plicata* 'Zebrina' used as a boundary feature, planted in 1954 on the west side. The deciduous azaleas at the south front of the house are estimated to be over 50 years old, and provide a spectacular display in May. They were purchased as large mature plants in 1950. Rhododendrons include a group of the large-leaved *R. calophytum*, *R. fulvum* and *R. fictolacteum* planted in 1948 as 5 ft plants. Shade and shelter for these come from a small pine copse. Bracken is used as an essential mulch.

The garden seems deceptively large for one acre, due to the clever design and the quality of the planting. No vegetables or fruit of any significance are grown, due to the sloping site and light soils. Maintenance is good.

Pinewood House

SU 970 563 (Sheet 186) Heath House Road, Worplesdon Hill. 3½ miles SW Woking off A322 Guildford–Bagshot road opposite Brookwood Cemetery. Owner: Mr and Mrs J. Van Zwanenberg. Open several Sundays in late April and May for the N.G.S.

A modern and unusual atrium-style house surrounded by seven acres of gardens and woodlands on acid, sandy soils. The atrium of the house has a good collection of conservatory plants.

Pinewood house lies on the light, Bagshot sandy loams in a seminatural setting of former pine, birch and beech heath, typical of this part of Surrey. The gardens merge almost imperceptibly into the Worplesdon Hill Golf Course to the south-east. A large Tudor-style Edwardian house once stood on this site and some of the mature ornamental species of pine, spruce, fir and cedar date from this period. The present owners replaced the old house with the present ingenious and unconventional new house about 11 years ago, designing the house on the Roman atrium principle. A light, spacious, glass-roofed central court is surrounded by the living-room and other accommodation on all four sides. The doors of all these rooms open into the court, where a luxurious setting of central pool and fountain – with pots and urns planted with exotic indoor plants, mostly collected by the owner in many parts of the world – is enlivened still further with tropical birds. The house is built of Cotswold stone, with a blue tiled roof. A wide stone terrace surrounds the house and links it to the gardens.

The gardens are well sheltered on all sides and secluded by dense evergreen and coniferous planting. The site is flat. Rainfall (see Merrist Wood). The gardens are largely informal and take the form of a large open glade with smaller glades in the enclosing copses of Scots Pine and beech, with some introduced exotic conifers. Around the house is more detailed, colourful planting, the wide paved house terraces attractively studded with carpeting subjects like thymes, thrift and campanulas. A large circular lawn is framed with massed perimeter plantings of acid-soil shrubs such as Japanese Maple varieties including some veteran *Acer palmatum* 'Dissectum' and many rhododendrons, magnolias, azaleas, dogwoods and heathers. A recently designed, oval herbaceous border area to the east of the house is intended to bring a succession of later colour into the garden when the spring flowering shrubs are over. A good selection of foliage and summer-flowering perennials have been planted here. A rose garden is a main feature in front of the terrace. The most recent feature observed in 1976 was the water garden created in about 1974, with an associated rock feature. Effective new planting is softening the new-looking lines of this area.

A woodland spinney of pine and beech to the south has been partially cleared to give glimpses of the golf course fairways, and the garden lawns flow into the smooth fairway swards without a break or ha-ha giving a splendid illusion of space. From a comfortable deckchair on the terrace, stooping golfers in the distance can even look like gardeners! The spinneys are bright with naturalized bulbs in March and April. A well-managed vegetable and fruit garden shows what can be done with light Bagshot sands given generous dressings of organic matter and good management. The gardens are very well maintained.

Polesden Lacey

TQ 135 524 (Sheet 187) 1½ miles S of Great Bookham (S of A246 Leatherhead–Guildford Road). 3½ miles from Leatherhead, 5 miles from Dorking. Elusively hidden away among the woods and hills NW of Ranmore Common. Owner: The National Trust. Open April–October usually every day, except Monday and Friday, 2–6 or sunset (if earlier). In winter months open weekends only. See National Trust publication or H.H.C.G. for latest details. Teas are available.

A large garden of over 30 acres set in beautiful historic parkland and the wooded hills of the chalk North Downs above Dorking. The garden extends for nearly half a mile along the side of a south-west slope. There are broad walks and fine lawns with mature trees, and a series of enclosed and walled gardens where roses, irises and perennials look particularly colourful from May onwards. There is also a good

collection of wall plants. The early-nineteenth-century house contains a superb collection of pictures and works of art.

The first house to stand on this site was built in 1632 by Anthony Ross. However, no trace remains of this house which survived with alterations until the early nineteenth century. An important owner in the late eighteenth century was Richard Brinsley Sheridan, who bought it in 1796 with 341 acres and gradually added to the estate. His main contribution to the gardens survives in the splendid long terraced walk which he must have extended from an earlier terrace dated 1761. Sheridan's son sold the house and estate in 1819 to Joseph Bonsor who demolished the old house without trace and between 1821–23 erected a large Regency villa to the design of Thomas Cubitt. Joseph Bonsor enlarged the estate and between 1824–25 planted 20,000 trees. He probably also built the arched gateway in the drive, the walled gardens and some of the cottages. After his death in 1835 Polesden Lacey changed hands many times until, in 1906, it was bought by Captain The Hon. Ronald Greville. It was his wife, who survived him by many years, who brought the valuable collections of pictures, furniture and other works of art to Polesden. She laid out the gardens in a spacious Edwardian style, adding many architectural and sculptural features, including a final flourish – a tomb for herself in the formal garden. On her death in 1942 she bequeathed the house and garden and estate of 1,000 acres to the National Trust, with her fine collection of works of art.

The house and garden lie on a high chalk ridge of the North Downs some 460 ft above sea level. The house is cleverly sited on a levelled terrace on the west-facing slope of the ridge, with good shelter from rising ground and tree planting to the north, north-east and east. There are magnificent views south-west and west from the house and the long terrace across farming landscape to beech and mixed woods on the skyline. Soils are rather thin and chalky and in need of constant enrichment. Rainfall 29–31 inches.

Few plans or records of the garden survive from any period and this short account is therefore necessarily sketchy. There are two distinct styles to be found at Polesden. First, the extensive and relatively informal parkland and grounds that lead up to the house and embellish it to the south-east, south and south-west. The lime avenue leading up to the entrance arch is of varying age, some limes being very old indeed. A policy of renewal is being adopted to perpetuate this fine feature. The car park is beneath the canopy of an ordered young tree plantation set in grass, but the feeling is of cool, restful woodland. Ash, beech and lime grow well here. The land forms around and below the house are interesting, with the great sweep of lawns sloping to the hedged boundary below, beyond which a lovely valley can be seen. On the house lawn are a number of fine specimen trees including Cedar of Lebanon, *Cedrus libani*, Atlas Cedar, *Cedrus atlantica*, Purple Beeches probably dating from the beginning of this century or earlier, and several 50 ft Colorado Blue Spruce, *Picea pungens glauca*, planted by George V in 1918. These, like many other exotic trees here, are growing surprisingly well on the chalky soils. Sheridan's long terrace walk is a splendid feature running nearly 500 yards in a north–south direction to the south-east of the house, a broad grass walk below the crest of the slope with delightful unspoilt views over the low yew hedge rampart, and backed on the north side by a long spinney of mature beech (now diseased and sadly to be felled), holly and yew. Seats here and there are ideal for basking and meditating in the sun in this delightful place.

For the gardener and plantsman the gardens of the second style will be of considerable interest. These are largely Mrs Greville's designs and consist of beds, borders and enclosed gardens within the large walled garden that lies to the north-west of the house; the winter garden and, below, the rock garden and croquet lawn area. Before exploring these, note the good use of wall plants on the house: the two massive early-flowering evergreen *Clematis armandii* 'Snowdrift'; (Graham Thomas notes: 'It is worth a special journey to see these with their thousands of *fragrant* white flowers against the glossy evergreen leaves in April').* There are also *Pyracantha coccinea*, *Magnolia grandiflora*, the blue *Ceanothus impressus*, and orange *Eccremocarpus scaber*. Beds beside the path are enlivened with seasonal scented flowers and foliage.

Before a wrought-iron gate to the great walled-garden complex one passes first the cool, shaded, almost sepulchral garden where Mrs Greville's tomb stands in a rectangle of grass guarded by statues of the Four Seasons and clustered with yew hedges, and with walls clothed by large-leaved Persian Ivy *Hedera colchica* 'Dentata Variegata'. From this somewhat austere place one emerges into the brightness, colour and fragrance of the main garden. The dominant feature down the central path, typical of Edwardian and 1920s fashion, is a long rose pergola clad with a great variety of climbing and rambling roses and other climbers. There are two long herbaceous and mixed borders which look magnificent in June and July. Irises and peonies do particularly well on these soils. The small, intimate iris garden is enclosed by yew hedges, and there is also a lavender garden, while on the rugged

---

* *Gardeners' Chronicle*, 16 October 1965.

stone and flint walls that enclose the whole garden *Aubrieta* spills in pale blue in April. New wall plants include clematis, jasmine, *Ceanothus* and honeysuckles. Notice the large wistaria-clad brick tower, the main water supply for the house and gardens dating from the Edwardian era. The wrought-iron gates leading out of this garden to the west are charming and finely constructed (see sketch).

The long axis of this walled garden ends at the western extremity with a curious thatched bridge in strong timber and thatch; it bridges a sunken estate road to the farm. The flint embankment of this road just north-east of the bridge carries the date 1861 but the bridge itself probably dates from the Edwardian era. Near the bridge is a small shaded winter garden dominated by a block of mature spreading Persian trees, *Parrotia persica*, that colour well in autumn. This garden is gradually being planted with winter-flowering shrubs and perennials like *Sarcococca*, *Helleborus*, *Viburnum* and *Daphne* and contains many bulbs and corms. The gardener's cottage behind the garden has a quaint crooked chimney built intentionally so for draught. From the bridge one can look further west to a tract of land, formerly the old vegetable garden, in which stands a thatched lodge as a terminal feature backed by woodland. This area is not yet open to the public but is being developed as a small orchard-like garden for quiet enjoyment.

The rock garden and rock bank lie to the south of the walled garden on a south-west slope and act as an ornamental break to the next level which is the croquet lawn. The rock garden in Westmorland stone is a monolithic affair of the early part of this century when one could buy masses of this now priceless stone and when transport was relatively cheap. It is of limited plant interest at present. The bank is massed with old veteran specimens of *Juniperus* × *media* 'Pfitzeriana', *Berberis*, *Cistus*, *Cotoneaster* and other shrubs. Those shrubs that grow well on the chalky soils at Polesden Lacey should be noted by gardeners with similar soils who wish to increase their collections. Particularly to note are *Viburnum* of all kinds; the grey-leaved, blue-flowered sub-shrubs: lavender, *Caryopteris* and *Perovskia*; *Cotinus coggygria* (*Rhus cotinus*) – barberries; buddleias; cotoneasters; forsythias; lilacs, *Syringa*; *Osmanthus delavayi* and × *Osmarea* 'Burkwoodii' (two fine medium-sized evergreens with white scented flowers); and many of the scented species of *Daphne*, especially *D.* × *burkwoodii* and the late winter-flowering *D. mezereum*. Flowering trees like Japanese cherries also do well, and the silvery-leaved Whitebeam, *Sorbus aria*, and its cultivars, and many climbers already mentioned.

The 30 acres of gardens are maintained to a realistic standard by five gardeners under the able headship of Mr Bob Hall. He tells me there used to be 15–20 gardeners in Mrs Greville's time. The policy of the Trust is to maintain Polesden Lacey as a part Edwardian and part eighteenth-century garden, to avoid bright modern colours and inappropriate innovations and to enhance the standard of cultivation and the atmosphere of quiet relaxation.

Deer and rabbits are an increasing problem in the garden, as are two-legged vandals who steal statuary, plants and labels. Visitor numbers have steadily increased to over 70,000 in 1976.

Ramster

SU 960 352 (Sheet 186) 1½ miles S of Chiddingfold on A283 Milford–Petworth road. Owner: Lady Burke. Open: Last week in April to second week in June, Sundays and Bank Holidays 2–6.

An extensive woodland garden with many fine and unusual trees and shrubs and good displays of rhododendrons and azaleas in late May and early June. The soils are moist and acid.

The house and garden were owned by Sir Harry Wechter, Bt, from about 1890–1920. He converted an Elizabethan farmhouse to the present mansion and created the gardens and lakes out of woodland in conjunction with the then well-known Gauntlett Nurseries, whose land adjoined Ramster. In 1920 the estate was bought by Sir Henry and Lady Norman. She was a sister of the first Lord Aberconway and, like him, a great horticulturist. She was responsible for completing the layout of the garden and introducing many of the fine rhododendrons and azaleas. Many of these were grown from her own crosses, and others came from Bodnant. The present owner is Lady Norman's daughter.

Although comparatively close to the main road, the garden is well concealed by thick arboretum-type planting including many mixed conifers and groups of flowering cherries and specimen trees in rough grass. There is an arrowed, recommended route round the gardens. The style is informal and of the woodland arboretum type with interesting winding paths through blocks and bold groups of shrubs opening into glades of scattered, mature, native and exotic trees. A dappled shade is cast by the canopy of fine oaks and some larches of 65–80 ft, and this, combined with moist, acidic, heavy clay soils, provides an ideal habitat for many choice and unusual plants.

There are good examples of Japanese Maples, rhododendrons and azaleas, and a camellia grove beneath large oaks with mostly *Camellia japonica* varieties up to 16–20 ft. Other ornamental trees include the elegant Japanese autumn-colouring *Cercidiphyllum japonicum, Parrotia persica* and many varieties of flowering cherries. There are a number of Wellingtonias over 50 ft high. The gardens merge on the western edge with more remote and wilder woodland with large ponds and more good native trees. There is a rather dark, silent pool not far from the house, created by damming a small valley, and occasional Japanese stone lanterns, fine old cut-leaf Japanese Maples, *Acer palmatum* 'Dissectum' and bamboo thickets add to the oriental effect. There is a fine magnolia bed with good examples of *M.denudata* and *M.× soulangiana*. A feature of the garden are the towering banks of *Rhododendron* 'Cynthia' lining the drive and the lake, reaching a height of 20–23 ft. *Rhododendron* species include *RR. calophytum, RR. thomsonii, RR. augustinii, RR. orbiculare, RR. wardii, RR. campylocarpum* and a fine tree of *RR.* 'Boddaertianum'. Bluebells carpet the woodland in May, and one may find the striking, large, rhubarb-like plant, *Gunnera manicata*, growing in the cool grassy glades.

Maintenance seems simple and effective and in keeping with the woodland character of the gardens.

Vann

SU 984 376 (Sheet 186). 1½ miles SE of Hambledon on a minor road to Chiddingfield and Dunsfold. 6 miles S of Godalming. A good map will help in finding this delightfully remote place. Owner: Mr and Mrs M. Cardoe. Opening is very limited. One or two Sundays early in the season. Parking is limited in a relatively narrow lane.

This is an outstanding example of one of the few Gertrude Jekyll gardens still perpetuated in her style. It was described in some detail by Mr Anthony Huxley in the 27 May 1976 issue of *Country Life*.

The name Vann derives from 'Fenne', a fen or bog, and the site is relatively low-lying on moist Wealden clay. The present house dates from the early sixteenth century and was extended in the seventeenth and eighteenth centuries. It was doubled in size in 1907–8 by W.D. Cardoe, the present owner's grandfather, who incorporated the existing barn and other buildings into the house. The pleasant country style of timber, brick and tile blends perfectly with the pastoral wooded countryside round about. In 1911 the Cardoes invited their friend and neighbour Gertrude Jekyll to advise on the layout of some of the gardens, and she undoubtedly had an influence on the design of the lower part of the garden. The complete scheme is very much in her style and typical of the early twentieth century. In 1948 the property passed to the next generation of the family who undertook a great renovation and reconstruction of the garden, which has been admirably continued by the present owners who came to Vann in 1969.

The setting is relatively sheltered and well-wooded, in unspoilt countryside. The soils are heavy Wealden acidic clays much improved by good management. The gardens lie about 195 ft above sea level. Climate (see Winkworth Arboretum). The gardens total about four-and-a-half acres, including orchards, woodland and vegetable garden, and the style is an attractive and effective blend of formal and informal.

The formal areas lie around the house. One enters by the old garden, which is the first garden of the original house, under a clipped yew arch. This is an enclosed rectangular garden divided up by paths and strips of lawn and attractively and informally planted with a cottage-garden blend of old roses, hardy fuchsias, Tree Peonies, campanulas and many more. There is a very effective border of grey/blue and yellow planting near the barn, comprising *Stachys lanata* and species of *Santolina, Ruta, Euphorbia, Ballota* and *Othonnopsis* among a ground pattern of ivies. The natural focal features of the garden are the clipped fastigiate yews.

The pergola, with piers of Bargate stone, is another fine feature of the more formal gardens bounding the north side of the formal lawn on the other side of the house. The borders flanking the pergola are richly planted with semi-shade-loving *Epimedium, Hosta, Iris, Helleborus, Geranium*, ferns and a fascinating blend of bulbous species. Climbers include clematis and the brilliant orange-flowered Trumpet Vine, *Campsis*. The borders facing the lawn area are richly planted with softly coloured and grey-foliaged plants, *Hebe, Artemisia, Ballota* and *Geranium renardii*, with the walls freely mantled with vines, roses and clematis. Another charming and simple formal feature is the front court, gravel surfaced and with a central old well-head. A variety of trees and shrubs surround the drive, particularly a large fig and large specimens of the climbing *Hydrangea petiolaris* on the walls.

A unique semi-formal feature to be found to the north of the large pond is the yew walk, created in 1910, which encloses a stone-lined ditch or damp-stream course whose banks are lined with bush roses emerging from a delightful blend of ferns, violas, primroses, cowslips and Mossy Saxifrages. At the western end are two massive Japanese Maples, *Acer palmatum*; a Medlar, *Mespilus germanica*; and a gnarled *Parrotia persica*, with a fine stone seat from which to contemplate this delightful part of the garden. A small winged statue is wreathed in wistarias.

The informal areas are to the east and north-east. The lower valley woodland garden is known to have been laid out by Gertrude Jekyll. A narrow stream runs through a lightly wooded valley and is enlarged here and there to create several small irregular pools. Stone paved paths cross and re-cross the course of the stream, and the natural oaks, ash and birch have been enriched with wild cherry, maples and other trees, while a selection of shrubs such as azaleas and low-growing *Gaultheria shallon* emerge from a groundwork of natural woodland plants – bluebells, celandines, Cow Parsley (Queen Anne's Lace) and fritillaries. By the pools are exotic associations of foliage perennials like *Rodgersia*, *Hosta*, with irises, ferns (including the shuttlecock fern *Matteuccia struthiopteris*) and the native kingcup, *Caltha palustris*. Nearer the house is the large, attractive old field pond, with water lilies, and edged with a natural blend of good native and exotic species.

To the north of the house is the business end of the garden. There is a large vegetable and fruit garden, glasshouses and beehives. An unusual serpentine, or 'crinkle-crankle', brick wall is a feature here, with wall fruit growing on it. There are also more ornamental trees and shrubs here, with a few remaining fine mature native trees.

To quote Anthony Huxley: 'Vann is a coherent garden, each part melting into the next but quite distinct, merging in turn with natural growth and the countryside beyond. Full of good plants, it is a fine example of relatively labour saving methods in successful operation'*

The gardens are largely maintained to a very commendable standard by the family with the help of a part-time man for nine hours or so a week. A visit is thoroughly recommended.

* *Country Life*, 27 May 1976.

Winkworth Arboretum

SU 995 413 (Sheet 186). 3 miles SE of Godalming, just off B2130 Godalming–Hascombe Road. Owner: The National Trust; maintained under a management agreement with three local authorities. Open all year round. Admission free. Shop and toilet facilities. Refreshments probably available in 1978.

A good collection of well-labelled ornamental trees and shrubs in early maturity on acid soils in very pleasant countryside; laid out as an informal hillside arboretum overlooking a lake. An ideal place for quiet relaxation.

The present site of the arboretum, covering about 100 acres, was purchased in 1938 by its founder and creator, Dr Wilfred Fox. He was immediately attracted by the site, a dramatic hillside overlooking a delightful valley where a small tributary of the River Wey had been dammed by a previous owner to form two small lakes (1). Dr Fox wrote an interesting account of the garden in the R.H.S. Journal of February 1954 and, in his own words, 'what originally attracted me to acquire the land and plant it, was the remarkable beauty of the valley, a valley quite unspoiled, of pastoral and wooded character.' At that time the land was covered with hazel, brambles and bracken. The first clearings were made by grubbing the scrub and unwanted vegetation in the winter of 1937–38, with the first plantings being made in that winter also. Wilfred Fox's plan was to create really bold groups of tree species in scale with the site and the land available. The plan of the arboretum today is still largely as Dr Fox laid it out.

The first main plantings (14) were of the larger maple species, *Acer platanoides* Norway Maple and its many cultivars; *A. rubrum*; *A. cappadocicum* (superb orange and gold in autumn); *A. hersii* for the attractive striped bark effects; and such rare species as *A. mono, A. lobelii, A. × dieckii, A. macrophyllum, A. trautvetteri, A. circinatum* and *A. carpinifolium*. Now about 40 years old, most of these can be seen today along the south end of the slope, providing particularly fine effects in autumn.

Dr Fox also planted the great central drift of nearly 100 Japanese Maples (3 and 4) – *Acer palmatum* and *A. japonicum* – including the brilliant autumn-tinted *A. palmatum* 'Heptalobum Osakazuki'. The winter of 1938–39 saw the planting of massed groups of Knap Hill azaleas (5), to flower in May with the natural carpet of bluebells, providing flamboyant colour combinations of gold, flame and yellow in a sea of blue. These are still mostly looking well after 40 years.

The fine groups of *Liquidambar styraciflua*, Sweet Gums, and *Quercus coccinea*, the Scarlet Oaks, give tremendous autumn effects, and for spring and autumn there are bold groups of the elegant Japanese Hill Cherry, *Prunus serrulata spontanea* (4 and 6). In siting these groups a deliberate attempt was made to avoid clear-cut hard lines by drifting them over the rather parallel lines of the paths that crossed the slope.

Planting was interrupted in the Second World War, although a little work was continued in this period, and then followed a ten-year period of more bold and widespread planting. The public was admitted to the young arboretum right from the start. In 1952 Dr Fox handed over the arboretum to the present joint committee which runs the garden with an agent and a small staff. Dr Fox died in 1962.

The setting, as already described is well wooded, sheltered and scenically very attractive. The soil lies in the belt of Lower Greensand, a deep but light, acid, sandy loam of forest origin. Springs rise in the cool north–north-west facing hillside that forms most of the arboretum and thus drought is seldom a problem. The altitude is about 320 ft above sea level at the highest point falling to 195 ft near the lake. Rainfall 31–33 inches. Sunshine 4–4.25 hrs.

The plan shows the main layout and some of the principal groups of trees and shrubs to be seen. Visitors should remember that the majority of the exotic species are between 30 and 40 years of age, that the area was planned for informal and natural groupings on a bold scale of foliage and textural plants, and that the soils and setting are ideal for the species chosen. There is a memorial to Dr Wilfred Fox in a glade recently planted with evergreens and hollies (18).

In areas 13–18 on the plan, the oaks and other main tree species are almost absent so that there is very little cover here, but in areas 20 and 22 there are many oaks. A summary only of the approximate location of the main genera and species to be seen at Winkworth is given here:

Lower path south end and The Bowl (3 and 4) – *Cedrus atlantica glauca*; *Sorbus*; *Acer*, maples; *Euonymus*; *Pyracantha*; *Viburnum*; Scarlet Oaks, *Quercus coccinea*; *Nyssa sylvatica*, Tupelo Tree. North end – *Cotoneaster*.

Middle path south end (5 and 14) – *Prunus*, cherries; *Malus*, crabs; *Liquidambar*; *Enkianthus*; *Rhus*; *Photinia*. Mid-area – Japanese Maples. North end – *Crataegus*, thorns.

Top path south end (6) – *Magnolia*; *Amelanchier*; tree maples;

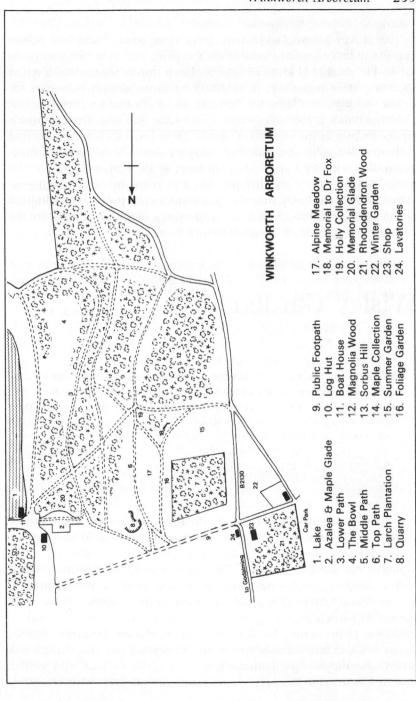

WINKWORTH ARBORETUM

1. Lake
2. Azalea & Maple Glade
3. Lower Path
4. The Bowl
5. Middle Path
6. Top Path
7. Larch Plantation
8. Quarry
9. Public Footpath
10. Log Hut
11. Boat House
12. Magnolia Wood
13. Sorbus Hill
14. Maple Collection
15. Summer Garden
16. Foliage Garden
17. Alpine Meadow
18. Memorial to Dr Fox
19. Holly Collection
20. Memorial Glade
21. Rhododendron Wood
22. Winter Garden
23. Shop
24. Lavatories

Viburnum; *Kalmia*; *Stranvaesia*; *Cornus*.

The cherry avenue specimens have now mostly died out. Other important collections are located on the plan. The area between paths (3) and (6) and (14) and (15) are all steep slopes, planted with many specimen trees including, in addition to those already summarized: *Betula, Nothofagus, Cladrastis, Parrotia, Fagus, Cedrus* and *Amelanchier*.

Maintenance is carried out by two full-time staff who are responsible for the upkeep of the entire 100 acres. Their tasks include fencing and path maintenance, tree planting, surgery and felling. Grass-cutting, much of it done by hand, takes up most of the summer months. An occasional very welcome helping hand is given by local volunteers. Management is in the hands of a committee comprising representatives of the local authorities, the R.H.S. and others, who are advised by the Gardens Advisory Staff of the National Trust.

Wisley Garden

TQ 065 584 (Sheet 187) 1 mile N of Ripley just W off A3 London–Portsmouth Road. The dual carriageway road has clear access signs to the gardens. 4 miles south of Cobham, 20 miles from central London. Owner: The Royal Horticultural Society. Open: Members of the R.H.S. (Fellows) can normally visit Wisley throughout the year (except Christmas Day) between 10 and early evening. The public are admitted on weekdays and after 2 on Sundays (admission fee). The excellent facilities for visitors include ample parking, a splendid garden shop (a wide range of gardening books and a plant centre) and an extremely good restaurant for refreshments and light meals.

The outstanding garden of the Royal Horticultural Society, ranking among the finest in Europe for its well-labelled, comprehensive collections of hardy plants and many new special demonstration areas aimed at the gardening public. The soil is a light, acidic, sandy loam.

The Anglo-Saxon name given to Wisley means a damp, marshy meadow-land. These characteristics have been exploited, in the wild garden in particular. The garden began in the 1870s when a former treasurer of the R.H.S., Mr G.F. Wilson, purchased 60 acres of wild, damp oak and birch woods and began to develop the area. In the oak wood near the western boundary he created his famous wild garden and he constructed the ponds and mass planted these with waterside plants. After Wilson's death, Sir Thomas Hanbury purchased the estate and garden in August 1903 and generously gave it in trust to the R.H.S. for its use in perpetuity. In 1904 the Society moved here from their overcrowded site in Chiswick. Mr S.T. Wright came from Chiswick as Superintendent and began developing the garden without delay. The wild garden was largely retained, with many of Wilson's specimen trees and shrubs and these still form the bulk of the mature planting in this area today. Staff cottages were built, and between 1914–16 the laboratory building was constructed in the comfortable Surrey country-house style of brick, timber and tiles reminiscent of a Lutyens house (see Hascombe Court).

In 1911 the rock garden was constructed by Messrs Pulham using Sussex sandstone and exploiting a natural north-facing slope. A series of pools at various levels, with waterfalls and rivulets, was created and supplied from a concealed tank supplemented by natural springs. The alpine house was built in 1926. The great collections of rhododendrons and azaleas were planted on Battleston Hill from 1937 onwards. The pinetum was created in the early 1900s and considerably extended from 1946 onwards, including the planting in 1948 of the first seedlings of the newly introduced Dawn Redwood, *Metasequoia glyptostroboides*. Many other additions and improvements have been made between 1946 and the present day, particularly in glasshouses, demonstration gardens, visitor facilities and extensive new trial grounds near the A3 road.

Wisley lies on the extreme south-eastern edge of the sandy heaths and woodlands that characterized much of north-west Surrey at one time. Extensive housing and road development are now eroding much of the secluded quality of Wisley and the A3, just south-west of the gardens, has caused noise and visual intrusion on this side. Soils are sandy, acidic Bagshot beds overlying heavier London clays. The soil in the gardens therefore varies from a very light, silvery sand in the upper parts, to a heavy retentive clay in the wild garden and near the pools. The climate is one of reasonable shelter and enclosure from the many sequences of planting, but frost pockets undoubtedly exist in the lower areas of the gardens and late spring frosts can be severe and damaging. There can be a difference of as much as 8°F between the higher Battleston Hill and the low-lying wild garden where frosts are frequent. Rainfall averages 26 inches. Sunshine 4 hrs. Wisley seems to be in an area of Surrey prone to sudden violent summer storms. On 16 July 1947, four inches of rain and hail fell in 1½ hours, devastating much of the planting and causing erosion canyons 3–4 ft deep in the sandy soils. Then on 21 July 1968 came the famous tornado which blazed a trail of destruction 60 yards wide across the fruit field, completely uprooting many established trees; 174 apple and plum trees were uprooted, some landing 40 feet away from their original site.

An excellent, up-to-date guide is available at the information centre, and as the garden is world famous and known to very many people this account takes the form of a summary highlighting the areas and features of particular interest. The plan, based on that reproduced in the guide, should help visitors on their way round, taking a circular route in a clockwise direction.

The entrance and information centre (1) – offers a good opportunity for all manner of horticultural diversions before entering the garden. On entering the garden, note the pair of wrought-iron gates erected in 1926 in memory of the Rev W. Wilks, Secretary of the R.H.S. from 1888 to 1920. He was responsible for raising the original stock of Shirley Poppies commemorated by the poppy motif on the gates. The main laboratory building lies to the right and its warm south-west and west walls have been used as a home for several exotic half-hardy plants. Note particularly the Silver Wattle, *Acacia dealbata* or Mimosa, the yellow-flowered Californian *Fremontodendron* 'California Glory', blue-flowered *Ceanothus* (also Californian), various camellias, several varieties of *Clematis montana*, *Actinidia kolomikta*, and climbing roses. The warm south walls and the light sandy soils are ideal for *Amaryllis belladonna* and *Nerine bowdenii*. Terraced lawns offset this building to the south-west with well-planted sandstone walls. A semi-formal terrace is reached either by a short flight of steps or by way of a gently sloping path designed to allow easy access for wheelchairs. To the left is the Broad Walk, a wide grass area forming one of the main axial vistas of the garden and flanked by two dramatic mixed borders (3), each 140 yards long and 6 yards wide. These are backed by hornbeam hedges and very well planted with a wide selection of perennials, shrubs and annuals. Ornamental grasses have been used to great effect here.

On either side of these borders are areas developed as demonstration areas. The summer garden is devoted to a range of shrubs, herbaceous plants, bulbs and annuals; and the garden for new roses (2) contains over 200 different new cultivars of bush and climbing roses introduced over the preceding five years and continuously replaced as new introductions are released. The hedge and ground-cover demonstration area (4) nearby comprises short lengths of over 100 different varieties of hedges as clipped and naturally grown plants, complemented by an equally large collection of good ground-cover species. The fine colour borders (5) are also good examples of colourful foliage and flower associations for all year round effects.

Battleston Hill (6) is an informal extensively planted ridge, growing a large collection and trial area of rhododendrons and azaleas. Daffodils are thick in the beds in April and exotic trees like Japanese Maples and Mountain Ashes are brilliantly coloured in the autumn. There are also many woodland flowering shrubs such as camellias and magnolias. The herb layer is enriched with many species of *Lilium* such as *martagon, regale, tigrinum* and *henryi*. Notice the banks made of peat blocks flanking the paths, an ideal place for such acid, shade-loving plants as *Soldanella, Shortia, Meconopsis* and *Cassiope*. The winter garden (7) lies close to the A3 highway and the Portsmouth trials field, now laid out as extensive trial grounds for flowers and vegetables. The glasshouses (9), completed in 1970, are a comprehensive complex of different houses where the visitor can see all manner of well-grown plants from exotic stove-house tropical species to extensive orchid, cactus and epiphyte collections and many others.

Continuing in a south-westerly direction one moves up the hill to the fruit collections (11) which cover 16 acres and include over 600 cultivars of apples, 90 pears, 90 plums, including gages and dessert plums, as well as soft and bush fruits and strawberries. The model gardens nearby provide excellent demonstrations of fruit-growing schemes for small gardens with particular emphasis on trained fruit and the use of dwarfing rootstocks. The model small gardens (12) are an enterprising new development aimed at the education of the garden-ing public by showing a number of examples of small garden layouts realistically designed to suit modern needs and limitations of size and budget. The garden for disabled people was opened in May 1977 and contains a wide range of gardening features to assist disabled and elderly people. It was designed in association with the Disabled Living Foundation. To the west, and separated from this garden by two borders containing plants of value to flower arrangers, is the recently established herb garden (13) planted with a wide range of culinary, medicinal and aromatic herbs.

The main rose borders (15) form the other arm of the two axial vistas arising from the colour border area. The terminal feature is the Bowes Lyon memorial pavilion (16) created as a memorial to the late Sir David Bowes Lyon, President of the R.H.S. from 1953—61. Two upright growing Dawyck Beeches add height to this scene, together with various other trees and shrubs. Note the large standard *Buddleia alternifolia* flowering in June. The superb alpine house (17) is alive with colour and variety, while nearby, but entirely different in emphasis, are the model vegetable gardens (18) with cropping plans based on the excellent R.H.S. booklet *The Vegetable Garden Displayed*.

The rock garden (19) is one of the older features of the gardens and is certainly one of the finest rock gardens of today. Many habitats have been created for the great variety of alpine shrubs, bulbs and perennials to be found here, and in recent years a special zig-zag path has been made to allow wheelchairs to be pushed up and down much of the rock garden without the problem of steps. The pools, streams and waterfalls eventually discharge into a long pond at the bottom of the rock garden, providing a fine habitat for waterside perennials like *Lysichitum americanum*, the Bog Arum; *Peltiphyllum peltatum*; *Trollius europaeus*, the Globe Flower; and many species of *Iris*.

The Alpine meadow (20) is one of the most unusual and attractive features of Wisley. A gently sloping area of grassland east of the rock garden and flowing towards the wild garden is composed essentially of the finer turf grasses that love the acid soils. These prove an ideal home for myriads of early spring-flowering bulbs dominated by the two dwarf species *Narcissus bulbocodium*, the pale yellow Hoop Petticoat and *N. cyclamineus* with its dainty, narrow, reflexed perianth looking something like a yellow-flowered cyclamen. Together these make a wonderful sight in late March and early April. The Alpine illusion is effectively maintained with scattered outcrops of rocks and a few sculptured mature mounds of the Japanese Maples *Acer palmatum* 'Dissectum', and a striking dwarf spreading form of the Colorado Blue Spruce, *Picea pungens glauca*. The meadow is cut in late June.

The wild garden (21) – The oldest part of the garden of Wisley. The natural, wet, acid woodland has proved an ideal home for many woodland shrubs introduced from North America and Asia, particularly of the genus Ericaceae. The old hybrid rhododendrons planted by Wilson have been mostly retained. More small spring-flowering bulbs mass the glades, and beside the streams are colourful colonies of May-flowering Asiatic candelabra primulas in pink, salmon, red and orange, the last to flower being the tall yellow *Primula florindae*. Look also in May for the brilliant blue Himalayan Poppies, *Meconopsis betonicifolia*, and other species that love these cool, lime-free soils. In June and July there are many magnificent lilies, including the huge 10 ft tall *Cardiocrinum giganteum*; and in autumn the fine colour and late flowers of the Sorrel Tree, *Oxydendrum arboreum*.

The heather garden and seven acres (22) – with the wild garden, this area, the pinetum and Howard's Field (30) all lie on the terrace of the River Wey that flows in a great arc on the north-western boundary of the garden. The soil is very sandy, overlying clays and gravels. The area here was developed from 1915 onwards, a gravel pit near the centre being enlarged and converted into a lake. Weeping Willows were planted beside the lake but unfortunately the largest of these

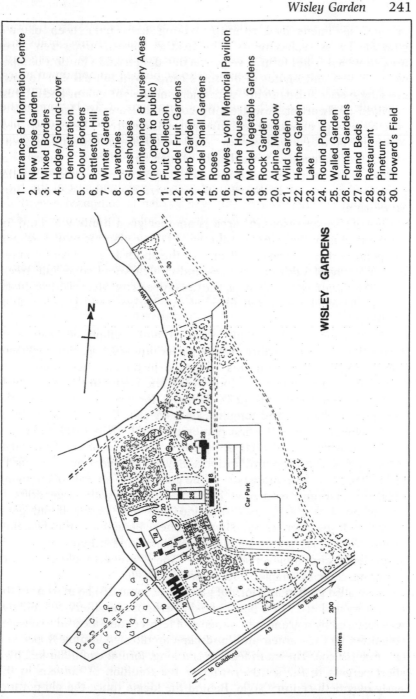

1. Entrance & Information Centre
2. New Rose Garden
3. Mixed Borders
4. Hedge/Ground-cover Demonstration
5. Colour Borders
6. Battleston Hill
7. Winter Garden
8. Lavatories
9. Glasshouses
10. Maintenance & Nursery Areas (not open to public)
11. Fruit Collection
12. Model Fruit Gardens
13. Herb Garden
14. Model Small Gardens
15. Roses
16. Bowes Lyon Memorial Pavilion
17. Alpine House
18. Model Vegetable Gardens
19. Rock Garden
20. Alpine Meadow
21. Wild Garden
22. Heather Garden
23. Lake
24. Round Pond
25. Walled Garden
26. Formal Gardens
27. Island Beds
28. Restaurant
29. Pinetum
30. Howard's Field

WISLEY GARDENS

original specimens died recently. Young trees have been planted strategically as replacements. The heather garden and seven acres area in which it lies form a very effective design and planting composition. Blocks and islands of heathers range from tall tree-like to low-growing species and cultivars, with additional height, colour and interest provided by dwarf or slow-growing conifers. Nearer the lake (23) are effective groups of autumn-colouring deciduous trees *Quercus coccinea*, *Nyssa sylvatica*, *Parrotia persica*, *Liquidambar styraciflua* and Norway Maple *Acer platanoides*. On a bright winter day there is a tapestry of colours from the stems of dogwoods, willows and birches and the persistent berries of barberries, *Cotoneaster*, *Pernettya*, *Skimmia* and *Stranvaesia*.

East of this very pleasant area is another good hunting-ground for the plantsman in the round pond area (24). The planting in and around the pond is rich and colourful and to the south is a series of planted beds, notably of *Viburnum* species and cultivars and some fine trees: Tulip Tree *Liriodendron tulipifera*, the Cucumber Tree *Magnolia acuminata*, and an unusual variegated form of the Turkey Oak, *Quercus cerris* 'Variegata'.

The restaurant (28) is an essential and well-placed feature to renew the inner man before plunging ever onwards; spacious, efficient and reasonably priced, it has earned a justifiably high reputation. While relaxing here one can look across the lawns to the island beds of herbaceous perennials (27) designed for low maintenance, the minimum of staking and long seasonal effects.

The pinetum (29) – the first planting began here in 1909 and today there is a wide and attractively planted collection of conifers, particularly pines, cypresses and junipers. Beyond the pinetum is Howard's Field (30), the most remote part of the garden and an area of changing uses and planting. It is now being re-designed with large drifts of sun-loving shrubs such as *Cistus* and *Halimium* among broad grass walks and specimen trees; silver birches, *Eucalyptus*, the fastigiate Locust Tree, *Robinia pseudoacacia* 'Fastigiata' and others. The soil is very sandy and impoverished here. There are also older, mature flowering cherries, maples and alders.

The walled garden and formal gardens (25 and 26) lie in front of the laboratory and in 1972 a block of old glasshouses and service buildings was replaced by a grand new scheme of terraces and a canal to designs submitted by the garden and landscape architects Lanning Roper and Geoffrey Jellicoe. The main feature is a long, formal canal flanked by a short pergola to the south, rather in the tradition of Lutyens in the early twentieth-century style. Behind the loggia (once the old potting-shed) lies a formal walled garden used for spring and summer bedding schemes. Herbs and foliage plants are prominent here, with good planting on the walls.

Maintenance of the 200 acres of the garden, which contains a number of intensive, time-consuming features, is a constant battle with diminishing experienced staff and rising costs. In the past ample labour was available to maintain the garden at a high level. In recent years a programme to rationalize and minimize the use of labour whilst making maximum use of machinery and weedkillers has been developed to maintain standards. Permanent gardening staff numbers 25 (1977).

The Society's constant aim is to encourage the spread of interest in gardening throughout the world, and in addition to the maintenance of the large collection of plants at Wisley there is also a very experienced staff of advisers on many aspects of gardening.

Supplement

A supplement of other gardens normally open in Surrey.

ABINGER MILL Abinger Hammer. Fairly recent planting of trees, shrubs and other plants in an old mill garden.

ANNESLEY Near Haslemere. 3 acres shrubs, roses and plants for floral arrangements.

ASHBURTON HOUSE Send, near Woking. 5 acres attractive garden with riverside lawns, water garden and rhododendrons and azaleas.

BELLASIS HOUSE 2 miles NE of Dorking. Fine trees, shrubs, rhododendrons and hydrangeas.

BRACKENBER LODGE Sunningdale. Flowering shrubs, water and rock gardens. Glasshouses.

CLAREMONT LANDSCAPE GARDEN 2 miles SW Esher off old A3. An historic early eighteenth-century garden at present undergoing an ambitious restoration programme by the National Trust. The main features include a lake with island pavilion; a grotto; a turf amphitheatre; viewpoints and very pleasant woodlands. A visit is recommended.

COLLIERS FARM Fernhurst. Medium-sized garden developed over last 4 years. Shrubs, mixed borders on a fine S slope. Woodland walk with rhododendrons in streamside setting.

DAWN HILL Wentworth. 3 acres rhododendrons, azaleas, water and rock gardens.

DUNSBOROUGH PARK Ripley. Fine glasshouses, conservatory plant collections, rose gardens.

IRON PEAR TREE HOUSE Tilburstow Hill, near Godstone. A fine spring garden stream, old trees and lawns.

LARKENSHAW Chobham. Wide variety of trees and shrubs, herbaceous plants. Glasshouses.

PARK LANE HOUSE Farnham. Medium-sized garden, shrubs, alpines, roses and borders.

ROBIN HILL Wentworth, Virginia Water. 8 acres of many attractive features: azaleas, rhododendrons, rare trees and shrubs, 1,000 varieties of roses; stream and woodlands.

SANDHILLS Blethingley. Flowering shrubs, azaleas and fine views.

SNOWDENHAM HOUSE Bramley, S Guildford. Woodland and formal garden with Georgian house.

SUTTON PLACE 3 miles N Guildford. Extensive formal gardens around Tudor mansion with parkland.

SUTTON PLACE FARM Abinger Hammer. Large garden in lovely setting with rhodendendrons, azaleas, heathers and conifers.

THANESCROFT Shamley Green, Guildford. Medium-sized old garden, shrubs and roses.

WINTERSHALL Bramley. 2½ acres of garden and 100 acres of park and woodlands. Pools, lakes, fine trees and shrubs.

WONERSH GARDENS Near Guildford. Two gardens usually open at Woodyers and Losiford House, showing contrasts in size, planting and setting.

YEW TREE COTTAGES Esher. Small, charming, old-world cottage garden with many attractive features. Visit recommended.

Index

magnificum 165
mallotum 122
mollyanum 122
obtusum 'Amoenum' 37, 71, 188
occidentale 188
orbiculare 230
ponticum 88, 209
'Princess Alice' 191
'Princess of Wales' 187
'Red Luscombei' 187
'Sapphire' 190
sinogrande 165
'Tally Ho' 141
thomsonii 230
wardii 230
yakushimanum 132, 152
'Yellow Hammer' 190
yunnanense 168
Roberts, Sir G. and Lady 161
Robinia pseudoacacia 32
  p. 'Fastigiata' 242
Robin Hill 244
Robinson, Mrs J.H. 137
Robinson, William 16, 38, 51, 98, 99, 110, 163
Rodgersia 36, 54, 57, 68, 71, 90, 134, 152, 232
Romneya coulteri 135, 139, 190
Rondel 99
Roper, Lanning 82, 83, 242
Rosa 'Alberic Barbier' 127, 128, 129
  'Allen Chandler' 99
  'Allgold' 28
  'Arthur Bell' 29
  'Austrian Copper' 52
  banksiae 29, 70, 76, 112, 155, 158, 168, 189
    b. 'Alboplena' 158
    b. 'Lutea' 158
    b. lutescens 158
    b. normalis 158
  'Blairi No I' 76
  'Blushing Lady' 94
  brunonii 128
  'Buff Beauty' 106, 128, 193
  californica 'Plena' 76, 94
  'Capitaine John Ingram' 128
  'Caroline Testout' 127
  'Cecile Brunner' 128
  'Celestial' 193
  'Cerise Bouquet' 128, 193
  'Chanelle' 27
  'Chapeau de Napoleon' 99
  'Charles de Mills' 76
  'Climbing Crimson Glory' 191
  'Cornelia' 128
  'Danse de Feu' 129
  'Day Break' 128
  'Dr Van Fleet' 76
  ecae 52
  'Elaine' 36
  'Elizabeth of Glamys' 82
  'Empress Josephine' (*R. francofurtana*) 128
  'Ena Harkness' 129
  'Etoile D'Hollande' 129, 191
  'Fantin Latour' 76, 106, 128
  filipes 'Kiftsgate' 172
  foetida 'Bicolor' 52
  gallica 'Versicolor' ('Rosa Mundi') 76
    g. 'Sissinghurst Castle' 102
  'Guinee' 129
  'Gold Bush' 128

'Golden Showers' 128, 191
'Gruss an Teplitz' 148
'Highdownensis' 193
'Hippolyte' 99, 128
'Iceberg' 83, 103
'Karen Poulsen' 82
'Kathleen' 100
'King Arthur' 82
laevigata 76
'Lawrence Johnston' 100
longicuspis 103
'Madame Alfred Carrière' 100, 127, 128, 129
'Madame Butterfly' 148
'Mme. E. Calvat' 148
'Maigold' 129
'Marguerite Hilling' 193
'Madame Grégoire Staechlin' 35, 129, 191
'Mme. Isaac Pereire' 148
'Meg' 191
'Mermaid' 191
moyesii 57, 154
'National Trust' 35
'Nevada' 57
'New Dawn' 128
'Nuits de Young' 99
'Peace' 28
'Penelope' 106, 128
'Pink Favourite' 27
'Rambling Rector' 94
'Rosa Mundii', see *R. gallica* 'Versicolor'
'Roseraie de l'Hay' 129
roxburghii 122, 135
rubrifolia 54, 83, 138, 193
rugosa 'Alba' 193
'Souvenir de Claudius Denoyel' 127
'Souvenir de la Malmaison' 128
spinossissima 'William III' 149
'Stephen Leyton' 27
'William Lobb' 76
'Wedding Day' 86
'Zigeuner Knabe' 52
Rosse, Earl and Countess of 163–165
Rother, River 130, 161
Royal Horticultural Society (R.H.S.) 14, 34, 236, 237
Rudbeckia 149
Rubus tricolor 150
  Tridel 138, 155
Russell, Bertrand 193
Ruta graveolens 47, 87, 231
Rymans 177–179
Sackville family 68
Sackville-West, Vita 69, 95–104
Sage, see *Phlomis* (Jerusalem), and *Salvia*
St John Jerusalem 84–85
St Leonard's Forest 121, 154, 156, 165, 186, 197
St Martha Hill 211
St Roche's Arboretum 179–180
Salix alba 'Chrysostella' 85, 109
  a. 'Tristis' 67, 85
  caprea 'Pendula' 111
  fragilis 85
  repens argentea 83
Saltwood Castle 14, 86–87
Salvia 59
  argentea 103
  nemorosa 'Superba' 149
  officinalis 133
  patens 112
  turkestanica 75, 139